SUPER HOROSCOPE
GEMINI

2009

MAY 21 – JUNE 20

BERKLEY BOOKS, NEW YORK

THE BERKLEY PUBLISHING GROUP
Published by the Penguin Group
Penguin Group (USA) Inc.
375 Hudson Street, New York, New York 10014, USA
Penguin Group (Canada), 90 Eglinton Avenue East, Suite 700, Toronto, Ontario M4P 2Y3, Canada
(a division of Pearson Penguin Canada Inc.)
Penguin Books Ltd., 80 Strand, London WC2R 0RL, England
Penguin Group Ireland, 25 St. Stephen's Green, Dublin 2, Ireland (a division of Penguin Books Ltd.)
Penguin Group (Australia), 250 Camberwell Road, Camberwell, Victoria 3124, Australia
(a division of Pearson Australia Group Pty. Ltd.)
Penguin Books India Pvt. Ltd., 11 Community Centre, Panchsheel Park, New Delhi—110 017, India
Penguin Group (NZ), 67 Apollo Drive, Rosedale, North Shore 0632, New Zealand
(a division of Pearson New Zealand Ltd.)
Penguin Books (South Africa) (Pty.) Ltd., 24 Sturdee Avenue, Rosebank, Johannesburg 2196,
South Africa

Penguin Books Ltd., Registered Offices: 80 Strand, London WC2R 0RL, England

2009 SUPER HOROSCOPE GEMINI

The publishers regret that they cannot answer individual letters requesting personal horoscope information.

PRINTING HISTORY
Berkley trade paperback edition / July 2008

Berkley trade paperback ISBN: 978-0-425-21999-7

Library of Congress Cataloging-in-Publication Data

ISSN: 1535-895X

PRINTED IN THE UNITED STATES OF AMERICA

10 9 8 7 6 5 4 3 2 1

CONTENTS

THE CUSP-BORN GEMINI

Are you *really* a Gemini? If your birthday falls during the third week of May, at the beginning of Gemini, will you still retain the traits of Taurus, the sign of the Zodiac before Gemini? And what if you were born late in June—are you more Cancer than Gemini? Many people born at the edge, or cusp, of a sign have difficulty determining exactly what sign they are. If you are one of these people, here's how you can figure it out, once and for all.

Consult the cusp table on the facing page, then locate the year of your birth. The table will tell you the precise days on which the Sun entered and left your sign for the year of your birth. In that way you can determine if you are a true Gemini—or whether you are a Taurus or Cancer—according to the variations in cusp dates from year to year (see also page 17).

If you were born at the beginning or end of Gemini, yours is a lifetime reflecting a process of subtle transformation. Your life on Earth will symbolize a significant change in consciousness, for you are either about to enter a whole new way of living or are leaving one behind.

If you were born during the third week of May, you may want to read the horoscope book for Taurus as well as for Gemini, for Taurus holds the key to a hidden and often perplexing side of your personality—yet one that is the seed of your cosmic uplift and unfolding.

Mobility is your aim and variety your purpose. Yet you are drawn again and again to fixed, immobile Taurus. Your compulsion to settle down, find stability, wealth, and constancy attracts you to Taurus, and this attraction is a dilemma. For where is your true commitment? To variety—that old spice of life—or to the solid, substantial promise of Taurus?

At best, you symbolize the birth of perception, the capacity of the mind to know and communicate information.

If you were born during the fourth week of June, you may want to read the horoscope book for Cancer, as well as Gemini, for in Cancer you find not only financial security but a way of making all your assets grow.

You are about to settle down, about to dock your ship in a port and stay awhile; but there is a restlessness in you that is irrepressible. You are preparing to make yourself secure. You can be shrewd, money-minded, and practical despite your moodiness, naivete, and sometimes irksome adolescent approach to life.

Above all, you are a skilled manipulator of language and design and your powers of reason lie behind everything you think and do.

THE CUSPS OF GEMINI

DATES SUN ENTERS GEMINI (LEAVES TAURUS)

May 21 every year from 1900 to 2010, except for the following:

	May 20			May 22
1948	1972	1988	2000	1903
52	76	89	2001	07
56	80	92	2004	11
60	81	93	2005	19
64	84	96	2008	
68	85	97	2009	

DATES SUN ENTERS GEMINI (LEAVES CANCER)

June 21 every year from 1900 to 2010, except for the following:

June 20	June 22		
1988	1902	1915	1931
1992	03	18	35
1996	06	19	39
2000	07	22	43
2004	10	23	47
2008	11	26	51
	14	27	55

THE ASCENDANT: GEMINI RISING

Could you be a "double" Gemini? That is, could you have Gemini as your Rising sign as well as your Sun sign? The tables on pages 8–9 will tell you Geminis what your Rising sign happens to be. Just find the hour of your birth, then find the day of your birth, and you will see which sign of the Zodiac is your Ascendant, as the Rising sign is called. The Ascendant is called that because it is the sign rising on the eastern horizon at the time of your birth. For a more detailed discussion of the Rising sign and the twelve houses of the Zodiac, see pages 17–20.

The Ascendant, or Rising sign, is placed on the 1st house in a horoscope, of which there are twelve houses. The 1st house represents your response to the environment—your unique response. Call it identity, personality, ego, self-image, facade, come-on, body-mind-spirit—whatever term best conveys to you the meaning of the you that acts and reacts in the world. It is a you that is always changing, discovering a new you. Your identity started with birth and early environment, over which you had little conscious control, and continues to experience, to adjust, to express itself. The 1st house also represents how others see you. Has anyone ever guessed your sign to be your Rising sign? People may respond to that personality, that facade, that body type governed by your Rising sign.

Your Ascendant, or Rising sign, modifies your basic Sun sign personality, and it affects the way you act out the daily predictions for your Sun sign. If your Rising sign indeed is Gemini, what follows is a description of its effect on your horoscope. If your Rising sign is not Gemini, but some other sign of the Zodiac, you may wish to read the horoscope book for that sign as well.

With Gemini on the Ascendant, that is, in the 1st house, your ruling planet Mercury is therefore in the 1st house. Mercury in this position gives you a restless spirit, pushing you on a constant search for knowledge. You are always alert for new information, and your quest may take you far afield to explore unfamiliar subjects and even foreign lands. Mercury confers a subtle wariness that could be your best defense when people try to fool you or cheat you. On the other hand, that trait could be aggressively used as a weapon against people, giving rise to unworthy actions, tricks, or disputes.

The desire to express yourself will be very strong in your personality. You tend to rely on logic rather than intuition, and you could

6

go to great lengths to prove to yourself and to others the validity of your ideas. This need for expression combined with an equal need for variety gives your life a lot of surface drama: you are endlessly changing your focus of experience. In your lifetime you may hold a series of seemingly unrelated jobs; move frequently to new residences in unusual surroundings; make friends, drop them, pick them up again; change your world view often. Although other people may judge you to lack seriousness, that is not really so. You seek ideas and experience to help you understand and order your environment because you want from it maximal comfort and constant ego satisfaction.

Human contact is another large need for Gemini Rising individuals. It gives your desire to express yourself an audience. Yours is the sign of brothers and sisters, relatives, family. If you do not have a closely knit blood family, you will create a familylike network among friends, workmates, neighbors, and community contacts. You like to keep up with distant acquaintances, even ex-lovers, just so you can invite them to participate in one of your shindigs. And of course your home will be the center of attraction. For you are more than just tidy and fashionable; you know how to arrange a setting and accommodate people in order to stimulate the greatest communication between them.

Your youthful appearance and pleasing speaking voice attract people to you, and you know it. You are not above heightening the effect of these natural assets. You have been known to adapt your costuming to suit the occasion, and you sometimes manipulate your speech patterns to display emotions you don't feel or to invoke emotions in other people. As a result, you can be accused of self-centeredness.

Charm is your great natural talent; you do it with words, words, words. Gemini teachers can fascinate bored students into enjoying, let alone learning, a boring subject. Gemini adults can sweet-talk unruly youngsters into rational behavior. Gemini people in general lighten the lives of their friends with endless small talk about clothes, things, events, places, other people. You also enlighten your friends when you talk on that deeper, more sophisticated level of patterns of experience and cause and effect.

Writing and public speaking are arts that you with Gemini Rising can rely on consistently. Scholarly work is a possibility in your lifetime. Intellect is the key word that will allow you to understand any environment. Although your financial fortunes may change, your mercurial talents will deepen and survive.

RISING SIGNS FOR GEMINI

Hour of Birth*	Day of Birth		
	May 21–25	Mary 26–30	May 31–June 4
Midnight	Aquarius	Aquarius	Aquarius; Pisces 6/3
1 AM	Pisces	Pisces	Pisces
2 AM	Pisces; Aries 5/23	Aries	Aries
3 AM	Aries	Taurus	Taurus
4 AM	Taurus	Taurus	Taurus; Gemini 6/3
5 AM	Gemini	Gemini	Gemini
6 AM	Gemini	Gemini	Gemini; Cancer 6/2
7 AM	Cancer	Cancer	Cancer
8 AM	Cancer	Cancer	Cancer
9 AM	Cancer; Leo 5/24	Leo	Leo
10 AM	Leo	Leo	Leo
11 AM	Leo	Leo	Virgo
Noon	Virgo	Virgo	Virgo
1 PM	Virgo	Virgo	Virgo
2 PM	Virgo	Libra	Libra
3 PM	Libra	Libra	Libra
4 PM	Libra	Libra; Scorpio 5/25	Scorpio
5 PM	Scorpio	Scorpio	Scorpio
6 PM	Scorpio	Scorpio	Scorpio
7 PM	Scorpio; Sagittarius 5/23	Sagittarius	Sagittarius
8 PM	Sagittarius	Sagittarius	Sagittarius
9 PM	Sagittarius	Sagittarius; Capricorn 5/28	Capricorn
10 PM	Capricorn	Capricorn	Capricorn
11 PM	Capricorn	Aquarius	Aquarius

*Hour of birth given here is for Standard Time in any time zone. If your hour of birth was recorded in Daylight Saving Time, subtract one hour from it and consult that hour in the table above. For example, if you were born at 6 AM. D.S.T., see 5 AM above.

Hour of Birth*	Day of Birth		
	June 5–10	June 11–15	June 16–21
Midnight	Pisces	Pisces	Pisces
1 AM	Pisces; Aries 6/7	Aries	Aries
2 AM	Aries	Taurus	Taurus
3 AM	Taurus	Taurus	Taurus; Gemini 6/18
4 AM	Gemini	Gemini	Gemini
5 AM	Gemini	Gemini	Gemini; Cancer 6/17
6 AM	Cancer	Cancer	Cancer
7 AM	Cancer	Cancer	Cancer
8 AM	Cancer; Leo 6/8	Leo	Leo
9 AM	Leo	Leo	Leo
10 AM	Leo	Leo; Virgo 6/15	Virgo
11 AM	Virgo	Virgo	Virgo
Noon	Virgo	Virgo	Virgo
1 PM	Virgo; Libra 6/7	Libra	Libra
2 PM	Libra	Libra	Libra
3 PM	Libra	Libra; Scorpio 6/14	Scorpio
4 PM	Scorpio	Scorpio	Scorpio
5 PM	Scorpio	Scorpio	Scorpio
6 PM	Scorpio; Sagittarius 6/7	Sagittarius	Sagittarius
7 PM	Sagittarius	Sagittarius	Sagittarius
8 PM	Sagittarius	Sagittarius; Capricorn 6/12	Sagittarius
9 PM	Capricorn	Capricorn	Capricorn
10 PM	Capricorn	Aquarius	Aquarius
11 PM	Aquarius	Aquarius	Pisces

*See note on facing page.

THE PLACE OF ASTROLOGY IN TODAY'S WORLD

Does astrology have a place in the fast-moving, ultra-scientific world we live in today? Can it be justified in a sophisticated society whose outriders are already preparing to step off the moon into the deep space of the planets themselves? Or is it just a hangover of ancient superstition, a psychological dummy for neurotics and dreamers of every historical age?

These are the kind of questions that any inquiring person can be expected to ask when they approach a subject like astrology which goes beyond, but never excludes, the materialistic side of life.

The simple, single answer is that astrology works. It works for many millions of people in the western world alone. In the United States there are 10 million followers and in Europe, an estimated 25 million. America has more than 4000 practicing astrologers, Europe nearly three times as many. Even down-under Australia has its hundreds of thousands of adherents. In the eastern countries, astrology has enormous followings, again, because it has been proved to work. In India, for example, brides and grooms for centuries have been chosen on the basis of their astrological compatibility.

Astrology today is more vital than ever before, more practicable because all over the world the media devotes much space and time to it, more valid because science itself is confirming the precepts of astrological knowledge with every new exciting step. The ordinary person who daily applies astrology intelligently does not have to wonder whether it is true nor believe in it blindly. He can see it working for himself. And, if he can use it—and this book is designed to help the reader to do just that—he can make living a far richer experience, and become a more developed personality and a better person.

Astrology and Relationships

Astrology is the science of relationships. It is not just a study of planetary influences on man and his environment. It is the study of man himself.

We are at the center of our personal universe, of all our relationships. And our happiness or sadness depends on how we act, how we relate to the people and things that surround us. The emotions that we generate have a distinct effect—for better or worse—on the world around us. Our friends and our enemies will confirm this. Just look in the mirror the next time you are angry. In other words, each of us is a kind of sun or planet or star radiating our feelings on the environment around us. Our influence on our personal universe, whether loving, helpful, or destructive, varies with our changing moods, expressed through our individual character.

Our personal "radiations" are potent in the way they affect our moods and our ability to control them. But we usually are able to throw off our emotion in some sort of action—we have a good cry, walk it off, or tell someone our troubles—before it can build up too far and make us physically ill. Astrology helps us to understand the universal forces working on us, and through this understanding, we can become more properly adjusted to our surroundings so that we find ourselves coping where others may flounder.

The Challenge of Love

The challenge of love lies in recognizing the difference between infatuation, emotion, sex, and, sometimes, the intentional deceit of the other person. Mankind, with its record of broken marriages, despair, and disillusionment, is obviously not very good at making these distinctions.

Can astrology help?

Yes. In the same way that advance knowledge can usually help in any human situation. And there is probably no situation as human, as poignant, as pathetic and universal, as the failure of man's love.

Love, of course, is not just between man and woman. It involves love of children, parents, home, and friends. But the big problems usually involve the choice of partner.

Astrology has established degrees of compatibility that exist between people born under the various signs of the Zodiac. Because people are individuals, there are numerous variations and modifications. So the astrologer, when approached on mate and marriage matters, makes allowances for them. But the fact remains that some groups of people are suited for each other and some are not, and astrology has expressed this in terms of characteristics we all can study and use as a personal guide.

No matter how much enjoyment and pleasure we find in the different aspects of each other's character, if it is not an overall compatibility, the chances of our finding fulfillment or enduring happiness in each other are pretty hopeless. And astrology can help us to find someone compatible.

Astrology and Science

Closely related to our emotions is the "other side" of our personal universe, our physical welfare. Our body, of course, is largely influenced by things around us over which we have very little control. The phone rings, we hear it. The train runs late. We snag our stocking or cut our face shaving. Our body is under a constant bombardment of events that influence our daily lives to varying degrees.

The question that arises from all this is, what makes each of us act so that we have to involve other people and keep the ball of activity and evolution rolling? This is the question that both science and astrology are involved with. The scientists have attacked it from different angles: anthropology, the study of human evolution as body, mind and response to environment; anatomy, the study of bodily structure; psychology, the science of the human mind; and so on. These studies have produced very impressive classifications and valuable information, but because the approach to the problem is fragmented, so is the result. They remain "branches" of science. Science generally studies effects. It keeps turning up wonderful answers but no lasting solutions. Astrology, on the other hand, approaches the question from the broader viewpoint. Astrology began its inquiry with the totality of human experience and saw it as an effect. It then looked to find the cause, or at least the prime movers, and during thousands of years of observation of man and his *universal* environment came up with the extraordinary principle of planetary influence—or astrology, which, from the Greek, means the science of the stars.

Modern science, as we shall see, has confirmed much of astrology's foundations—most of it unintentionally, some of it reluctantly, but still, indisputably.

It is not difficult to imagine that there must be a connection between outer space and Earth. Even today, scientists are not too sure how our Earth was created, but it is generally agreed that it is only a tiny part of the universe. And as a part of the universe, people on Earth see and feel the influence of heavenly bodies in almost every aspect of our existence. There is no doubt that the Sun has the greatest influence on life on this planet. Without it there would be no life, for without it there would be no warmth, no division into day and night, no cycles of time or season at all. This is clear and easy to see. The influence of the Moon, on the other hand, is more subtle, though no less definite.

There are many ways in which the influence of the Moon manifests itself here on Earth, both on human and animal life. It is a well-known fact, for instance, that the large movements of water on our planet—that is the ebb and flow of the tides—are caused by the Moon's gravitational pull. Since this is so, it follows that these water movements do not occur only in the oceans, but that all bodies of water are affected, even down to the tiniest puddle.

The human body, too, which consists of about 70 percent water, falls within the scope of this lunar influence. For example the menstrual cycle of most women corresponds to the 28-day lunar month; the period of pregnancy in humans is 273 days, or equal to nine lunar months. Similarly, many illnesses reach a crisis at the change of the Moon, and statistics in many countries have shown that the crime rate is highest at the time of the Full Moon. Even human sexual desire has been associated with the phases of the Moon. But it is in the movement of the tides that we get the clearest demonstration of planetary influence, which leads to the irresistible correspondence between the so-called metaphysical and the physical.

Tide tables are prepared years in advance by calculating the future positions of the Moon. Science has known for a long time that the Moon is the main cause of tidal action. But only in the last few years has it begun to realize the possible extent of this influence on mankind. To begin with, the ocean tides do not rise and fall as we might imagine from our personal observations of them. The Moon as it orbits around Earth sets up a circular wave of attraction which pulls the oceans of the world after it, broadly in an east to west direction. This influence is like a phantom wave crest, a loop of power stretching from pole to pole which passes over and around the Earth like an invisible shadow. It travels with equal effect across the land masses and, as scientists were recently amazed to observe, caused oysters placed in the dark in the middle of the United States where there is no sea to open their shells to receive the nonexistent tide. If the land-locked oysters react to this invisible signal, what effect does it have on us who not so long ago in evolutionary time came out of the sea and still have its salt in our blood and sweat?

Less well known is the fact that the Moon is also the primary force behind the circulation of blood in human beings and animals, and the movement of sap in trees and plants. Agriculturists have established that the Moon has a distinct influence on crops, which explains why for centuries people have planted according to Moon cycles. The habits of many animals, too, are directed by the movement of the Moon. Migratory birds, for instance, depart only at or near the time of the Full Moon. And certain sea creatures, eels in particular, move only in accordance with certain phases of the Moon.

Know Thyself—Why?

In today's fast-changing world, everyone still longs to know what the future holds. It is the one thing that everyone has in common: rich and poor, famous and infamous, all are deeply concerned about tomorrow.

But the key to the future, as every historian knows, lies in the past. This is as true of individual people as it is of nations. You cannot understand your future without first understanding your past, which is simply another way of saying that you must first of all know yourself.

The motto "know thyself" seems obvious enough nowadays, but it was originally put forward as the foundation of wisdom by the ancient Greek philosophers. It was then adopted by the "mystery religions" of the ancient Middle East, Greece, Rome, and is still used in all genuine schools of mind training or mystical discipline, both in those of the East, based on yoga, and those of the West. So it is universally accepted now, and has been through the ages.

But how do you go about discovering what sort of person you are? The first step is usually classification into some sort of system of types. Astrology did this long before the birth of Christ. Psychology has also done it. So has modern medicine, in its way.

One system classifies people according to the source of the impulses they respond to most readily: the muscles, leading to direct bodily action; the digestive organs, resulting in emotion; or the brain and nerves, giving rise to thinking. Another such system says that character is determined by the endocrine glands, and gives us such labels as "pituitary," "thyroid," and "hyperthyroid" types. These different systems are neither contradictory nor mutually exclusive. In fact, they are very often different ways of saying the same thing.

Very popular, useful classifications were devised by Carl Jung, the eminent disciple of Freud. Jung observed among the different faculties of the mind, four which have a predominant influence on character. These four faculties exist in all of us without exception, but not in perfect balance. So when we say, for instance, that someone is a "thinking type," it means that in any situation he or she tries to be rational. Emotion, which may be the opposite of thinking, will be his or her weakest function. This thinking type can be sensible and reasonable, or calculating and unsympathetic. The emotional type, on the other hand, can often be recognized by exaggerated language—everything is either marvelous or terrible—and in extreme cases they even invent dramas and quarrels out of nothing just to make life more interesting.

The other two faculties are intuition and physical sensation. The sensation type does not only care for food and drink, nice clothes and furniture; he or she is also interested in all forms of physical experience. Many scientists are sensation types as are athletes and nature-lovers. Like sensation, intuition is a form of perception and we all possess it. But it works through that part of the mind which is not under conscious control—consequently it sees meanings and connections which are not obvious to thought or emotion. Inventors and original thinkers are always intuitive, but so, too, are superstitious people who see meanings where none exist.

Thus, sensation tells us what is going on in the world, feeling (that is, emotion) tells us how important it is to ourselves, thinking enables us to interpret it and work out what we should do about it, and intuition tells us what it means to ourselves and others. All four faculties are essential, and all are present in every one of us. But some people are guided chiefly by one, others by another. In addition, Jung also observed a division of the human personality into the extrovert and the introvert, which cuts across these four types.

A disadvantage of all these systems of classification is that one cannot tell very easily where to place oneself. Some people are reluctant to admit that they act to please their emotions. So they deceive themselves for years by trying to belong to whichever type they think is the "best." Of course, there is no best; each has its faults and each has its good points.

The advantage of the signs of the Zodiac is that they simplify classification. Not only that, but your date of birth is personal—

it is unarguably yours. What better way to know yourself than by going back as far as possible to the very moment of your birth? And this is precisely what your horoscope is all about, as we shall see in the next section.

WHAT IS A HOROSCOPE?

If you had been able to take a picture of the skies at the moment of your birth, that photograph would be your horoscope. Lacking such a snapshot, it is still possible to recreate the picture—and this is at the basis of the astrologer's art. In other words, your horoscope is a representation of the skies with the planets in the exact positions they occupied at the time you were born.

The year of birth tells an astrologer the positions of the distant, slow-moving planets Jupiter, Saturn, Uranus, Neptune, and Pluto. The month of birth indicates the Sun sign, or birth sign as it is commonly called, as well as indicating the positions of the rapidly moving planets Venus, Mercury, and Mars. The day and time of birth will locate the position of our Moon. And the moment—the exact hour and minute—of birth determines the houses through what is called the Ascendant, or Rising sign.

With this information the astrologer consults various tables to calculate the specific positions of the Sun, Moon, and other planets relative to your birthplace at the moment you were born. Then he or she locates them by means of the Zodiac.

The Zodiac

The Zodiac is a band of stars (constellations) in the skies, centered on the Sun's apparent path around the Earth, and is divided into twelve equal segments, or signs. What we are actually dividing up is the Earth's path around the Sun. But from our point of view here on Earth, it seems as if the Sun is making a great circle around our planet in the sky, so we say it is the Sun's apparent path. This twelvefold division, the Zodiac, is a reference system for the astrologer. At any given moment the planets—and in astrology both the Sun and Moon are considered to be planets—can all be located at a specific point along this path.

Now where in all this are you, the subject of the horoscope? Your character is largely determined by the sign the Sun is in. So that is where the astrologer looks first in your horoscope, at your Sun sign.

The Sun Sign and the Cusp

There are twelve signs in the Zodiac, and the Sun spends approximately one month in each sign. But because of the motion of the Earth around the Sun—the Sun's apparent motion—the dates when the Sun enters and leaves each sign may change from year to year. Some people born near the cusp, or edge, of a sign have difficulty determining which is their Sun sign. But in this book a Table of Cusps is provided for the years 1900 to 2010 (page 5) so you can find out what your true Sun sign is.

Here are the twelve signs of the Zodiac, their ancient zodiacal symbol, and the dates when the Sun enters and leaves each sign for the year 2009. Remember, these dates may change from year to year.

ARIES	Ram	March 20–April 19
TAURUS	Bull	April 19–May 20
GEMINI	Twins	May 20–June 21
CANCER	Crab	June 21–July 22
LEO	Lion	July 22–August 22
VIRGO	Virgin	August 22–September 22
LIBRA	Scales	September 22–October 23
SCORPIO	Scorpion	October 23–November 22
SAGITTARIUS	Archer	November 22–December 21
CAPRICORN	Sea Goat	December 21–January 19
AQUARIUS	Water Bearer	January 19–February 18
PISCES	Fish	February 18–March 20

It is possible to draw significant conclusions and make meaningful predictions based simply on the Sun sign of a person. There are many people who have been amazed at the accuracy of the description of their own character based only on the Sun sign. But an astrologer needs more information than just your Sun sign to interpret the photograph that is your horoscope.

The Rising Sign and the Zodiacal Houses

An astrologer needs the exact time and place of your birth in order to construct and interpret your horoscope. The illustration on the next page shows the flat chart, or natural wheel, an astrologer uses. Note the inner circle of the wheel labeled 1 through 12. These 12 divisions are known as the houses of the Zodiac.

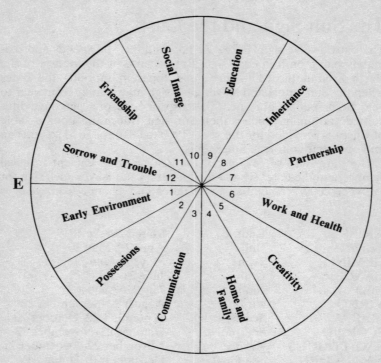

The 1st house always starts from the position marked E, which corresponds to the eastern horizon. The rest of the houses 2 through 12 follow around in a "counterclockwise" direction. The point where each house starts is known as a cusp, or edge.

The cusp, or edge, of the 1st house (point E) is where an astrologer would place your Rising sign, the Ascendant. And, as already noted, the exact time of your birth determines your Rising sign. Let's see how this works.

As the Earth rotates on its axis once every 24 hours, each one of the twelve signs of the Zodiac appears to be "rising" on the horizon, with a new one appearing about every 2 hours. Actually it is the turning of the Earth that exposes each sign to view, but in our astrological work we are discussing apparent motion. This Rising sign marks the Ascendant, and it colors the whole orientation of a horoscope. It indicates the sign governing the 1st house of the chart, and will thus determine which signs will govern all the other houses.

To visualize this idea, imagine two color wheels with twelve divisions superimposed upon each other. For just as the Zodiac is divided into twelve constellations that we identify as the signs, another twelvefold division is used to denote the houses. Now imagine one wheel (the signs) moving slowly while the other wheel (the houses) remains still. This analogy may help you see how the signs keep shifting the "color" of the houses as the Rising sign continues to change every two hours. To simplify things, a Table of Rising Signs has been provided (pages 8–9) for your specific Sun sign.

Once your Rising sign has been placed on the cusp of the 1st house, the signs that govern the rest of the 11 houses can be placed on the chart. In any individual's horoscope the signs do not necessarily correspond with the houses. For example, it could be that a sign covers part of two adjacent houses. It is the interpretation of such variations in an individual's horoscope that marks the professional astrologer.

But to gain a workable understanding of astrology, it is not necessary to go into great detail. In fact, we just need a description of the houses and their meanings, as is shown in the illustration above and in the table below.

THE 12 HOUSES OF THE ZODIAC

1st	Individuality, body appearance, general outlook on life	Personality house
2nd	Finance, possessions, ethical principles, gain or loss	Money house
3rd	Relatives, communication, short journeys, writing, education	Relatives house
4th	Family and home, parental ties, land and property, security	Home house
5th	Pleasure, children, creativity, entertainment, risk	Pleasure house
6th	Health, harvest, hygiene, work and service, employees	Health house
7th	Marriage and divorce, the law, partnerships and alliances	Marriage house
8th	Inheritance, secret deals, sex, death, regeneration	Inheritance house
9th	Travel, sports, study, philosophy Ω house	Travel house
10th	Career, social standing, success and honor	Business house
11th	Friendship, social life, hopes and wishes	Friends house
12th	Troubles, illness, secret enemies, hidden agendas	Trouble house

The Planets in the Houses

An astrologer, knowing the exact time and place of your birth, will use tables of planetary motion in order to locate the planets in your horoscope chart. He or she will determine which planet or planets are in which sign and in which house. It is not uncommon, in an individual's horoscope, for there to be two or more planets in the same sign and in the same house.

The characteristics of the planets modify the influence of the Sun according to their natures and strengths.

Sun: Source of life. Basic temperament according to the Sun sign. The conscious will. Human potential.

Moon: Emotions. Moods. Customs. Habits. Changeable. Adaptive. Nurturing.

Mercury: Communication. Intellect. Reasoning power. Curiosity. Short travels.

Venus: Love. Delight. Charm. Harmony. Balance. Art. Beautiful possessions.

Mars: Energy. Initiative. War. Anger. Adventure. Courage. Daring. Impulse.

Jupiter: Luck. Optimism. Generous. Expansive. Opportunities. Protection.

Saturn: Pessimism. Privation. Obstacles. Delay. Hard work. Research. Lasting rewards after long struggle.

Uranus: Fashion. Electricity. Revolution. Independence. Freedom. Sudden changes. Modern science.

Neptune: Sensationalism. Theater. Dreams. Inspiration. Illusion. Deception.

Pluto: Creation and destruction. Total transformation. Lust for power. Strong obsessions.

Superimpose the characteristics of the planets on the functions of the house in which they appear. Express the result through the character of the Sun sign, and you will get the basic idea.

Of course, many other considerations have been taken into account in producing the carefully worked out predictions in this book: the aspects of the planets to each other; their strength according to position and sign; whether they are in a house of exaltation or decline; whether they are natural enemies or not; whether a planet occupies its own sign; the position of a planet in relation to its own house or sign; whether the sign is male or female; whether the sign is a fire, earth, water, or air sign. These are only a few of the colors on the astrologer's pallet which he or she must mix with the inspiration of the artist and the accuracy of the mathematician.

How To Use These Predictions

A person reading the predictions in this book should understand that they are produced from the daily position of the planets for a group of people and are not, of course, individually specialized. To get the full benefit of them our readers should relate the predictions to their own character and circumstances, coordinate them, and draw their own conclusions from them.

If you are a serious observer of your own life, you should find a definite pattern emerging that will be a helpful and reliable guide.

The point is that we always retain our free will. The stars indicate certain directional tendencies but we are not compelled to follow. We can do or not do, and wisdom must make the choice.

We all have our good and bad days. Sometimes they extend into cycles of weeks. It is therefore advisable to study daily predictions in a span ranging from the day before to several days ahead.

Daily predictions should be taken very generally. The word "difficult" does not necessarily indicate a whole day of obstruction or inconvenience. It is a warning to you to be cautious. Your caution will often see you around the difficulty before you are involved. This is the correct use of astrology.

In another section (pages 78–84), detailed information is given about the influence of the Moon as it passes through each of the twelve signs of the Zodiac. There are instructions on how to use the Moon Tables (pages 85–92), which provide Moon Sign Dates throughout the year as well as the Moon's role in health and daily affairs. This information should be used in conjunction with the daily forecasts to give a fuller picture of the astrological trends.

HISTORY OF ASTROLOGY

The origins of astrology have been lost far back in history, but we do know that reference is made to it as far back as the first written records of the human race. It is not hard to see why. Even in primitive times, people must have looked for an explanation for the various happenings in their lives. They must have wanted to know why people were different from one another. And in their search they turned to the regular movements of the Sun, Moon, and stars to see if they could provide an answer.

It is interesting to note that as soon as man learned to use his tools in any type of design, or his mind in any kind of calculation, he turned his attention to the heavens. Ancient cave dwellings reveal dim crescents and circles representative of the Sun and Moon, rulers of day and night. Mesopotamia and the civilization of Chaldea, in itself the foundation of those of Babylonia and Assyria, show a complete picture of astronomical observation and well-developed astrological interpretation.

Humanity has a natural instinct for order. The study of anthropology reveals that primitive people—even as far back as prehistoric times—were striving to achieve a certain order in their lives. They tried to organize the apparent chaos of the universe. They had the desire to attach meaning to things. This demand for order has persisted throughout the history of man. So that observing the regularity of the heavenly bodies made it logical that primitive peoples should turn heavenward in their search for an understanding of the world in which they found themselves so random and alone.

And they did find a significance in the movements of the stars. Shepherds tending their flocks, for instance, observed that when the cluster of stars now known as the constellation Aries was in sight, it was the time of fertility and they associated it with the Ram. And they noticed that the growth of plants and plant life corresponded with different phases of the Moon, so that certain times were favorable for the planting of crops, and other times were not. In this way, there grew up a tradition of seasons and causes connected with the passage of the Sun through the twelve signs of the Zodiac.

Astrology was valued so highly that the king was kept informed of the daily and monthly changes in the heavenly bodies, and the results of astrological studies regarding events of the future. Head astrologers were clearly men of great rank and position, and the office was said to be a hereditary one.

Omens were taken, not only from eclipses and conjunctions of the Moon or Sun with one of the planets, but also from storms and earthquakes. In the eastern civilizations, particularly, the reverence inspired by astrology appears to have remained unbroken since the very earliest days. In ancient China, astrology, astronomy, and religion went hand in hand. The astrologer, who was also an astronomer, was part of the official government service and had his own corner in the Imperial Palace. The duties of the Imperial astrologer, whose office was one of the most important in the land, were clearly defined, as this extract from early records shows:

> This exalted gentleman must concern himself with the stars in the heavens, keeping a record of the changes and movements of the Planets, the Sun and the Moon, in order to examine the movements of the terrestrial world with the object of prognosticating good and bad fortune. He divides the territories of the nine regions of the empire in accordance with their dependence on particular celestial bodies. All the fiefs and principalities are connected with the stars and from this their prosperity or misfortune should be ascertained. He makes prognostications according to the twelve years of the Jupiter cycle of good and evil of the terrestrial world. From the colors of the five kinds of clouds, he determines the coming of floods or droughts, abundance or famine. From the twelve winds, he draws conclusions about the state of harmony of heaven and earth, and takes note of good and bad signs that result from their accord or disaccord. In general, he concerns himself with five kinds of phenomena so as to warn the Emperor to come to the aid of the government and to allow for variations in the ceremonies according to their circumstances.

The Chinese were also keen observers of the fixed stars, giving them such unusual names as Ghost Vehicle, Sun of Imperial Concubine, Imperial Prince, Pivot of Heaven, Twinkling Brilliance, Weaving Girl. But, great astrologers though they may have been, the Chinese lacked one aspect of mathematics that the Greeks applied to astrology—deductive geometry. Deductive geometry was the basis of much classical astrology in and after the time of the Greeks, and this explains the different methods of prognostication used in the East and West.

Down through the ages the astrologer's art has depended, not so much on the uncovering of new facts, though this is important, as on the interpretation of the facts already known. This is the essence of the astrologer's skill.

But why should the signs of the Zodiac have any effect at all on the formation of human character? It is easy to see why people thought they did, and even now we constantly use astrological expressions in our everyday speech. The thoughts of "lucky star," "ill-fated," "star-crossed," "mooning around," are interwoven into the very structure of our language.

Wherever the concept of the Zodiac is understood and used, it could well appear to have an influence on the human character. Does this mean, then, that the human race, in whose civilization the idea of the twelve signs of the Zodiac has long been embedded, is divided into only twelve types? Can we honestly believe that it is really as simple as that? If so, there must be pretty wide ranges of variation within each type. And if, to explain the variation, we call in heredity and environment, experiences in early childhood, the thyroid and other glands, and also the four functions of the mind together with extroversion and introversion, then one begins to wonder if the original classification was worth making at all. No sensible person believes that his favorite system explains everything. But even so, he will not find the system much use at all if it does not even save him the trouble of bothering with the others.

In the same way, if we were to put every person under only one sign of the Zodiac, the system becomes too rigid and unlike life. Besides, it was never intended to be used like that. It may be convenient to have only twelve types, but we know that in practice there is every possible gradation between aggressiveness and timidity, or between conscientiousness and laziness. How, then, do we account for this?

A person born under any given Sun sign can be mainly influenced by one or two of the other signs that appear in their individual horoscope. For instance, famous persons born under the sign of Gemini include Henry VIII, whom nothing and no one could have induced to abdicate, and Edward VIII, who did just that. Obviously, then, the sign Gemini does not fully explain the complete character of either of them.

Again, under the opposite sign, Sagittarius, were both Stalin, who was totally consumed with the notion of power, and Charles V, who freely gave up an empire because he preferred to go into a monastery. And we find under Scorpio many uncompromising characters such as Luther, de Gaulle, Indira Gandhi, and Montgomery, but also Petain, a successful commander whose name later became synonymous with collaboration.

A single sign is therefore obviously inadequate to explain the differences between people; it can only explain resemblances, such as the combativeness of the Scorpio group, or the far-reaching devotion of Charles V and Stalin to their respective ideals—the Christian heaven and the Communist utopia.

But very few people have only one sign in their horoscope chart.

In addition to the month of birth, the day and, even more, the hour to the nearest minute if possible, ought to be considered. Without this, it is impossible to have an actual horoscope, for the word horoscope literally means "a consideration of the hour."

The month of birth tells you only which sign of the Zodiac was occupied by the Sun. The day and hour tell you what sign was occupied by the Moon. And the minute tells you which sign was rising on the eastern horizon. This is called the Ascendant, and, as some astrologers believe, it is supposed to be the most important thing in the whole horoscope.

The Sun is said to signify one's heart, that is to say, one's deepest desires and inmost nature. This is quite different from the Moon, which signifies one's superficial way of behaving. When the ancient Romans referred to the Emperor Augustus as a Capricorn, they meant that he had the Moon in Capricorn. Or, to take another example, a modern astrologer would call Disraeli a Scorpion because he had Scorpio Rising, but most people would call him Sagittarius because he had the Sun there. The Romans would have called him Leo because his Moon was in Leo.

So if one does not seem to fit one's birth month, it is always worthwhile reading the other signs, for one may have been born at a time when any of them were rising or occupied by the Moon. It also seems to be the case that the influence of the Sun develops as life goes on, so that the month of birth is easier to guess in people over the age of forty. The young are supposed to be influenced mainly by their Ascendant, the Rising sign, which characterizes the body and physical personality as a whole.

It is nonsense to assume that all people born at a certain time will exhibit the same characteristics, or that they will even behave in the same manner. It is quite obvious that, from the very moment of its birth, a child is subject to the effects of its environment, and that this in turn will influence its character and heritage to a decisive extent. Also to be taken into account are education and economic conditions, which play a very important part in the formation of one's character as well.

People have, in general, certain character traits and qualities which, according to their environment, develop in either a positive or a negative manner. Therefore, selfishness (inherent selfishness, that is) might emerge as unselfishness; kindness and consideration as cruelty and lack of consideration toward others. In the same way, a naturally constructive person may, through frustration, become destructive, and so on. The latent characteristics with which people are born can, therefore, through environment and good or bad training, become something that would appear to be its opposite, and so give the lie to the astrologer's description of their character.

But this is not the case. The true character is still there, but it is buried deep beneath these external superficialities.

Careful study of the character traits of various signs of the Zodiac are of immeasurable help, and can render beneficial service to the intelligent person. Undoubtedly, the reader will already have discovered that, while he is able to get on very well with some people, he just "cannot stand" others. The causes sometimes seem inexplicable. At times there is intense dislike, at other times immediate sympathy. And there is, too, the phenomenon of love at first sight, which is also apparently inexplicable. People appear to be either sympathetic or unsympathetic toward each other for no apparent reason.

Now if we look at this in the light of the Zodiac, we find that people born under different signs are either compatible or incompatible with each other. In other words, there are good and bad interrelating factors among the various signs. This does not, of course, mean that humanity can be divided into groups of hostile camps. It would be quite wrong to be hostile or indifferent toward people who happen to be born under an incompatible sign. There is no reason why everybody should not, or cannot, learn to control and adjust their feelings and actions, especially after they are aware of the positive qualities of other people by studying their character analyses, among other things.

Every person born under a certain sign has both positive and negative qualities, which are developed more or less according to our free will. Nobody is entirely good or entirely bad, and it is up to each of us to learn to control ourselves on the one hand and at the same time to endeavor to learn about ourselves and others.

It cannot be emphasized often enough that it is free will that determines whether we will make really good use of our talents and abilities. Using our free will, we can either overcome our failings or allow them to rule us. Our free will enables us to exert sufficient willpower to control our failings so that they do not harm ourselves or others.

Astrology can reveal our inclinations and tendencies. Astrology can tell us about ourselves so that we are able to use our free will to overcome our shortcomings. In this way astrology helps us do our best to become needed and valuable members of society as well as helpmates to our family and our friends. Astrology also can save us a great deal of unhappiness and remorse.

Yet it may seem absurd that an ancient philosophy could be a prop to modern men and women. But below the materialistic surface of modern life, there are hidden streams of feeling and thought. Symbology is reappearing as a study worthy of the scholar; the psychosomatic factor in illness has passed from the writings of the crank to those of the specialist; spiritual healing in all its forms is no longer a pious hope but an accepted phenomenon. And it is into this context that we consider astrology, in the sense that it is an analysis of human types.

Astrology and medicine had a long journey together, and only parted company a couple of centuries ago. There still remain in medical language such astrological terms as "saturnine," "choleric," and "mercurial," used in the diagnosis of physical tendencies. The herbalist, for long the handyman of the medical profession, has been dominated by astrology since the days of the Greeks. Certain herbs traditionally respond to certain planetary influences, and diseases must therefore be treated to ensure harmony between the medicine and the disease.

But the stars are expected to foretell and not only to diagnose.

Astrological forecasting has been remarkably accurate, but often it is wide of the mark. The brave person who cares to predict world events takes dangerous chances. Individual forecasting is less clear cut; it can be a help or a disillusionment. Then we come to the nagging question: if it is possible to foreknow, is it right to foretell? This is a point of ethics on which it is hard to pronounce judgment. The doctor faces the same dilemma if he finds that symptoms of a mortal disease are present in his patient and that he can only prognosticate a steady decline. How much to tell an individual in a crisis is a problem that has perplexed many distinguished scholars. Honest and conscientious astrologers in this modern world, where so many people are seeking guidance, face the same problem.

Five hundred years ago it was customary to call in a learned man who was an astrologer who was probably also a doctor and a philosopher. By his knowledge of astrology, his study of planetary influences, he felt himself qualified to guide those in distress. The world has moved forward at a fantastic rate since then, and yet people are still uncertain of themselves. At first sight it seems fantastic in the light of modern thinking that they turn to the most ancient of all studies, and get someone to calculate a horoscope for them. But is it really so fantastic if you take a second look? For astrology is concerned with tomorrow, with survival. And in a world such as ours, tomorrow and survival are the keywords for the twenty-first century.

ASTROLOGICAL BRIDGE TO THE 21st CENTURY

Themes connecting past, present, and future are in play as the first decade reveals hidden paths and personal hints for achieving your potential. Make the most of the messages from the planets.

With the dawning of the twenty-first century look first to Jupiter, the planet of good fortune. Each new yearly Jupiter cycle follows the natural progression of the Zodiac. First is Jupiter in Aries and in Taurus through spring 2000, next Jupiter is in Gemini to summer 2001, then in Cancer to midsummer 2002, in Leo to late summer 2003, in Virgo to early autumn 2004, in Libra to midautumn 2005, and so on through Jupiter in Pisces through June 2010. The beneficent planet Jupiter promotes your professional and educational goals while urging informed choice and deliberation, providing a rich medium for creativity. Planet Jupiter's influence is protective, the generous helper that comes to the rescue just in the nick of time. And while safeguarding good luck, Jupiter can turn unusual risks into achievable aims.

In order to take advantage of luck and opportunity, to gain wisdom from experience, to persevere against adversity, look to beautiful planet Saturn. Saturn, planet of reason and responsibility, began a new cycle in earthy Taurus at the turn of the century. Saturn in Taurus until spring 2001 inspires industry and affection, blends practicality and imagination, all the while inviting caution and care. Saturn in Taurus lends beauty, order, and structure to your life. Then Saturn is in Gemini, the sign of mind and communication, until June 2003. Saturn in Gemini gives a lively intellectual capacity, so the limits of creativity can be stretched and boundaries broken. Saturn in Gemini holds the promise of fruitful endeavor through sustained study, learning, and application. Saturn in Cancer from early June 2003 to mid-July 2005 poses issues of long-term security versus immediate gratification. Rely on deliberation and choice to make sense out of diversity and change. Saturn in Cancer can be a revealing cycle, leading to the desired outcomes of growth and maturity. Saturn in Leo from mid-July 2005 to early September 2007 can be a test of boldness versus caution. Here every challenge must be met with benevolent authority, matched by a caring and generous outlook. Saturn in Virgo early September 2007 into October 2009 sharpens and deepens the mind. Saturn in Virgo presents chances to excel, to gain prominence through good words and good works. Saturn in Libra end of October 2009 into November 2012 promotes artistry, balance, goodwill, and peace.

Uranus, planet of innovation and surprise, started an important new cycle in January of 1996. At that time Uranus entered its natural home in airy Aquarius. Uranus in Aquarius into the year 2003 has a profound effect on your personality and the lens through which you see the world. A basic change in the way you project yourself is just one impact of Uranus in Aquarius. More significantly, a whole new consciousness is evolving. Winds of change blowing your way emphasize movement and freedom. Uranus in Aquarius poses involvement in the larger community beyond self, family, friends, lovers, associates. Radical ideas and progressive thought signal a journey of liberation. As the new century begins, follow Uranus on the path of humanitarianism. A new Uranus cycle begins March 2003 when Uranus visits Pisces, briefly revisits Aquarius, then returns late in 2003 to Pisces where it will stay into May 2010. Uranus in Pisces, a strongly intuitive force, urges work and service for the good of humankind to make the world a better place for all people.

Neptune, planet of vision and mystery, is enjoying a long cycle that excites creativity and imaginative thinking. Neptune is in airy Aquarius from November 1998 to February of 2012. Neptune in Aquarius, the sign of the Water Bearer, represents two sides of the coin of wisdom: inspiration and reason. Here Neptune stirs powerful currents bearing a rich and varied harvest, the fertile breeding ground for idealistic aims and practical considerations. Neptune's fine intuition tunes in to your dreams, your imagination, your spirituality. You can never turn your back on the mysteries of life. Uranus and Neptune, the planets of enlightenment and idealism, give you glimpses into the future, letting you peek through secret doorways into the twenty-first century.

Pluto, dwarf planet of beginnings and endings, started a new cycle of transformative power in the year 2008. Pluto entered the earthy sign of Capricorn and journeys there for sixteen years until 2024. Pluto in Capricorn over the course of this extensive journey has the capacity to change the landscape as well as the humanscape. The transforming energy of Pluto combines with the persevering power of Capricorn to give depth and character to potential change. Pluto in Capricorn can bring focus and cohesion to disparate, diverse creativities. As new forms arise and take root, Pluto in Capricorn organizes the rebuilding process. Freedom versus limitation, freedom versus authority is part of the picture. Reasonableness struggles with recklessness to solve divisive issues. Pluto in Capricorn can teach important lessons about adversity, and the lessons will be learned.

THE SIGNS OF THE ZODIAC

Dominant Characteristics

Aries: March 21–April 20

The Positive Side of Aries

The Aries has many positive points to his character. People born under this first sign of the Zodiac are often quite strong and enthusiastic. On the whole, they are forward-looking people who are not easily discouraged by temporary setbacks. They know what they want out of life and they go out after it. Their personalities are strong. Others are usually quite impressed by the Ram's way of doing things. Quite often they are sources of inspiration for others traveling the same route. Aries men and women have a special zest for life that can be contagious; for others, they are a fine example of how life should be lived.

The Aries person usually has a quick and active mind. He is imaginative and inventive. He enjoys keeping busy and active. He generally gets along well with all kinds of people. He is interested in mankind, as a whole. He likes to be challenged. Some would say he thrives on opposition, for it is when he is set against that he often does his best. Getting over or around obstacles is a challenge he generally enjoys. All in all, Aries is quite positive and young-thinking. He likes to keep abreast of new things that are happening in the world. Aries are often fond of speed. They like things to be done quickly, and this sometimes aggravates their slower colleagues and associates.

The Aries man or woman always seems to remain young. Their whole approach to life is youthful and optimistic. They never say die, no matter what the odds. They may have an occasional setback, but it is not long before they are back on their feet again.

The Negative Side of Aries

Everybody has his less positive qualities—and Aries is no exception. Sometimes the Aries man or woman is not very tactful in communicating with others; in his hurry to get things done he is apt to be a little callous or inconsiderate. Sensitive people are likely to find him somewhat sharp-tongued in some situations. Often in his eagerness to get the show on the road, he misses the mark altogether and cannot achieve his aims.

At times Aries can be too impulsive. He can occasionally be stubborn and refuse to listen to reason. If things do not move quickly enough to suit the Aries man or woman, he or she is apt to become rather nervous or irritable. The uncultivated Aries is not unfamiliar with moments of doubt and fear. He is capable of being destructive if he does not get his way. He can overcome some of his emotional problems by steadily trying to express himself as he really is, but this requires effort.

Taurus: April 21–May 20

The Positive Side of Taurus

The Taurus person is known for his ability to concentrate and for his tenacity. These are perhaps his strongest qualities. The Taurus man or woman generally has very little trouble in getting along with others; it's his nature to be helpful toward people in need. He can always be depended on by his friends, especially those in trouble.

Taurus generally achieves what he wants through his ability to persevere. He never leaves anything unfinished but works on something until it has been completed. People can usually take him at his word; he is honest and forthright in most of his dealings. The Taurus person has a good chance to make a success of his life because of his many positive qualities. The Taurus who aims high seldom falls short of his mark. He learns well by experience. He is thorough and does not believe in shortcuts of any kind. The Bull's thoroughness pays off in the end, for through his deliberateness he learns how to rely on himself and what he has learned. The Taurus person tries to get along with others, as a rule. He is not overly critical and likes people to be themselves. He is a tolerant person and enjoys peace and harmony—especially in his home life.

Taurus is usually cautious in all that he does. He is not a person

who believes in taking unnecessary risks. Before adopting any one line of action, he will weigh all of the pros and cons. The Taurus person is steadfast. Once his mind is made up it seldom changes. The person born under this sign usually is a good family person—reliable and loving.

The Negative Side of Taurus

Sometimes the Taurus man or woman is a bit too stubborn. He won't listen to other points of view if his mind is set on something. To others, this can be quite annoying. Taurus also does not like to be told what to do. He becomes rather angry if others think him not too bright. He does not like to be told he is wrong, even when he is. He dislikes being contradicted.

Some people who are born under this sign are very suspicious of others—even of those persons close to them. They find it difficult to trust people fully. They are often afraid of being deceived or taken advantage of. The Bull often finds it difficult to forget or forgive. His love of material things sometimes makes him rather avaricious and petty.

Gemini: May 21–June 20

The Positive Side of Gemini

The person born under this sign of the Heavenly Twins is usually quite bright and quick-witted. Some of them are capable of doing many different things. The Gemini person very often has many different interests. He keeps an open mind and is always anxious to learn new things.

Gemini is often an analytical person. He is a person who enjoys making use of his intellect. He is governed more by his mind than by his emotions. He is a person who is not confined to one view; he can often understand both sides to a problem or question. He knows how to reason, how to make rapid decisions if need be.

He is an adaptable person and can make himself at home almost anywhere. There are all kinds of situations he can adapt to. He is a person who seldom doubts himself; he is sure of his talents and his ability to think and reason. Gemini is generally most satisfied when he is in a situation where he can make use of his intellect. Never

short of imagination, he often has strong talents for invention. He is rather a modern person when it comes to life; Gemini almost always moves along with the times—perhaps that is why he remains so youthful throughout most of his life.

Literature and art appeal to the person born under this sign. Creativity in almost any form will interest and intrigue the Gemini man or woman.

The Gemini is often quite charming. A good talker, he often is the center of attraction at any gathering. People find it easy to like a person born under this sign because he can appear easygoing and usually has a good sense of humor.

The Negative Side of Gemini

Sometimes the Gemini person tries to do too many things at one time—and as a result, winds up finishing nothing. Some Twins are easily distracted and find it rather difficult to concentrate on one thing for too long a time. Sometimes they give in to trifling fancies and find it rather boring to become too serious about any one thing. Some of them are never dependable, no matter what they promise.

Although the Gemini man or woman often appears to be well-versed on many subjects, this is sometimes just a veneer. His knowledge may be only superficial, but because he speaks so well he gives people the impression of erudition. Some Geminis are sharp-tongued and inconsiderate; they think only of themselves and their own pleasure.

Cancer: June 21–July 20

The Positive Side of Cancer

The Moon Child's most positive point is his understanding nature. On the whole, he is a loving and sympathetic person. He would never go out of his way to hurt anyone. The Cancer man or woman is often very kind and tender; they give what they can to others. They hate to see others suffering and will do what they can to help someone in less fortunate circumstances than themselves. They are often very concerned about the world. Their interest in people generally goes beyond that of just their own families and close friends; they have a deep sense of community and respect humanitarian values. The Moon Child means what he says, as a rule; he is honest about his feelings.

The Cancer man or woman is a person who knows the art of patience. When something seems difficult, he is willing to wait until the situation becomes manageable again. He is a person who knows how to bide his time. Cancer knows how to concentrate on one thing at a time. When he has made his mind up he generally sticks with what he does, seeing it through to the end.

Cancer is a person who loves his home. He enjoys being surrounded by familiar things and the people he loves. Of all the signs, Cancer is the most maternal. Even the men born under this sign often have a motherly or protective quality about them. They like to take care of people in their family—to see that they are well loved and well provided for. They are usually loyal and faithful. Family ties mean a lot to the Cancer man or woman. Parents and in-laws are respected and loved. Young Cancer responds very well to adults who show faith in him. The Moon Child has a strong sense of tradition. He is very sensitive to the moods of others.

The Negative Side of Cancer

Sometimes Cancer finds it rather hard to face life. It becomes too much for him. He can be a little timid and retiring, when things don't go too well. When unfortunate things happen, he is apt to just shrug and say, "Whatever will be will be." He can be fatalistic to a fault. The uncultivated Cancer is a bit lazy. He doesn't have very much ambition. Anything that seems a bit difficult he'll gladly leave to others. He may be lacking in initiative. Too sensitive, when he feels he's been injured, he'll crawl back into his shell and nurse his imaginary wounds. The immature Moon Child often is given to crying when the smallest thing goes wrong.

Some Cancers find it difficult to enjoy themselves in environments outside their homes. They make heavy demands on others, and need to be constantly reassured that they are loved. Lacking such reassurance, they may resort to sulking in silence.

Leo: July 21–August 21

The Positive Side of Leo

Often Leos make good leaders. They seem to be good organizers and administrators. Usually they are quite popular with others. Whatever group it is that they belong to, the Leo man or woman is almost sure to be or become the leader. Loyalty, one of the Lion's noblest traits, enables him or her to maintain this leadership position.

Leo is generous most of the time. It is his best characteristic. He or she likes to give gifts and presents. In making others happy, the Leo person becomes happy himself. He likes to splurge when spending money on others. In some instances it may seem that the Lion's generosity knows no boundaries. A hospitable person, the Leo man or woman is very fond of welcoming people to his house and entertaining them. He is never short of company.

Leo has plenty of energy and drive. He enjoys working toward some specific goal. When he applies himself correctly, he gets what he wants most often. The Leo person is almost never unsure of himself. He has plenty of confidence and aplomb. He is a person who is direct in almost everything he does. He has a quick mind and can make a decision in a very short time.

He usually sets a good example for others because of his ambitious manner and positive ways. He knows how to stick to something once he's started. Although Leo may be good at making a joke, he is not superficial or glib. He is a loving person, kind and thoughtful.

There is generally nothing small or petty about the Leo man or woman. He does what he can for those who are deserving. He is a person others can rely upon at all times. He means what he says. An honest person, generally speaking, he is a friend who is valued and sought out.

The Negative Side of Leo

Leo, however, does have his faults. At times, he can be just a bit too arrogant. He thinks that no one deserves a leadership position except him. Only he is capable of doing things well. His opinion of himself is often much too high. Because of his conceit, he is

sometimes rather unpopular with a good many people. Some Leos are too materialistic; they can only think in terms of money and profit.

Some Leos enjoy lording it over others—at home or at their place of business. What is more, they feel they have the right to. Egocentric to an impossible degree, this sort of Leo cares little about how others think or feel. He can be rude and cutting.

Virgo: August 22–September 22

The Positive Side of Virgo

The person born under the sign of Virgo is generally a busy person. He knows how to arrange and organize things. He is a good planner. Above all, he is practical and is not afraid of hard work.

Often called the sign of the Harvester, Virgo knows how to attain what he desires. He sticks with something until it is finished. He never shirks his duties, and can always be depended upon. The Virgo person can be thoroughly trusted at all times.

The man or woman born under this sign tries to do everything to perfection. He doesn't believe in doing anything halfway. He always aims for the top. He is the sort of a person who is always learning and constantly striving to better himself—not because he wants more money or glory, but because it gives him a feeling of accomplishment.

The Virgo man or woman is a very observant person. He is sensitive to how others feel, and can see things below the surface of a situation. He usually puts this talent to constructive use.

It is not difficult for the Virgo to be open and earnest. He believes in putting his cards on the table. He is never secretive or underhanded. He's as good as his word. The Virgo person is generally plainspoken and down to earth. He has no trouble in expressing himself.

The Virgo person likes to keep up to date on new developments in his particular field. Well-informed, generally, he sometimes has a keen interest in the arts or literature. What he knows, he knows well. His ability to use his critical faculties is well-developed and sometimes startles others because of its accuracy.

Virgos adhere to a moderate way of life; they avoid excesses. Virgo is a responsible person and enjoys being of service.

The Negative Side of Virgo

Sometimes a Virgo person is too critical. He thinks that only he can do something the way it should be done. Whatever anyone else does is inferior. He can be rather annoying in the way he quibbles over insignificant details. In telling others how things should be done, he can be rather tactless and mean.

Some Virgos seem rather emotionless and cool. They feel emotional involvement is beneath them. They are sometimes too tidy, too neat. With money they can be rather miserly. Some Virgos try to force their opinions and ideas on others.

Libra: September 23–October 22

The Positive Side of Libra

Libras love harmony. It is one of their most outstanding character traits. They are interested in achieving balance; they admire beauty and grace in things as well as in people. Generally speaking, they are kind and considerate people. Libras are usually very sympathetic. They go out of their way not to hurt another person's feelings. They are outgoing and do what they can to help those in need.

People born under the sign of Libra almost always make good friends. They are loyal and amiable. They enjoy the company of others. Many of them are rather moderate in their views; they believe in keeping an open mind, however, and weighing both sides of an issue fairly before making a decision.

Alert and intelligent, Libra, often known as the Lawgiver, is always fair-minded and tries to put himself in the position of the other person. They are against injustice; quite often they take up for the underdog. In most of their social dealings, they try to be tactful and kind. They dislike discord and bickering, and most Libras strive for peace and harmony in all their relationships.

The Libra man or woman has a keen sense of beauty. They appreciate handsome furnishings and clothes. Many of them are artistically inclined. Their taste is usually impeccable. They know how to use color. Their homes are almost always attractively arranged and inviting. They enjoy entertaining people and see to it that their guests always feel at home and welcome.

Libra gets along with almost everyone. He is well-liked and socially much in demand.

The Negative Side of Libra

Some people born under this sign tend to be rather insincere. So eager are they to achieve harmony in all relationships that they will even go so far as to lie. Many of them are escapists. They find facing the truth an ordeal and prefer living in a world of make-believe.

In a serious argument, some Libras give in rather easily even when they know they are right. Arguing, even about something they believe in, is too unsettling for some of them.

Libras sometimes care too much for material things. They enjoy possessions and luxuries. Some are vain and tend to be jealous.

Scorpio: October 23–November 22

The Positive Side of Scorpio

The Scorpio man or woman generally knows what he or she wants out of life. He is a determined person. He sees something through to the end. Scorpio is quite sincere, and seldom says anything he doesn't mean. When he sets a goal for himself he tries to go about achieving it in a very direct way.

The Scorpion is brave and courageous. They are not afraid of hard work. Obstacles do not frighten them. They forge ahead until they achieve what they set out for. The Scorpio man or woman has a strong will.

Although Scorpio may seem rather fixed and determined, inside he is often quite tender and loving. He can care very much for others. He believes in sincerity in all relationships. His feelings about someone tend to last; they are profound and not superficial.

The Scorpio person is someone who adheres to his principles no matter what happens. He will not be deterred from a path he believes to be right.

Because of his many positive strengths, the Scorpion can often achieve happiness for himself and for those that he loves.

He is a constructive person by nature. He often has a deep understanding of people and of life, in general. He is perceptive and unafraid. Obstacles often seem to spur him on. He is a positive person who enjoys winning. He has many strengths and resources; challenge of any sort often brings out the best in him.

The Negative Side of Scorpio

The Scorpio person is sometimes hypersensitive. Often he imagines injury when there is none. He feels that others do not bother to recognize him for his true worth. Sometimes he is given to excessive boasting in order to compensate for what he feels is neglect.

Scorpio can be proud, arrogant, and competitive. They can be sly when they put their minds to it and they enjoy outwitting persons or institutions noted for their cleverness.

Their tactics for getting what they want are sometimes devious and ruthless. They don't care too much about what others may think. If they feel others have done them an injustice, they will do their best to seek revenge. The Scorpion often has a sudden, violent temper; and this person's interest in sex is sometimes quite unbalanced or excessive.

Sagittarius: November 23–December 20

The Positive Side of Sagittarius

People born under this sign are honest and forthright. Their approach to life is earnest and open. Sagittarius is often quite adult in his way of seeing things. They are broad-minded and tolerant people. When dealing with others the person born under the sign of the Archer is almost always open and forthright. He doesn't believe in deceit or pretension. His standards are high. People who associate with Sagittarius generally admire and respect his tolerant viewpoint.

The Archer trusts others easily and expects them to trust him. He is never suspicious or envious and almost always thinks well of others. People always enjoy his company because he is so friendly and easygoing. The Sagittarius man or woman is often good-humored. He can always be depended upon by his friends, family, and coworkers.

The person born under this sign of the Zodiac likes a good joke every now and then. Sagittarius is eager for fun and laughs, which makes him very popular with others.

A lively person, he enjoys sports and outdoor life. The Archer is fond of animals. Intelligent and interesting, he can begin an

animated conversation with ease. He likes exchanging ideas and discussing various views.

He is not selfish or proud. If someone proposes an idea or plan that is better than his, he will immediately adopt it. Imaginative yet practical, he knows how to put ideas into practice.

The Archer enjoys sport and games, and it doesn't matter if he wins or loses. He is a forgiving person, and never sulks over something that has not worked out in his favor.

He is seldom critical, and is almost always generous.

The Negative Side of Sagittarius

Some Sagittarius are restless. They take foolish risks and seldom learn from the mistakes they make. They don't have heads for money and are often mismanaging their finances. Some of them devote much of their time to gambling.

Some are too outspoken and tactless, always putting their feet in their mouths. They hurt others carelessly by being honest at the wrong time. Sometimes they make promises which they don't keep. They don't stick close enough to their plans and go from one failure to another. They are undisciplined and waste a lot of energy.

Capricorn: December 21–January 19

The Positive Side of Capricorn

The person born under the sign of Capricorn, known variously as the Mountain Goat or Sea Goat, is usually very stable and patient. He sticks to whatever tasks he has and sees them through. He can always be relied upon and he is not averse to work.

An honest person, Capricorn is generally serious about whatever he does. He does not take his duties lightly. He is a practical person and believes in keeping his feet on the ground.

Quite often the person born under this sign is ambitious and knows how to get what he wants out of life. The Goat forges ahead and never gives up his goal. When he is determined about something, he almost always wins. He is a good worker—a hard worker. Although things may not come easy to him, he will not complain, but continue working until his chores are finished.

He is usually good at business matters and knows the value of money. He is not a spendthrift and knows how to put something away for a rainy day; he dislikes waste and unnecessary loss.

Capricorn knows how to make use of his self-control. He can apply himself to almost anything once he puts his mind to it. His ability to concentrate sometimes astounds others. He is diligent and does well when involved in detail work.

The Capricorn man or woman is charitable, generally speaking, and will do what is possible to help others less fortunate. As a friend, he is loyal and trustworthy. He never shirks his duties or responsibilities. He is self-reliant and never expects too much of the other fellow. He does what he can on his own. If someone does him a good turn, then he will do his best to return the favor.

The Negative Side of Capricorn

Like everyone, Capricorn, too, has faults. At times, the Goat can be overcritical of others. He expects others to live up to his own high standards. He thinks highly of himself and tends to look down on others.

His interest in material things may be exaggerated. The Capricorn man or woman thinks too much about getting on in the world and having something to show for it. He may even be a little greedy.

He sometimes thinks he knows what's best for everyone. He is too bossy. He is always trying to organize and correct others. He may be a little narrow in his thinking.

Aquarius: January 20–February 18

The Positive Side of Aquarius

The Aquarius man or woman is usually very honest and forthright. These are his two greatest qualities. His standards for himself are generally very high. He can always be relied upon by others. His word is his bond.

Aquarius is perhaps the most tolerant of all the Zodiac personalities. He respects other people's beliefs and feels that everyone is entitled to his own approach to life.

He would never do anything to injure another's feelings. He is never unkind or cruel. Always considerate of others, the Water

Bearer is always willing to help a person in need. He feels a very strong tie between himself and all the other members of mankind.

The person born under this sign, called the Water Bearer, is almost always an individualist. He does not believe in teaming up with the masses, but prefers going his own way. His ideas about life and mankind are often quite advanced. There is a saying to the effect that the average Aquarius is fifty years ahead of his time.

Aquarius is community-minded. The problems of the world concern him greatly. He is interested in helping others no matter what part of the globe they live in. He is truly a humanitarian sort. He likes to be of service to others.

Giving, considerate, and without prejudice, Aquarius have no trouble getting along with others.

The Negative Side of Aquarius

Aquarius may be too much of a dreamer. He makes plans but seldom carries them out. He is rather unrealistic. His imagination has a tendency to run away with him. Because many of his plans are impractical, he is always in some sort of a dither.

Others may not approve of him at all times because of his unconventional behavior. He may be a bit eccentric. Sometimes he is so busy with his own thoughts that he loses touch with the realities of existence.

Some Aquarius feel they are more clever and intelligent than others. They seldom admit to their own faults, even when they are quite apparent. Some become rather fanatic in their views. Their criticism of others is sometimes destructive and negative.

Pisces: February 19–March 20

The Positive Side of Pisces

Known as the sign of the Fishes, Pisces has a sympathetic nature. Kindly, he is often dedicated in the way he goes about helping others. The sick and the troubled often turn to him for advice and assistance. Possessing keen intuition, Pisces can easily understand people's deepest problems.

He is very broad-minded and does not criticize others for their faults. He knows how to accept people for what they are. On the whole, he is a trustworthy and earnest person. He is loyal to his friends and will do what he can to help them in time of need. Generous and good-natured, he is a lover of peace; he is often willing to help others solve their differences. People who have taken a wrong turn in life often interest him and he will do what he can to persuade them to rehabilitate themselves.

He has a strong intuitive sense and most of the time he knows how to make it work for him. Pisces is unusually perceptive and often knows what is bothering someone before that person, himself, is aware of it. The Pisces man or woman is an idealistic person, basically, and is interested in making the world a better place in which to live. Pisces believes that everyone should help each other. He is willing to do more than his share in order to achieve cooperation with others.

The person born under this sign often is talented in music or art. He is a receptive person; he is able to take the ups and downs of life with philosophic calm.

The Negative Side of Pisces

Some Pisces are often depressed; their outlook on life is rather glum. They may feel that they have been given a bad deal in life and that others are always taking unfair advantage of them. Pisces sometimes feel that the world is a cold and cruel place. The Fishes can be easily discouraged. The Pisces man or woman may even withdraw from the harshness of reality into a secret shell of his own where he dreams and idles away a good deal of his time.

Pisces can be lazy. He lets things happen without giving the least bit of resistance. He drifts along, whether on the high road or on the low. He can be lacking in willpower.

Some Pisces people seek escape through drugs or alcohol. When temptation comes along they find it hard to resist. In matters of sex, they can be rather permissive.

Sun Sign Personalities

ARIES: Hans Christian Andersen, Pearl Bailey, Marlon Brando, Wernher Von Braun, Charlie Chaplin, Joan Crawford, Da Vinci, Bette Davis, Doris Day, W.C. Fields, Alec Guinness, Adolf Hitler, William Holden, Thomas Jefferson, Nikita Khrushchev, Elton John, Arturo Toscanini, J.P. Morgan, Paul Robeson, Gloria Steinem, Sarah Vaughn, Vincent van Gogh, Tennessee Williams

TAURUS: Fred Astaire, Charlotte Brontë, Carol Burnett, Irving Berlin, Bing Crosby, Salvador Dali, Tchaikovsky, Queen Elizabeth II, Duke Ellington, Ella Fitzgerald, Henry Fonda, Sigmund Freud, Orson Welles, Joe Louis, Lenin, Karl Marx, Golda Meir, Eva Peron, Bertrand Russell, Shakespeare, Kate Smith, Benjamin Spock, Barbra Streisand, Shirley Temple, Harry Truman

GEMINI: Ruth Benedict, Josephine Baker, Rachel Carson, Carlos Chavez, Walt Whitman, Bob Dylan, Ralph Waldo Emerson, Judy Garland, Paul Gauguin, Allen Ginsberg, Benny Goodman, Bob Hope, Burl Ives, John F. Kennedy, Peggy Lee, Marilyn Monroe, Joe Namath, Cole Porter, Laurence Olivier, Harriet Beecher Stowe, Queen Victoria, John Wayne, Frank Lloyd Wright

CANCER: "Dear Abby," Lizzie Borden, David Brinkley, Yul Brynner, Pearl Buck, Marc Chagall, Princess Diana, Babe Didrikson, Mary Baker Eddy, Henry VIII, John Glenn, Ernest Hemingway, Lena Horne, Oscar Hammerstein, Helen Keller, Ann Landers, George Orwell, Nancy Reagan, Rembrandt, Richard Rodgers, Ginger Rogers, Rubens, Jean-Paul Sartre, O.J. Simpson

LEO: Neil Armstrong, James Baldwin, Lucille Ball, Emily Brontë, Wilt Chamberlain, Julia Child, William J. Clinton, Cecil B. De Mille, Ogden Nash, Amelia Earhart, Edna Ferber, Arthur Goldberg, Alfred Hitchcock, Mick Jagger, George Meany, Annie Oakley, George Bernard Shaw, Napoleon, Jacqueline Onassis, Henry Ford, Francis Scott Key, Andy Warhol, Mae West, Orville Wright

VIRGO: Ingrid Bergman, Warren Burger, Maurice Chevalier, Agatha Christie, Sean Connery, Lafayette, Peter Falk, Greta Garbo, Althea Gibson, Arthur Godfrey, Goethe, Buddy Hackett, Michael Jackson, Lyndon Johnson, D.H. Lawrence, Sophia Loren, Grandma Moses, Arnold Palmer, Queen Elizabeth I, Walter Reuther, Peter Sellers, Lily Tomlin, George Wallace

LIBRA: Brigitte Bardot, Art Buchwald, Truman Capote, Dwight D. Eisenhower, William Faulkner, F. Scott Fitzgerald, Gandhi, George Gershwin, Micky Mantle, Helen Hayes, Vladimir Horowitz, Doris Lessing, Martina Navratalova, Eugene O'Neill, Luciano Pavarotti, Emily Post, Eleanor Roosevelt, Bruce Springsteen, Margaret Thatcher, Gore Vidal, Barbara Walters, Oscar Wilde

SCORPIO: Vivien Leigh, Richard Burton, Art Carney, Johnny Carson, Billy Graham, Grace Kelly, Walter Cronkite, Marie Curie, Charles de Gaulle, Linda Evans, Indira Gandhi, Theodore Roosevelt, Rock Hudson, Katherine Hepburn, Robert F. Kennedy, Billie Jean King, Martin Luther, Georgia O'Keeffe, Pablo Picasso, Jonas Salk, Alan Shepard, Robert Louis Stevenson

SAGITTARIUS: Jane Austen, Louisa May Alcott, Woody Allen, Beethoven, Willy Brandt, Mary Martin, William F. Buckley, Maria Callas, Winston Churchill, Noel Coward, Emily Dickinson, Walt Disney, Benjamin Disraeli, James Doolittle, Kirk Douglas, Chet Huntley, Jane Fonda, Chris Evert Lloyd, Margaret Mead, Charles Schulz, John Milton, Frank Sinatra, Steven Spielberg

CAPRICORN: Muhammad Ali, Isaac Asimov, Pablo Casals, Dizzy Dean, Marlene Dietrich, James Farmer, Ava Gardner, Barry Goldwater, Cary Grant, J. Edgar Hoover, Howard Hughes, Joan of Arc, Gypsy Rose Lee, Martin Luther King, Jr., Rudyard Kipling, Mao Tse-tung, Richard Nixon, Gamal Nasser, Louis Pasteur, Albert Schweitzer, Stalin, Benjamin Franklin, Elvis Presley

AQUARIUS: Marian Anderson, Susan B. Anthony, Jack Benny, John Barrymore, Mikhail Baryshnikov, Charles Darwin, Charles Dickens, Thomas Edison, Clark Gable, Jascha Heifetz, Abraham Lincoln, Yehudi Menuhin, Mozart, Jack Nicklaus, Ronald Reagan, Jackie Robinson, Norman Rockwell, Franklin D. Roosevelt, Gertrude Stein, Charles Lindbergh, Margaret Truman

PISCES: Edward Albee, Harry Belafonte, Alexander Graham Bell, Chopin, Adelle Davis, Albert Einstein, Golda Meir, Jackie Gleason, Winslow Homer, Edward M. Kennedy, Victor Hugo, Mike Mansfield, Michelangelo, Edna St. Vincent Millay, Liza Minelli, John Steinbeck, Linus Pauling, Ravel, Renoir, Diana Ross, William Shirer, Elizabeth Taylor, George Washington

The Signs and Their Key Words

		POSITIVE	NEGATIVE
ARIES	self	courage, initiative, pioneer instinct	brash rudeness, selfish impetuosity
TAURUS	money	endurance, loyalty, wealth	obstinacy, gluttony
GEMINI	mind	versatility	capriciousness, unreliability
CANCER	family	sympathy, homing instinct	clannishness, childishness
LEO	children	love, authority, integrity	egotism, force
VIRGO	work	purity, industry, analysis	faultfinding, cynicism
LIBRA	marriage	harmony, justice	vacillation, superficiality
SCORPIO	sex	survival, regeneration	vengeance, discord
SAGITTARIUS	travel	optimism, higher learning	lawlessness
CAPRICORN	career	depth	narrowness, gloom
AQUARIUS	friends	human fellowship, genius	perverse unpredictability
PISCES	confine-ment	spiritual love, universality	diffusion, escapism

The Elements and Qualities of The Signs

Every sign has both an *element* and a *quality* associated with it. The element indicates the basic makeup of the sign, and the quality describes the kind of activity associated with each.

Element	Sign	Quality	Sign
FIRE	ARIES LEO SAGITTARIUS	CARDINAL	ARIES LIBRA CANCER CAPRICORN
EARTH	TAURUS VIRGO CAPRICORN	FIXED	TAURUS LEO SCORPIO AQUARIUS
AIR	GEMINI LIBRA AQUARIUS		
WATER	CANCER SCORPIO PISCES	MUTABLE	GEMINI VIRGO SAGITTARIUS PISCES

Signs can be grouped together according to their element and quality. Signs of the same element share many basic traits in common. They tend to form stable configurations and ultimately harmonious relationships. Signs of the same quality are often less harmonious, but they share many dynamic potentials for growth as well as profound fulfillment.

Further discussion of each of these sign groupings is provided on the following pages.

The Fire Signs

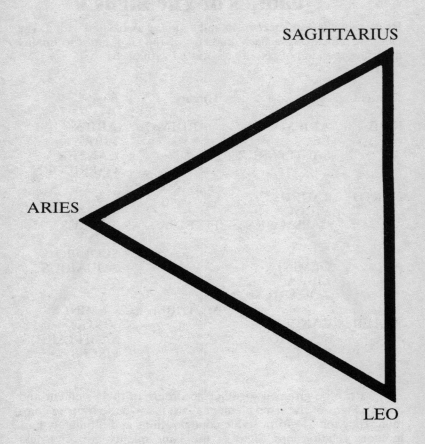

This is the fire group. On the whole these are emotional, volatile types, quick to anger, quick to forgive. They are adventurous, powerful people and act as a source of inspiration for everyone. They spark into action with immediate exuberant impulses. They are intelligent, self-involved, creative, and idealistic. They all share a certain vibrancy and glow that outwardly reflects an inner flame and passion for living.

The Earth Signs

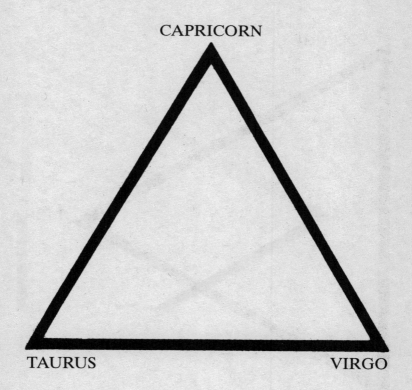

CAPRICORN

TAURUS

VIRGO

This is the earth group. They are in constant touch with the material world and tend to be conservative. Although they are all capable of spartan self-discipline, they are earthy, sensual people who are stimulated by the tangible, elegant, and luxurious. The thread of their lives is always practical, but they do fantasize and are often attracted to dark, mysterious, emotional people. They are like great cliffs overhanging the sea, forever married to the ocean but always resisting erosion from the dark, emotional forces that thunder at their feet.

The Air Signs

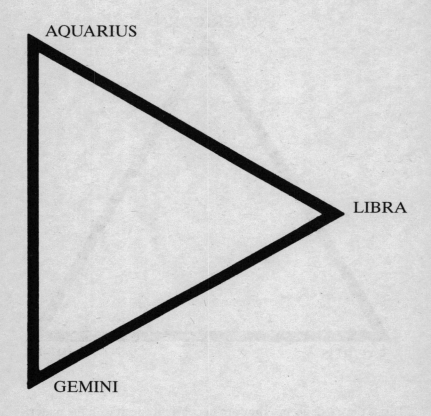

This is the air group. They are light, mental creatures desirous of contact, communication, and relationship. They are involved with people and the forming of ties on many levels. Original thinkers, they are the bearers of human news. Their language is their sense of word, color, style, and beauty. They provide an atmosphere suitable and pleasant for living. They add change and versatility to the scene, and it is through them that we can explore new territory of human intelligence and experience.

The Water Signs

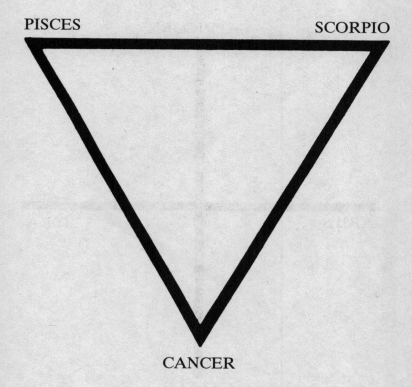

PISCES

SCORPIO

CANCER

This is the water group. Through the water people, we are all joined together on emotional, nonverbal levels. They are silent, mysterious types whose magic hypnotizes even the most determined realist. They have uncanny perceptions about people and are as rich as the oceans when it comes to feeling, emotion, or imagination. They are sensitive, mystical creatures with memories that go back beyond time. Through water, life is sustained. These people have the potential for the depths of darkness or the heights of mysticism and art.

The Cardinal Signs

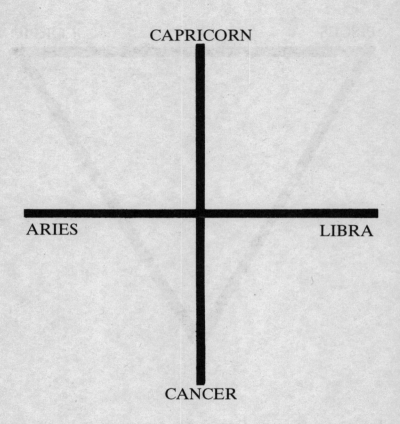

Put together, this is a clear-cut picture of dynamism, activity, tremendous stress, and remarkable achievement. These people know the meaning of great change since their lives are often characterized by significant crises and major successes. This combination is like a simultaneous storm of summer, fall, winter, and spring. The danger is chaotic diffusion of energy; the potential is irrepressible growth and victory.

The Fixed Signs

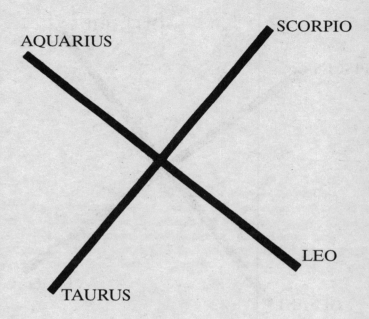

Fixed signs are always establishing themselves in a given place or area of experience. Like explorers who arrive and plant a flag, these people claim a position from which they do not enjoy being deposed. They are staunch, stalwart, upright, trusty, honorable people, although their obstinacy is well-known. Their contribution is fixity, and they are the angels who support our visible world.

The Mutable Signs

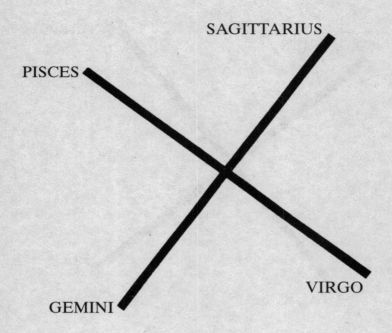

Mutable people are versatile, sensitive, intelligent, nervous, and deeply curious about life. They are the translators of all energy. They often carry out or complete tasks initiated by others. Combinations of these signs have highly developed minds; they are imaginative and jumpy and think and talk a lot. At worst their lives are a Tower of Babel. At best they are adaptable and ready creatures who can assimilate one kind of experience and enjoy it while anticipating coming changes.

THE PLANETS
OF THE SOLAR SYSTEM

This section describes the planets of the solar system. In astrology, both the Sun and the Moon are considered to be planets. Because of the Moon's influence in our day-to-day lives, the Moon is described in a separate section following this one.

The Planets and the Signs They Rule

The signs of the Zodiac are linked to the planets in the following way. Each sign is governed or ruled by one or more planets. No matter where the planets are located in the sky at any given moment, they still rule their respective signs, and when they travel through the signs they rule, they have special dignity and their effects are stronger.

Following is a list of the planets and the signs they rule. After looking at the list, read the definitions of the planets and see if you can determine how the planet ruling *your* Sun sign has affected your life.

SIGNS	RULING PLANETS
Aries	Mars, Pluto
Taurus	Venus
Gemini	Mercury
Cancer	Moon
Leo	Sun
Virgo	Mercury
Libra	Venus
Scorpio	Mars, Pluto
Sagittarius	Jupiter
Capricorn	Saturn
Aquarius	Saturn, Uranus
Pisces	Jupiter, Neptune

Characteristics of the Planets

The following pages give the meaning and characteristics of the planets of the solar system. They all travel around the Sun at different speeds and different distances. Taken with the Sun, they all distribute individual intelligence and ability throughout the entire chart.

The planets modify the influence of the Sun in a chart according to their own particular natures, strengths, and positions. Their positions must be calculated for each year and day, and their function and expression in a horoscope will change as they move from one area of the Zodiac to another.

We start with a description of the sun.

THE SUN

SUN

This is the center of existence. Around this flaming sphere all the planets revolve in endless orbits. Our star is constantly sending out its beams of light and energy without which no life on Earth would be possible. In astrology it symbolizes everything we are trying to become, the center around which all of our activity in life will always revolve. It is the symbol of our basic nature and describes the natural and constant thread that runs through everything that we do from birth to death on this planet.

To early astrologers, the Sun seemed to be another planet because it crossed the heavens every day, just like the rest of the bodies in the sky.

It is the only star near enough to be seen well—it is, in fact, a dwarf star. Approximately 860,000 miles in diameter, it is about ten times as wide as the giant planet Jupiter. The next nearest star is nearly 300,000 times as far away, and if the Sun were located as far away as most of the bright stars, it would be too faint to be seen without a telescope.

Everything in the horoscope ultimately revolves around this singular body. Although other forces may be prominent in the charts of some individuals, still the Sun is the total nucleus of being and symbolizes the complete potential of every human being alive. It is vitality and the life force. Your whole essence comes from the position of the Sun.

You are always trying to express the Sun according to its position by house and sign. Possibility for all development is found in the Sun, and it marks the fundamental character of your personal radiations all around you.

It is the symbol of strength, vigor, wisdom, dignity, ardor, and generosity, and the ability for a person to function as a mature individual. It is also a creative force in society. It is consciousness of the gift of life.

The underdeveloped solar nature is arrogant, pushy, undependable, and proud, and is constantly using force.

MERCURY

Mercury is the planet closest to the Sun. It races around our star, gathering information and translating it to the rest of the system. Mercury represents your capacity to understand the desires of your own will and to translate those desires into action.

In other words it is the planet of mind and the power of communication. Through Mercury we develop an ability to think, write, speak, and observe—to become aware of the world around us. It colors our attitudes and vision of the world, as well as our capacity to communicate our inner responses to the outside world. Some people who have serious disabilities in their power of verbal communication have often wrongly been described as people lacking intelligence.

Although this planet (and its position in the horoscope) indicates your power to communicate your thoughts and perceptions to the world, intelligence is something deeper. Intelligence is distributed throughout all the planets. It is the relationship of the planets to each other that truly describes what we call intelligence. Mercury rules speaking, language, mathematics, draft and design, students, messengers, young people, offices, teachers, and any pursuits where the mind of man has wings.

VENUS

Venus is beauty. It symbolizes the harmony and radiance of a rare and elusive quality: beauty itself. It is refinement and delicacy, softness and charm. In astrology it indicates grace, balance, and the aesthetic sense. Where Venus is we see beauty, a gentle drawing in of energy and the need for satisfaction and completion. It is a special touch that finishes off rough edges. It is sensitivity, and affection, and it is always the place for that other elusive phenomenon: love. Venus describes our sense of what is beautiful and loving. Poorly developed, it is vulgar, tasteless, and self-indulgent. But its ideal is the flame of spiritual love—Aphrodite, goddess of love, and the sweetness and power of personal beauty.

MARS

Mars is raw, crude energy. The planet next to Earth but outward from the Sun is a fiery red sphere that charges through the horoscope with force and fury. It represents the way you reach out for new adventure and new experience. It is energy and drive, initiative, courage, and daring. It is the power to start something and see it through. It can be thoughtless, cruel and wild, angry and hostile, causing cuts, burns, scalds, and wounds. It can stab its way through a chart, or it can be the symbol of healthy spirited adventure, well-channeled constructive power to begin and keep up the drive. If you have trouble starting things, if you lack the get-up-and-go to start the ball rolling, if you lack aggressiveness and self-confidence, chances are there's another planet influencing your Mars. Mars rules soldiers, butchers, surgeons, salesmen—any field that requires daring, bold skill, operational technique, or self-promotion.

JUPITER

This is the largest planet of the solar system. Scientists have recently learned that Jupiter reflects more light than it receives from the Sun. In a sense it is like a star itself. In astrology it rules good luck and good cheer, health, wealth, optimism, happiness, success, and joy. It is the symbol of opportunity and always opens the way for new possibilities in your life. It rules exuberance, enthusiasm, wisdom, knowledge, generosity, and all forms of expansion in general. It rules actors, statesmen, clerics, professional people, religion, publishing, and the distribution of many people over large areas.

Sometimes Jupiter makes you think you deserve everything, and you become sloppy, wasteful, careless and rude, prodigal and lawless, in the illusion that nothing can ever go wrong. Then there is the danger of overconfidence, exaggeration, undependability, and overindulgence.

Jupiter is the minimization of limitation and the emphasis on spirituality and potential. It is the thirst for knowledge and higher learning.

SATURN

Saturn circles our system in dark splendor with its mysterious rings, forcing us to be awakened to whatever we have neglected in the past. It will present real puzzles and problems to be solved, causing delays, obstacles, and hindrances. By doing so, Saturn stirs our own sensitivity to those areas where we are laziest.

Here we must patiently develop *method*, and only through painstaking effort can our ends be achieved. It brings order to a horoscope and imposes reason just where we are feeling least reasonable. By creating limitations and boundary, Saturn shows the consequences of being human and demands that we accept the changing cycles inevitable in human life. Saturn rules time, old age, and sobriety. It can bring depression, gloom, jealousy, and greed, or serious acceptance of responsibilities out of which success will develop. With Saturn there is nothing to do but face facts. It rules laborers, stones, granite, rocks, and crystals of all kinds.

THE OUTER PLANETS:
URANUS, NEPTUNE, PLUTO

Uranus, Neptune, Pluto are the outer planets. They liberate human beings from cultural conditioning, and in that sense are the law-breakers. In early times it was thought that Saturn was the last planet of the system—the outer limit beyond which we could never go. The discovery of the next three planets ushered in new phases of human history, revolution, and technology.

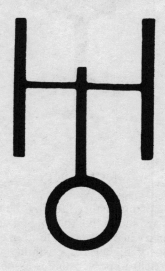

URANUS

Uranus rules unexpected change, upheaval, revolution. It is the symbol of total independence and asserts the freedom of an individual from all restriction and restraint. It is a breakthrough planet and indicates talent, originality, and genius in a horoscope. It usually causes last-minute reversals and changes of plan, unwanted separations, accidents, catastrophes, and eccentric behavior. It can add irrational rebelliousness and perverse bohemianism to a personality or a streak of unaffected brilliance in science and art. It rules technology, aviation, and all forms of electrical and electronic advancement. It governs great leaps forward and topsy-turvy situations, and *always* turns things around at the last minute. Its effects are difficult to predict, since it rules sudden last-minute decisions and events that come like lightning out of the blue.

NEPTUNE

Neptune dissolves existing reality the way the sea erodes the cliffs beside it. Its effects are subtle like the ringing of a buoy's bell in the fog. It suggests a reality higher than definition can usually describe. It awakens a sense of higher responsibility often causing guilt, worry, anxieties, or delusions. Neptune is associated with all forms of escape and can make things seem a certain way so convincingly that you are absolutely sure of something that eventually turns out to be quite different.

It is the planet of illusion and therefore governs the invisible realms that lie beyond our ordinary minds, beyond our simple factual ability to prove what is "real." Treachery, deceit, disillusionment, and disappointment are linked to Neptune. It describes a vague reality that promises eternity and the divine, yet in a manner so complex that we cannot really fathom it at all. At its worst Neptune is a cheap intoxicant; at its best it is the poetry, music, and inspiration of the higher planes of spiritual love. It has dominion over movies, photographs, and much of the arts.

PLUTO

Pluto lies at the outpost of our system and therefore rules finality in a horoscope—the final closing of chapters in your life, the passing of major milestones and points of development from which there is no return. It is a final wipeout, a closeout, an evacuation. It is a distant, subtle but powerful catalyst in all transformations that occur. It creates, destroys, then recreates. Sometimes Pluto starts its influence with a minor event or insignificant incident that might even go unnoticed. Slowly but surely, little by little, everything changes, until at last there has been a total transformation in the area of your life where Pluto has been operating. It rules mass thinking and the trends that society first rejects, then adopts, and finally outgrows.

Pluto rules the dead and the underworld—all the powerful forces of creation and destruction that go on all the time beneath, around, and above us. It can bring a lust for power with strong obsessions.

It is the planet that rules the metamorphosis of the caterpillar into a butterfly, for it symbolizes the capacity to change totally and forever a person's lifestyle, way of thought, and behavior.

THE MOON IN EACH SIGN

The Moon is the nearest planet to the Earth. It exerts more observable influence on us from day to day than any other planet. The effect is very personal, very intimate, and if we are not aware of how it works it can make us quite unstable in our ideas. And the annoying thing is that at these times we often see our own instability but can do nothing about it. A knowledge of what can be expected may help considerably. We can then be prepared to stand strong against the Moon's negative influences and use its positive ones to help us to get ahead. Who has not heard of going with the tide?

The Moon reflects, has no light of its own. It reflects the Sun—the life giver—in the form of vital movement. The Moon controls the tides, the blood rhythm, the movement of sap in trees and plants. Its nature is inconstancy and change so it signifies our moods, our superficial behavior—walking, talking, and especially thinking. Being a true reflector of other forces, the Moon is cold, watery like the surface of a still lake, brilliant and scintillating at times, but easily ruffled and disturbed by the winds of change.

The Moon takes about 27⅓ days to make a complete transit of the Zodiac. It spends just over 2¼ days in each sign. During that time it reflects the qualities, energies, and characteristics of the sign and, to a degree, the planet which rules the sign. When the Moon in its transit occupies a sign incompatible with our own birth sign, we can expect to feel a vague uneasiness, perhaps a touch of irritableness. We should not be discouraged nor let the feeling get us down, or, worse still, allow ourselves to take the discomfort out on others. Try to remember that the Moon has to change signs within 55 hours and, provided you are not physically ill, your mood will probably change with it. It is amazing how frequently depression lifts with the shift in the Moon's position. And, of course, when the Moon is transiting a sign compatible or sympathetic to yours, you will probably feel some sort of stimulation or just be plain happy to be alive.

In the horoscope, the Moon is such a powerful indicator that competent astrologers often use the sign it occupied at birth as the birth sign of the person. This is done particularly when the Sun is on the cusp, or edge, of two signs. Most experienced astrologers, however, coordinate both Sun and Moon signs by reading and confirming from one to the other and secure a far more accurate and personalized analysis.

For these reasons, the Moon tables which follow this section (see pages 86–92) are of great importance to the individual. They show the days and the exact times the Moon will enter each sign of the Zodiac for the year. Remember, you have to adjust the indicated times to local time. The corrections, already calculated for most of the main cities, are at the beginning of the tables. What follows now is a guide to the influences that will be reflected to the Earth by the Moon while it transits each of the twelve signs. The influence is at its peak about 26 hours after the Moon enters a sign. As you read the daily forecast, check the Moon sign for any given day and glance back at this guide.

MOON IN ARIES

This is a time for action, for reaching out beyond the usual self-imposed limitations and faint-hearted cautions. If you have plans in your head or on your desk, put them into practice. New ventures, applications, new jobs, new starts of any kind—all have a good chance of success. This is the period when original and dynamic impulses are being reflected onto Earth. Such energies are extremely vital and favor the pursuit of pleasure and adventure in practically every form. Sick people should feel an improvement. Those who are well will probably find themselves exuding confidence and optimism. People fond of physical exercise should find their bodies growing with tone and well-being. Boldness, strength, determination should characterize most of your activities with a readiness to face up to old challenges. Yesterday's problems may seem petty and exaggerated—so deal with them. Strike out alone. Self-reliance will attract others to you. This is a good time for making friends. Business and marriage partners are more likely to be impressed with the man and woman of action. Opposition will be overcome or thrown aside with much less effort than usual. CAUTION: Be dominant but not domineering.

MOON IN TAURUS

The spontaneous, action-packed person of yesterday gives way to the cautious, diligent, hardworking "thinker." In this period ideas will probably be concentrated on ways of improving finances. A great deal of time may be spent figuring out and going over schemes and plans. It is the right time to be careful with detail. People will find themselves working longer than usual at their desks. Or devoting more time to serious thought about the future. A strong desire to put order into business and financial arrangements may cause extra work. Loved ones may complain of being neglected and may fail to appreciate that your efforts are for their ultimate benefit. Your desire for system may extend to criticism of arrangements in the home and lead to minor upsets. Health may be affected through overwork. Try to secure a reasonable amount of rest and relaxation, although the tendency will be to "keep going" despite good advice. Work done conscientiously in this period should result in a solid contribution to your future security. CAUTION: Try not to be as serious with people as the work you are engaged in.

MOON IN GEMINI

The humdrum of routine and too much work should suddenly end. You are likely to find yourself in an expansive, quicksilver world of change and self-expression. Urges to write, to paint, to experience the freedom of some sort of artistic outpouring, may be very strong. Take full advantage of them. You may find yourself finishing something you began and put aside long ago. Or embarking on something new which could easily be prompted by a chance meeting, a new acquaintance, or even an advertisement. There may be a yearning for a change of scenery, the feeling to visit another country (not too far away), or at least to get away for a few days. This may result in short, quick journeys. Or, if you are planning a single visit, there may be some unexpected changes or detours on the way. Familiar activities will seem to give little satisfaction unless they contain a fresh element of excitement or expectation. The inclination will be toward untried pursuits, particularly those that allow you to express your inner nature. The accent is on new faces, new places. CAUTION: Do not be too quick to commit yourself emotionally.

MOON IN CANCER

Feelings of uncertainty and vague insecurity are likely to cause problems while the Moon is in Cancer. Thoughts may turn frequently to the warmth of the home and the comfort of loved ones. Nostalgic impulses could cause you to bring out old photographs and letters and reflect on the days when your life seemed to be much more rewarding and less demanding. The love and understanding of parents and family may be important, and, if it is not forthcoming, you may have to fight against bouts of self-pity. The cordiality of friends and the thought of good times with them that are sure to be repeated will help to restore you to a happier frame of mind. The desire to be alone may follow minor setbacks or rebuffs at this time, but solitude is unlikely to help. Better to get on the telephone or visit someone. This period often causes peculiar dreams and upsurges of imaginative thinking which can be helpful to authors of occult and mystical works. Preoccupation with the personal world of simple human needs can overshadow any material strivings. CAUTION: Do not spend too much time thinking—seek the company of loved ones or close friends.

MOON IN LEO
New horizons of exciting and rather extravagant activity open up. This is the time for exhilarating entertainment, glamorous and lavish parties, and expensive shopping sprees. Any merrymaking that relies upon your generosity as a host has every chance of being a spectacular success. You should find yourself right in the center of the fun, either as the life of the party or simply as a person whom happy people like to be with. Romance thrives in this heady atmosphere and friendships are likely to explode unexpectedly into serious attachments. Children and younger people should be attracted to you and you may find yourself organizing a picnic or a visit to a fun-fair, the movies, or the beach. The sunny company and vitality of youthful companions should help you to find some unsuspected energy. In career, you could find an opening for promotion or advancement. This should be the time to make a direct approach. The period favors those engaged in original research. CAUTION: Bask in popularity, not in flattery.

MOON IN VIRGO
Off comes the party cap and out steps the busy, practical worker. He wants to get his personal affairs straight, to rearrange them, if necessary, for more efficiency, so he will have more time for more work. He clears up his correspondence, pays outstanding bills, makes numerous phone calls. He is likely to make inquiries, or sign up for some new insurance and put money into gilt-edged investment. Thoughts probably revolve around the need for future security—to tie up loose ends and clear the decks. There may be a tendency to be "finicky," to interfere in the routine of others, particularly friends and family members. The motive may be a genuine desire to help with suggestions for updating or streamlining their affairs, but these will probably not be welcomed. Sympathy may be felt for less fortunate sections of the community and a flurry of some sort of voluntary service is likely. This may be accompanied by strong feelings of responsibility on several fronts and health may suffer from extra efforts made. CAUTION: Everyone may not want your help or advice.

MOON IN LIBRA

These are days of harmony and agreement and you should find yourself at peace with most others. Relationships tend to be smooth and sweet-flowing. Friends may become closer and bonds deepen in mutual understanding. Hopes will be shared. Progress by cooperation could be the secret of success in every sphere. In business, established partnerships may flourish and new ones get off to a good start. Acquaintances could discover similar interests that lead to congenial discussions and rewarding exchanges of some sort. Love, as a unifying force, reaches its optimum. Marriage partners should find accord. Those who wed at this time face the prospect of a happy union. Cooperation and tolerance are felt to be stronger than dissension and impatience. The argumentative are not quite so loud in their bellowings, nor as inflexible in their attitudes. In the home, there should be a greater recognition of the other point of view and a readiness to put the wishes of the group before selfish insistence. This is a favorable time to join an art group. CAUTION: Do not be too independent—let others help you if they want to.

MOON IN SCORPIO

Driving impulses to make money and to economize are likely to cause upsets all around. No area of expenditure is likely to be spared the ax, including the household budget. This is a time when the desire to cut down on extravagance can become near fanatical. Care must be exercised to try to keep the aim in reasonable perspective. Others may not feel the same urgent need to save and may retaliate. There is a danger that possessions of sentimental value will be sold to realize cash for investment. Buying and selling of stock for quick profit is also likely. The attention turns to organizing, reorganizing, tidying up at home and at work. Neglected jobs could suddenly be done with great bursts of energy. The desire for solitude may intervene. Self-searching thoughts could disturb. The sense of invisible and mysterious energies in play could cause some excitability. The reassurance of loves ones may help. CAUTION: Be kind to the people you love.

MOON IN SAGITTARIUS

These are days when you are likely to be stirred and elevated by discussions and reflections of a religious and philosophical nature. Ideas of faraway places may cause unusual response and excitement. A decision may be made to visit someone overseas, perhaps a person whose influence was important to your earlier character development. There could be a strong resolution to get away from present intellectual patterns, to learn new subjects, and to meet more interesting people. The superficial may be rejected in all its forms. An impatience with old ideas and unimaginative contacts could lead to a change of companions and interests. There may be an upsurge of religious feeling and metaphysical inquiry. Even a new insight into the significance of astrology and other occult studies is likely under the curious stimulus of the Moon in Sagittarius. Physically, you may express this need for fundamental change by spending more time outdoors: sports, gardening, long walks appeal. CAUTION: Try to channel any restlessness into worthwhile study.

MOON IN CAPRICORN
Life in these hours may seem to pivot around the importance of gaining prestige and honor in the career, as well as maintaining a spotless reputation. Ambitious urges may be excessive and could be accompanied by quite acquisitive drives for money. Effort should be directed along strictly ethical lines where there is no possibility of reproach or scandal. All endeavors are likely to be characterized by great earnestness, and an air of authority and purpose which should impress those who are looking for leadership or reliability. The desire to conform to accepted standards may extend to sharp criticism of family members. Frivolity and unconventional actions are unlikely to amuse while the Moon is in Capricorn. Moderation and seriousness are the orders of the day. Achievement and recognition in this period could come through community work or organizing for the benefit of some amateur group. CAUTION: Dignity and esteem are not always self-awarded.

MOON IN AQUARIUS
Moon in Aquarius is in the second last sign of the Zodiac where ideas can become disturbingly fine and subtle. The result is often a mental "no-man's land" where imagination cannot be trusted with the same certitude as other times. The dangers for the individual are the extremes of optimism and pessimism. Unless the imagination is held in check, situations are likely to be misread, and rosy conclusions drawn where they do not exist. Consequences for the unwary can be costly in career and business. Best to think twice and not speak or act until you think again. Pessimism can be a cruel self-inflicted penalty for delusion at this time. Between the two extremes are strange areas of self-deception which, for example, can make the selfish person think he is actually being generous. Eerie dreams which resemble the reality and even seem to continue into the waking state are also possible. CAUTION: Look for the fact and not just for the image in your mind.

MOON IN PISCES

Everything seems to come to the surface now. Memory may be crystal clear, throwing up long-forgotten information which could be valuable in the career or business. Flashes of clairvoyance and intuition are possible along with sudden realizations of one's own nature, which may be used for self-improvement. A talent, never before suspected, may be discovered. Qualities not evident before in friends and marriage partners are likely to be noticed. As this is a period in which the truth seems to emerge, the discovery of false characteristics is likely to lead to disenchantment or a shift in attachments. However, when qualities are accepted, it should lead to happiness and deeper feeling. Surprise solutions could bob up for old problems. There may be a public announcement of the solving of a crime or mystery. People with secrets may find someone has "guessed" correctly. The secrets of the soul or the inner self also tend to reveal themselves. Religious and philosophical groups may make some interesting discoveries. CAUTION: Not a time for activities that depend on secrecy.

NOTE: When you read your daily forecasts, use the Moon Sign Dates that are provided in the following section of Moon Tables. Then you may want to glance back here for the Moon's influence in a given sign.

MOON TABLES

Atlanta, Boston, Detroit, Miami, Washington, Montreal,
  Ottawa, Quebec, Bogota,Havana, Lima, Santiago ... Same time
Chicago, New Orleans, Houston, Winnipeg, Churchill,
  Mexico City .... Deduct 1 hour
Albuquerque, Denver, Phoenix, El Paso, Edmonton,
  Helena .... Deduct 2 hours
Los Angeles, San Francisco, Reno, Portland,
  Seattle, Vancouver .... Deduct 3 hours
Honolulu, Anchorage, Fairbanks, Kodiak .... Deduct 5 hours
Nome, Samoa, Tonga, Midway .... Deduct 6 hours
Halifax, Bermuda, San Juan, Caracas, La Paz,
  Barbados .... Add 1 hour
St. John's, Brasilia, Rio de Janeiro, Sao Paulo,
  Buenos Aires, Montevideo .... Add 2 hours
Azores, Cape Verde Islands .... Add 3 hours
Canary Islands, Madeira, Reykjavik .... Add 4 hours
London, Paris, Amsterdam, Madrid, Lisbon,
  Gibraltar, Belfast, Raba .... Add 5 hours
Frankfurt, Rome, Oslo, Stockholm, Prague,
  Belgrade .... Add 6 hours
Bucharest, Beirut, Tel Aviv, Athens, Istanbul, Cairo,
  Alexandria, Cape Town, Johannesburg .... Add 7 hours
Moscow, Leningrad, Baghdad, Dhahran,
  Addis Ababa, Nairobi, Teheran, Zanzibar .... Add 8 hours
Bombay, Calcutta, Sri Lanka .... Add $10\frac{1}{2}$
Hong Kong, Shanghai, Manila, Peking, Perth ...... Add 13 hours
Tokyo, Okinawa, Darwin, Pusan .... Add 14 hours
Sydney, Melbourne, Port Moresby, Guam .... Add 15 hours
Auckland, Wellington, Suva, Wake .... Add 17 hours

2009 MOON SIGN DATES—
NEW YORK TIME

JANUARY		FEBRUARY		MARCH	
Day Moon Enters		**Day Moon Enters**		**Day Moon Enters**	
1. Pisces		1. Taurus	5:10 pm	1. Taurus	
2. Pisces		2. Taurus		2. Taurus	
3. Aries	4:51 am	3. Gemini	9:16 pm	3. Gemini	3:00 pm
4. Aries		4. Gemini		4. Gemini	
5. Taurus	10:47 am	5. Cancer	11:07 pm	5. Cancer	6:08 am
6. Taurus		6. Cancer		6. Cancer	
7. Gemini	1:13 pm	7. Leo	11:44 pm	7. Leo	8:25 am
8. Gemini		8. Leo		8. Leo	
9. Cancer	1:15 pm	9. Leo		9. Virgo	10:35 am
10. Cancer		10. Virgo	12:39 am	10. Virgo	
11. Leo	12:42 pm	11. Virgo		11. Libra	1:47 pm
12. Leo		12. Libra	3:34 am	12. Libra	
13. Virgo	1:34 pm	13. Libra		13. Scorp.	7:24 pm
14. Virgo		14. Scorp.	9:52 am	14. Scorp.	
15. Libra	5:31 pm	15. Scorp.		15. Scorp.	
16. Libra		16. Sagitt.	7:54 pm	16. Sagitt.	4:23 am
17. Libra		17. Sagitt.		17. Sagitt.	
18. Scorp.	1:21 am	18. Sagitt.		18. Capric.	4:20 pm
19. Scorp.		19. Capric.	8:26 am	19. Capric.	
20. Sagitt.	12:31 pm	20. Capric.		20. Capric.	
21. Sagitt.		21. Aquar.	9:07 pm	21. Aquar.	5:08 am
22. Sagitt.		22. Aquar.		22. Aquar.	
23. Capric.	1:19 am	23. Aquar.		23. Pisces	4:09 pm
24. Capric.		24. Pisces	8:01 am	24. Pisces	
25. Aquar.	1:58 pm	25. Pisces		25. Pisces	
26. Aquar.		26. Aries	4:25 pm	26. Aries	12:04 am
27. Aquar.		27. Aries		27. Aries	
28. Pisces	1:13 am	28. Taurus	10:34 pm	28. Taurus	10:10 am
29. Pisces				29. Taurus	
30. Aries	10:26 am			30. Gemini	8:37 am
31. Aries				31. Gemini	

Daylight saving time to be considered where applicable.

2009 MOON SIGN DATES—
NEW YORK TIME

APRIL Day Moon Enters		MAY Day Moon Enters		JUNE Day Moon Enters	
1. Cancer	11:31 am	1. Leo		1. Libra	10:18 am
2. Cancer		2. Virgo	11:38 pm	2. Libra	
3. Leo	2:34 pm	3. Virgo		3. Scorp.	5:45 pm
4. Leo		4. Virgo		4. Scorp.	
5. Virgo	6:02 pm	5. Libra	4:52 am	5. Scorp.	
6. Virgo		6. Libra		6. Sagitt.	3:25 am
7. Libra	10:23 pm	7. Scorp.	11:49 am	7. Sagitt.	
8. Libra		8. Scorp.		8. Capric.	3:01 pm
9. Libra		9. Sagitt.	8:50 pm	9. Capric.	
10. Scorp.	4:24 am	10. Sagitt.		10. Capric.	
11. Scorp.		11. Sagitt.		11. Aquar.	3:54 am
12. Sagitt.	1:02 pm	12. Capric.	8:10 am	12. Aquar.	
13. Sagitt.		13. Capric.		13. Pisces	4:33 pm
14. Sagitt.		14. Aquar.	9:02 pm	14. Pisces	
15. Capric.	12:28 am	15. Aquar.		15. Pisces	
16. Capric.		16. Aquar.		16. Aries	2:53 am
17. Aquar.	1:20 pm	17. Pisces	9:18 am	17. Aries	
18. Aquar.		18. Pisces		18. Taurus	9:21 am
19. Aquar.		19. Aries	6:31 pm	19. Taurus	
20. Pisces	12:56 am	20. Aries		20. Gemini	12:01 pm
21. Pisces		21. Taurus	11:41 pm	21. Gemini	
22. Aries	9:10 am	22. Taurus		22. Cancer	12:13 pm
23. Aries		23. Taurus		23. Cancer	
24. Taurus	1:47 pm	24. Gemini	1:35 am	24. Leo	11:51 am
25. Taurus		25. Gemini		25. Leo	
26. Gemini	4:03 pm	26. Cancer	1:59 am	26. Virgo	12:48 pm
27. Gemini		27. Cancer		27. Virgo	
28. Cancer	5:39 pm	28. Leo	2:45 am	28. Libra	4:26 pm
29. Cancer		29. Leo		29. Libra	
30. Leo	7:57 pm	30. Virgo	5:19 am	30. Scorp.	11:20 pm
		31. Virgo			

Daylight saving time to be considered where applicable.

2009 MOON SIGN DATES—
NEW YORK TIME

JULY Day Moon Enters		AUGUST Day Moon Enters		SEPTEMBER Day Moon Enters	
1. Scorp.		1. Sagitt.		1. Aquar.	
2. Scorp.		2. Capric.	3:09 am	2. Aquar.	
3. Sagitt.	9:12 am	3. Capric.		3. Pisces	10:59 am
4. Sagitt.		4. Aquar.	5:09 pm	4. Pisces	
5. Capric.	9:09 pm	5. Aquar.		5. Aries	9:15 pm
6. Capric.		6. Aquar.		6. Aries	
7. Capric.		7. Pisces	4:35 pm	7. Aries	
8. Aquar.	10:04 am	8. Pisces		8. Taurus	5:19 am
9. Aquar.		9. Aries	3:24 pm	9. Taurus	
10. Pisces	10:45 pm	10. Aries		10. Gemini	11:18 am
11. Pisces		11. Taurus	11:51 pm	11. Gemini	
12. Pisces		12. Taurus		12. Cancer	3:21 pm
13. Aries	9:41 am	13. Taurus		13. Cancer	
14. Aries		14. Gemini	5:27 am	14. Leo	5:40 pm
15. Taurus	5:31 pm	15. Gemini		15. Leo	
16. Taurus		16. Cancer	8:14 am	16. Virgo	6:57 pm
17. Gemini	9:42 pm	17. Cancer		17. Virgo	
18. Gemini		18. Leo	8:58 am	18. Libra	8:27 pm
19. Cancer	10:52 pm	19. Leo		19. Libra	
20. Cancer		20. Virgo	9:02 am	20. Scorp.	11:53 pm
21. Leo	10:29 pm	21. Virgo		21. Scorp.	
22. Leo		22. Libra	10:13 am	22. Scorp.	
23. Virgo	10:24 pm	23. Libra		23. Sagitt.	6:44 am
24. Virgo		24. Scorp.	2:17 pm	24. Sagitt.	
25. Virgo		25. Scorp.		25. Capric.	5:20 pm
26. Libra	12:27 am	26. Sagitt.	10:17 pm	26. Capric.	
27. Libra		27. Sagitt.		27. Capric.	
28. Scorp.	5:57 am	28. Sagitt.		28. Aquar.	6:08 am
29. Scorp.		29. Capric.	9:45 am	29. Aquar.	
30. Sagitt.	3:11 pm	30. Capric.		30. Pisces	6:27 pm
31. Sagitt.		31. Aquar.	10:44 pm		

Daylight saving time to be considered where applicable.

2009 MOON SIGN DATES—
NEW YORK TIME

OCTOBER Day Moon Enters		NOVEMBER Day Moon Enters		DECEMBER Day Moon Enters	
1. Pisces		1. Taurus	7:46 pm	1. Gemini	9:25 am
2. Pisces		2. Taurus		2. Gemini	
3. Aries	4:22 am	3. Gemini	11:54 pm	3. Cancer	11:02 am
4. Aries		4. Gemini		4. Cancer	
5. Taurus	11:34 am	5. Gemini		5. Leo	12:06 pm
6. Taurus		6. Cancer	2:44 am	6. Leo	
7. Gemini	4:48 pm	7. Cancer		7. Virgo	2:07 pm
8. Gemini		8. Leo	5:24 am	8. Virgo	
9. Cancer	8:49 pm	9. Leo		9. Libra	5:48 pm
10. Cancer		10. Virgo	8:31 am	10. Libra	
11. Cancer		11. Virgo		11. Scorp.	11:33 pm
12. Leo	12:04 am	12. Libra	12:23 pm	12. Scorp.	
13. Leo		13. Libra		13. Scorp.	
14. Virgo	2:46 am	14. Scorp.	5:25 pm	14. Sagitt.	7:26 am
15. Virgo		15. Scorp.		15. Sagitt.	
16. Libra	5:31 am	16. Scorp.		16. Capric.	5:33 pm
17. Libra		17. Sagitt.	12:23 am	17. Capric.	
18. Scorp.	9:24 am	18. Sagitt.		18. Capric.	
19. Scorp.		19. Capric.	10:02 am	19. Aquar.	5:40 am
20. Sagitt.	3:50 pm	20. Capric.		20. Aquar.	
21. Sagitt.		21. Aquar.	10:12 pm	21. Pisces	6:43 pm
22. Sagitt.		22. Aquar.		22. Pisces	
23. Capric.	1:40 am	23. Aquar.		23. Pisces	
24. Capric.		24. Pisces	11:09 am	24. Aries	6:41 am
25. Aquar.	2:09 pm	25. Pisces		25. Aries	
26. Aquar.		26. Aries	10:12 pm	26. Taurus	3:27 pm
27. Aquar.		27. Aries		27. Taurus	
28. Pisces	2:46 am	28. Aries		28. Gemini	8:14 pm
29. Pisces		29. Taurus	5:35 am	29. Gemini	
30. Aries	12:58 pm	30. Taurus		30. Cancer	9:46 pm
31. Aries				31. Cancer	

Daylight saving time to be considered where applicable.

2009 PHASES OF THE MOON—
NEW YORK TIME

New Moon	First Quarter	Full Moon	Last Quarter
Dec. 27 ('08)	Jan. 4	Jan. 10	Jan. 17
Jan. 26	Feb. 2	Feb. 9	Feb. 16
Feb. 24	March 4	March 10	March 18
March 26	April 2	April 9	April 17
April 24	May 1	May 9	May 17
May 24	May 30	June 7	June 15
June 22	June 29	July 7	July 15
July 21	July 28	August 5	August 13
August 20	August 27	Sept. 4	Sept. 11
Sept. 18	Sept. 26	Oct. 4	Oct. 11
Oct. 18	Oct. 25	Nov. 2	Nov. 9
Nov. 16	Nov. 24	Dec. 2	Dec. 8
Dec. 15	Dec. 24	Dec. 31	Jan. 7 ('10)

Each phase of the Moon lasts approximately seven to eight days, during which the Moon's shape gradually changes as it comes out of one phase and goes into the next.

There will be a solar eclipse during the New Moon phase on January 26 and July 21.

There will be a lunar eclipse during the Full Moon phase on February 9, July 7, August 5, and December 31.

2009 FISHING GUIDE

	Good	Best
January	4-8-9-11-12-13-14-26	10-18
February	8-9-10-11-17	2-6-7-25
March	4-9-10-11-19-26	12-13-14-15
April	7-8-13-17-18	2-8-9-10-11-25
May	1-10-11-17-24-31	5-6-7-8-9
June	6-7-8-16-22	4-5-9-10-29
July	4-5-8-9-10-15-21	6-7-28
August	4-5-6-20-27	2-3-7-8-13
September	2-3-6-7-8-11	4-5-19-26
October	1-3-4-5-7-26-31	2-6-11-18-29
November	1-4-5-9-16-29	2-3-25-30
December	1-2-3-5-9-16-25-29-30	4-27-31

2009 PLANTING GUIDE

	Aboveground Crops	Root Crops
January	1-2-6-10-29	16-17-18-19-23-24
February	2-3-6-7-24-25	12-13-14-15-20-21
March	1-2-5-6-29	13-14-15-16-19-20-24-25
April	2-8-9-25-29-30	10-11-15-16-21
May	5-6-7-8-26-27	13-14-18-19-22-23
June	2-3-4-5-23-29-30	9-10-14-15-19
July	1-2-6-27-28-29	7-11-16-17-20-21
August	2-3-23-24-25-26-30	7-8-12-13-17
September	4-19-20-21-22-26-27	5-9-13
October	2-18-19-23-24-28-29	6-10-11-17
November	2-19-20-25-30	3-6-7-13-14-15-16
December	17-18-22-23-27-28	4-10-11-12-13

	Pruning	Weeds and Pests
January	18-10	12-13-14-15-21-22
February	14-15	1-11-17-18-22
March	14-15-24-25	16-17-21-22
April	10-11-21	13-14-18-23
May	17-18	10-11-15-16-20-21
June	14-15	11-12-17-21
July	12-20-21	9-10-13-14-18-19
August	8-9-17	10-11-14-15-19
September	4-13	6-7-11-15-16-17
October	10-11	8-12-13-14-15
November	6-7-15-16	4-5-8-9-10-11
December	4-12-13	1-5-6-7-8-14-15

MOON'S INFLUENCE OVER PLANTS

Centuries ago it was established that seeds planted when the Moon is in signs and phases called Fruitful will produce more growth than seeds planted when the Moon is in a Barren sign.

Fruitful Signs: Taurus, Cancer, Libra, Scorpio, Capricorn, Pisces
Barren Signs: Aries, Gemini, Leo, Virgo, Sagittarius, Aquarius
Dry Signs: Aries, Gemini, Sagittarius, Aquarius

Activity	Moon In
Mow lawn, trim plants	**Fruitful sign:** 1st & 2nd quarter
Plant flowers	**Fruitful sign:** 2nd quarter; best in Cancer and Libra
Prune	**Fruitful sign:** 3rd & 4th quarter
Destroy pests; spray	**Barren sign:** 4th quarter
Harvest potatoes, root crops	**Dry sign:** 3rd & 4th quarter; Taurus, Leo, and Aquarius

MOON'S INFLUENCE OVER YOUR HEALTH

ARIES   Head, brain, face, upper jaw
TAURUS   Throat, neck, lower jaw
GEMINI   Hands, arms, lungs, shoulders, nervous system
CANCER   Esophagus, stomach, breasts, womb, liver
LEO   Heart, spine
VIRGO   Intestines, liver
LIBRA   Kidneys, lower back
SCORPIO   Sex and eliminative organs
SAGITTARIUS   Hips, thighs, liver
CAPRICORN   Skin, bones, teeth, knees
AQUARIUS   Circulatory system, lower legs
PISCES   Feet, tone of being

Try to avoid work being done on that part of the body when the Moon is in the sign governing that part.

MOON'S INFLUENCE OVER DAILY AFFAIRS

The Moon makes a complete transit of the Zodiac every 27 days 7 hours and 43 minutes. In making this transit the Moon forms different aspects with the planets and consequently has favorable or unfavorable bearings on affairs and events for persons according to the sign of the Zodiac under which they were born.

When the Moon is in conjunction with the Sun it is called a New Moon; when the Moon and Sun are in opposition it is called a Full Moon. From New Moon to Full Moon, first and second quarter—which takes about two weeks—the Moon is increasing or waxing. From Full Moon to New Moon, third and fourth quarter, the Moon is decreasing or waning.

Activity	Moon In
Business: buying and selling	Sagittarius, Aries, Gemini, Virgo
new, requiring public support	1st and 2nd quarter
meant to be kept quiet	3rd and 4th quarter
Investigation	3rd and 4th quarter
Signing documents	1st & 2nd quarter, Cancer, Scorpio, Pisces
Advertising	2nd quarter, Sagittarius
Journeys and trips	1st & 2nd quarter, Gemini, Virgo
Renting offices, etc.	Taurus, Leo, Scorpio, Aquarius
Painting of house/apartment	3rd & 4th quarter, Taurus, Scorpio, Aquarius
Decorating	Gemini, Libra, Aquarius
Buying clothes and accessories	Taurus, Virgo
Beauty salon or barber shop visit	1st & 2nd quarter, Taurus, Leo, Libra, Scorpio, Aquarius
Weddings	1st & 2nd quarter

Gemini

GEMINI

Character Analysis

People born under this third sign of the Zodiac are generally known for their versatility, their duality. Quite often they are able to manage several things at the same time. Some of them have two or more sides to their personalities. At one moment they can be happy and fun-loving, the next they can be sullen and morose. For the outsider, this sudden change may be difficult to understand or appreciate.

The Gemini man or woman is interested in all sorts of things and in different ways. Many of the subjects that attract them seem contrary and dissimilar. To Gemini, they're not.

The person born under the sign of the Twins has a mercurial nature. He can fly into a rage one moment, then be absolutely lovable the next. Chances are he won't remember what all the fuss was about after a few moments have passed.

The Gemini man or woman is spiritual in nature. Intellectual challenges whet his appetite. He's a sensitive person. His mind is active, alert. He could even be described as idea-hungry, always on the lookout for new concepts, new ways of doing things. He is always moving along with the times. On the whole, Gemini is very energetic. However, he is apt to bite off more than he can chew at times. He may begin a dozen different projects at once—and never finish any. It's often the doing—starting something—that he finds interesting. As soon as something becomes too familiar or humdrum, he may drop it like a hot coal and begin something else. The cultivated Gemini, however, does not have this problem. He has learned by experience that constancy pays off. He knows how to limit his interests—no matter how great the temptation may be to take on more—and how to finish the work that he has begun. It's a hard lesson for the natural Gemini to learn, but it can be done.

In school, the Twins are quite popular and often at the top of their class. They learn quickly, and when they apply themselves, they can make good use of their powers of concentration. Many do well in languages. They are clever conversationalists; they can keep an audience entranced for hours. Still and all, the depth of their knowledge may be slight. They know how to phrase things well, and this gives the impression of deep learning. They read things too quickly at times and often miss important points. Sometimes they will insist that something is right when in fact it isn't.

Generally, Gemini has a good sense of humor. He knows how to appreciate a good joke, which is apt to make him popular. He seldom fails to see the humorous side of life. In fact, he may irritate others by not acknowledging the serious side of a situation when it is necessary.

All in all, Gemini is open-minded. He is tolerant of others no matter what their views are. He can get along well with various types of people. He's a great mixer. He never has much trouble understanding another's viewpoint.

It is held that the Gemini person is one who prefers to work with concrete things. To him, facts are more important than fantasy. He's practical—or at least attempts to be. He can be quite goal-directed; there is always a reason for what he does. An ambitious person, on the whole, he is never short on projects; there is always something that he has to get done. He could be described as restless; he doesn't like sitting still for long periods of time. He's got to be on the go.

Health

Gemini usually is an active person. He has plenty of energy stored up. Still, he has to be careful at times because he is apt to strain himself emotionally. He gets too wound up and finds it difficult to relax. Troubles, small and large, can turn him into a high-strung person, if he doesn't look out for himself. Weak points of his body are his lungs, arms, and nervous system. During the winter months, some Twins develop one cold after another. Sore throats are sometimes a common Gemini complaint.

On the whole, however, Gemini has a pretty good constitution. He's healthy, but he has to learn how to take care of his health. People often think of Gemini as being weak and sickly, but this isn't so. His physique is often thin and wiry. He may not look like he can endure too much pressure, but his powers for endurance are amazing. He is not delicate, by any stretch of the imagination.

Although the Twins may be bothered by one minor ailment or another, they seldom contract serious illnesses—if they take proper care of themselves. The wise Gemini acknowledges his limits and never tries to exceed them. He will never take on more work than he can comfortably handle. It is important that the Gemini man or woman learns how to relax. Sleep is also an important ingredient for good health. Some Twins feel they have to be constantly on the go; it is as if they were on a treadmill. Of course, they can only keep it up for a short while, then they have to pay the consequences.

The Gemini man or woman is often gifted with handsome looks. Others find them winsome and attractive. Their faces are very lively and expressive, their smiles charming. Most of them tend to be on the slim side. They may seem restless or fidgety from time to time.

Occupation

Geminis are ambitious; they have plenty of drive. They like to keep busy. Most of them do well in jobs that give them a chance to make full use of their intellects. They like to use their minds more than their hands. They are good talkers, generally, and do well in positions where they have to deal directly with the public. They are clever with words and are persuasive in their arguments. Also, they know how to make people feel at ease by making use of their sense of humor. A well-placed joke can work wonders when dealing with the public.

The Twins know how to turn a disadvantage to advantage. They know how to bargain. They are seldom made fools of when it comes to trading. Some of them make excellent salespeople and it is little wonder. Because they can juggle words so well and they have a deep interest in facts, they often become capable journalists. Some of them make good theater or film critics. Writing is one of their chief talents. They generally do well in the arts.

Anything to do with negotiating or bargaining is something in which Gemini is apt to excel. They know how to phrase things, to put them in a favorable light. The Twins fit in almost anywhere in business or profession.

One also finds Geminis in such professions as dentistry, medicine, law, engineering. They excel at logic and reasoning. Some of them have a head for mathematics and make good accountants.

When working with others, they will do what is necessary to make the project successful. However, they do like to go their own way. They do not like someone looking over their shoulder constantly, advising them how something should be done. They like to move around; nothing pleases them more than a job where they are free to come and go as they please. They generally find it difficult to sit at a desk for long stretches at a time. Geminis like movement for its own sake. They are not particularly interested in destinations. It's getting there that absorbs their interest.

They are generally not contented being busy with just one thing. They are apt to try to hold down two jobs at the same time just to be active. Their hobbies are varied; some they manage to develop into side occupations. They abhor dull routine and are creative in their approach to a familiar scheme. They will do what they can to make their work interesting. If they are placed in the wrong position—that is, a position that does not coincide with their interests—they can be grumpy and difficult to get along with.

They like to be attached to a modern, progressive concern that provides a chance to learn new technology. They dislike job situations that are old-fashioned and tiresome.

Geminis aren't money-hungry, generally, but somehow or other they always manage to find jobs that are well-paying. They are not willing to work for nothing. They value their own skills and know how much they are worth.

Money interests the Gemini man or woman because it represents security. The uncultivated Gemini, however, spends his earnings carelessly. He doesn't run out of money, but he mismanages what he has. When he has learned how to economize, he does quite well. He's always looking for a way to better his financial situation. Some Geminis are job hoppers; they are never satisfied with the position they have and they go from one job to another looking for their "proper niche," they think. It is the Gemini who knows how to make the best out of a job situation he already has who wins the day. Job hopping never seems to stop, and in the end the job hopper has nothing to show for all the changing.

People born under this sign usually know how to win the sympathy of influential people. The Twins are often helped, advised, and encouraged by people who hold important positions. People find it easy to believe in Gemini.

The Gemini man or woman is generous with what he has; he does not mind sharing. He can be expansive and doesn't mind paying for others if he can afford it. Once in a while, he may do something unwise with his finances, but, all in all, he manages to keep his financial head above water.

Home and Family

Gemini is adaptable. He is willing to do without if it is necessary. But if he can have his own way, he likes to be surrounded by comfortable and harmonious things. Home is important to him. He likes a house that radiates beauty and calm.

He likes to invite people to his home; he likes entertaining. It is important to Gemini that people feel at home while visiting him. Because he is such a ready host, his house is often full of people— of all description. Although he may be at a loss how he should handle some household matters, he always seems to manage in one way or another. His home is likely to be modern—equipped with the latest conveniences and appliances. He is often amused by gadgets.

Although his home may be important to him, he also likes to pick up and go somewhere whenever the mood strikes. He doesn't like the feeling of being tied down. Home is where he hangs his hat, he likes to think. A Gemini is apt to change his address more than once in his lifetime. This may or may not upset family ties to a certain extent. Still, if they understand him, they will give in to his plans. No one is more difficult to live with than a dissatisfied Gemini. Still, more than likely Gemini has his family conditioned to his moods and there is enough understanding to make life together possible. The cultivated Gemini learns to stay put and make the most of the home he has.

The Gemini man or woman is a great fixer. He likes to make minor repairs, changing appliances, painting, wallpapering, and so on. He will do many things to make improvements on his home. Sometimes he will go ahead and make changes without consulting those he lives with, which can cause discord.

Outsiders may not think of Gemini as the ideal parent or family man. In fact, they may be open in their criticism. Gemini might resent this strongly because he feels it just isn't true. Children may get on the Gemini man or woman's nerves now and again. They like the kids to be expressive and creative. But the Twins do enjoy moments of peace and quiet. Generally, they know how to get along well with their children. This may be because they do have a youthful streak themselves. They understand the ups and downs of childhood, the trials and tribulations of growing up—also the joys. They may scold once in a while, but children who know them will never pay too much attention to them. The Gemini parent is generally a pushover for the willful child.

Gemini children are usually filled with restless, nervous energy. It comes from their minds, which are like delicately tuned electronic instruments. Mercury, Gemini's planet, is the planet of mind and communication, which bestows the ability to think, speak, write, and observe. So these young sons and daughters of Mercury cannot keep still, mentally or physically. They must be constantly engaged in something that interests them.

Young Gemini is an exceptionally bright child. He or she learns almost instantaneously and has an alert, inquiring mind that demands to know the reason behind anything that catches his or her attention. Parents and teachers of Geminis may find this an exhausting business, mainly because these lovable imps lose interest more quickly than most children. When that happens, and no one is around, their capacity for mischief is unbelievable.

Gemini children are sometimes difficult to manage. They usually don't like to be hampered by parental guidance. They like to be allowed to do as they please when they please. They often show signs of artistic ability at a very early age. The perceptive parent knows how to encourage them and to help them develop the characteristics that will help them later on in life.

Social Relationships

Gemini is usually easy to get along with. He likes people and knows how to make them like him. He seldom has serious enemies; he's too friendly for that. Because of his lighthearted ways many people are drawn to him. He is generally sincere in his friendships and expects that sincerity to be reciprocated. A sensitive person, he never forgets or forgives an offense.

The Twins like to be in a crowd—a friendly crowd. They seldom like to be alone for long stretches. They like their friends to be as active and as enthusiastic as they are. Social involvement is important to them. They are apt to throw a party at the drop of a hat. The Gemini man or woman enjoys making others feel good. They are excellent hosts and try to anticipate their guests' needs. Gemini could never be called inhospitable.

Their friends are apt be very different from each other. Gemini gets along well with all types of people. Their social needs may seem contradictory to someone who does not understand the Gemini nature. The cultivated person born under this sign knows how to keep apart those friends who are not likely to get along. He'll avoid social conflict among his friends at all costs.

Meeting new people is important to the man or woman born under the third sign of the Zodiac. He thrives on social activities. He likes exchanging views and ideas.

Gemini does not demand that his friends be his intellectual equal. He can be content discussing trivial matters as well as profound ones. He likes people he can relax with.

Friends may like Gemini but find him hard to understand. The Twins seem to have so many different personas at the same time. They are difficult to pin down.

People are always inviting Geminis to parties; any social affair would seem incomplete without them. Their charm and liveliness are contagious. People enjoy being around them. They can be loose-tongued at social gatherings, and sometimes divulge information about themselves or others that they shouldn't. They can be severe, too, in their criticisms. A Gemini's sharp tongue has cut many a social tie.

Love and Marriage

Gemini longs for affection and understanding. He doesn't always find it, though. Although he's honest in his search, Gemini is apt to be too critical. Once he's won someone, he finds fault with them. The cultivated Gemini learns to take the bitter with the sweet. He realizes that no one is perfect, and he accepts the love of his life for what she is.

It is quite possible for Gemini to have many love relationships before he ever thinks of settling down with one person. He may not be an intense lover. He loves being affectionate, however. Flattery can turn his head.

Gemini does not like to feel that he is tied down. He likes someone who will give him the freedom he needs. He doesn't like to feel imprisoned by love. He is often attracted to someone who is as independent in spirit as he is. He likes a witty and intelligent companion, someone who can discuss things rationally.

It is sometimes difficult for the natural Gemini to give himself to any one person. He does not like being limited in his affections. He flirts just for the pleasure of flirting. He enjoys attention and at times will go to great lengths to get it. He likes variety in romance. The same love diet is apt to bore him after a while.

In spite of his changeability, the intelligent Gemini can settle down to one partner, once he puts his mind to it. The person who wins a Gemini is usually gifted and clever, someone adaptable who knows how to change with his moods. Gemini is not difficult to get along with. He is pleasant and gentle, for the most part. He likes people who are responsive to his moods. If he really loves someone, he sees to it that his demands are not too unreasonable. He's willing to make compromises.

Even after he's married, the average Gemini is given to flirting, but it's nothing for his mate to be concerned about. He'll keep it at a harmless level. He will not risk a love relationship that contains the benefits he appreciates.

Marriage for Gemini is a relationship that should be lively and exciting. He's not the kind of person who accepts a humdrum home life. He wants a family that is as active as he is.

Romance and the Gemini Woman

The Gemini woman has no trouble attracting members of the opposite sex. They find her dazzling and glamorous. Her disposition is almost always gay and fun-loving. She knows how to make her suitors feel appreciated and wanted. However, she is restless and easily changes from one mood to another. This often mystifies and disappoints admirers. Sometimes she seems easy to please, other times not. People who don't understand her think she is difficult and egocentric.

The Gemini woman likes variety in her love relationships. She may go through many romances before she thinks of marrying and settling down. She admires a man who can accept her as an equal, intellectually and emotionally. She is not too fond of domestic duties. After marriage, she wants to pursue her various interests just as she did when she was single.

An intellectual man is apt to appeal to her when she is interested in a serious love relationship. A man who can win her mind can win her heart. Gemini seldom marries someone she considers her inferior intellectually. She wants someone she can respect.

The single Gemini woman can be quite flirtatious. She may even toy with the affections of someone she is not seriously interested in. When she feels a romance has come to an end, she'll say so bluntly and move on. She likes her love relationships to be an adventure—full of amusement and excitement. Men looking for a housekeeper instead of a partner are wasting their time when courting a Gemini woman. She'll never tie herself to the kitchen for the love of a man. She is interested in too many other things.

The considerate Gemini woman, however, will cut down on her interests and confine most of her activities to the home if she feels the love of her man is worth the sacrifice.

The Gemini woman has good taste in decorating a home. She knows how to arrange rooms and how to use color tastefully. She can become a good homemaker once she puts her mind to it. She likes things tidy and neat but is not too fond of domestic chores. If possible, she will see to it that she has some help in carrying out household duties.

Romance and the Gemini Man

The Gemini man is interested in change and adventure in his romantic activities. The woman who desires to keep up with him has to be quick on her feet. His restlessness is apt to puzzle even those who love him. He is quick-witted and fond of challenge. Someone who is likely to drag him into a life of humdrum domesticity will not win him.

In spite of the fact that he may go from romance to romance quite easily, the Gemini man is really in search of a true and lasting love relationship. He is popular with women. They like him because of his charm and intelligence. If he cares for a woman, he can make her feel like the most important person in his life. He is capable of steadfastness in his affections, but there is no guarantee how long this will last.

A girl interested in home and a family—and nothing else—is not one who will appeal to him. He wants someone who is a good companion, someone who can share his interests as well as his moods. He wants someone he can talk with as an equal, someone whose interests go beyond the trivial.

In love, he can be either passionate or mild; it depends on his partner and the circumstances. Some Geminis are easily distracted in romance, and their interests travel from one woman to the other with appalling ease.

When he does meet the ideal mate, Gemini proves himself to be loving and responsible. He does his best to protect the interests of his family and is willing to make the sacrifices necessary to keep his home life in order. He may flirt occasionally after marriage, but it seldom goes beyond that. The woman who marries him must allow him his romantic fantasies. He can become unreasonable if he is reproached for flirting harmlessly.

He will be faithful to the woman who allows him his freedom— the woman who is not suspicious and trusts him.

Life with a Gemini man can be a happy one indeed, but the woman who plans to go through life at his side has to be as adaptable and active as he is.

Woman—Man

GEMINI WOMAN
ARIES MAN
The man born under the sign of Aries is often attracted to the Gemini woman. In you he can find that mixture of intellect and charm that is so often difficult to find in a woman. Like you, he has many interests and is always seeking one adventure after another. He has an insatiable thirst for knowledge of all kinds.

He can do with a woman like you—someone attractive, quick-witted, and intelligent. He'll admire you for your independence. He's not interested in a clinging vine. He wants someone who is there when he needs her; someone who listens and understands what he says; someone who can give advice if he should ever happen to ask for it, which is not likely to be often.

The Aries man wants a woman who is a good companion and a good sport. He is looking for a woman who will look good on his arm without hanging on it too heavily. He is looking for a woman who has both feet on the ground and yet is mysterious and enticing, a modern Helen of Troy whose face or fine speech can launch a thousand business deals, if need be. That woman he is in search of sounds a little like you. If the shoe fits, put it on. You won't be sorry.

The Aries man makes a good husband. He is faithful and attentive. He is an affectionate man. He'll make you feel needed and loved. Love is a serious matter for Aries. He does not believe in flirting or playing the field—especially after he's found the woman of his dreams. He'll expect you to be as constant in your affection as he is in his. Try to curb your bent for harmless flirting if you have your heart set on an Aries. He'll expect you to be a hundred percent his; he won't put up with any nonsense while romancing you.

The Aries man may be progressive and modern about many things, but when it comes to pants wearing, he's downright conventional: it's strictly male attire. The best role you can take in the relationship is a supporting one. He's the boss and that's that. If you can accept it, you'll find the going easy.

The Aries man, with his endless energy and drive, likes to relax in comfort at the end of the day. The Gemini woman who is a good homemaker can be sure of his undying affection. If you see to it that everything in the house is where he expects to find it, you'll have no difficulty keeping the relationship on an even keel.

Aries is generally a good provider. He'll see to it that you never want. Although he is interested in security, he's a man who is not afraid to take risks. Often his gambling pays off.

Aries fathers, while affectionate and playful, sometimes have trouble seeing things through the eyes of a child. Your innate understanding of youth will always come in handy.

GEMINI WOMAN
TAURUS MAN

If your heart is set on a man born under the sign of Taurus, you'll have to learn the art of being patient. Taurus take their time about everything—even love.

The steady and deliberate Taurus is a little slow on the draw; it may take him quite a while before he gets around to popping that question. For the Gemini woman who is adaptable, the waiting and anticipating almost always pays off in the end. Taurus men want to make sure that every step they take is right, especially if the path they're on could lead to the altar.

If you are in the mood for a whirlwind romance, better cast your net in shallower waters. Moreover, most Taurus prefer to do the angling themselves. They are not keen on women taking the lead. Once she does, he may drop her immediately. If the Gemini woman lets herself get caught on his terms, she'll find that her Taurus has fallen for her—hook, line, and sinker.

The Taurus man is fond of a comfortable home life. It is very important to him. If you keep those home fires burning you will have no trouble keeping that flame in the Taurus heart aglow. You have a talent for homemaking. You are an old hand at harmony and color. Your taste in furnishings is excellent. Perhaps, with your moodiness, sense of adventure, and love of change, you could turn out to be a challenging mate for the strong, steady, and protective Bull. Perhaps he could be the anchor for your dreams and plans. He could help you acquire a more balanced outlook and approach to your life. Not one for wild schemes, himself, Taurus can help you to curb your impulsiveness. He's the man who is always there when you need him.

The Taurus man is steady—the kind of man the Gemini woman often needs.

When you tie the knot with a Bull, you can put away fears about creditors pounding on the front door. Taurus is practical about everything including bill paying. When he carries you over the threshold, you can be certain the entire house is paid for.

Married to a Taurus man, you need not worry about having to put aside your many interests for the sake of back-breaking household chores. He'll see to it that you have all the latest time-saving appliances and comforts.

You also can forget about acquiring premature gray hairs due to unruly, ruckus-raising children under your feet. Papa Taurus is a master at keeping youngsters in line. He's crazy about kids but he also knows what's good for them.

GEMINI WOMAN
GEMINI MAN
The Gemini man and the Gemini woman are a couple who understand each other. They are so much alike. Both are intelligent, witty, outgoing, and versatile. The Gemini man could easily turn out to be your better half. One thing that causes a Twin's mind and affection to wander is a bore, and it's highly unlikely that an active Gemini woman would ever allow herself to be accused of that.

The Gemini man who has caught your heart will admire you for your ideas and intellect—perhaps even more than for your good cooking and flawless talent for homemaking. The Gemini woman needn't feel that once she's made her marriage vows she'll have to put her interests and ambition in storage. The Gemini man will admire you for your zeal and liveliness. He's the kind of guy who won't pout and scowl if you let him shift for himself in the kitchen once in a while. In fact, he'll enjoy the challenge of wrestling with pots and pans for a change. Chances are, too, that he might turn out to be a better cook than you—that is, if he isn't already.

The man born under the sign of the Twins is very active. There aren't many women who have enough pep to keep up with him. But this doesn't set a problem for the spry Gemini woman. You are both dreamers, planners, and idealists. The strong Gemini woman can easily fill the role of rudder for her Gemini man's ship-without-a-sail. If you happen to be a cultivated Gemini, he won't mind it too much. The intelligent Twin is often aware of his shortcomings. He doesn't resent it if someone with better bearings gives him a shove in the right direction. The average Gemini does not have serious ego hang-ups and will gracefully accept a well-deserved chewing out from his mate.

When you and your Gemini man team up, you'll probably always have a houseful of people to entertain—interesting people, too. Geminis find it hard to tolerate sluggish minds.

Gemini men are always attractive to the opposite sex. You'll perhaps have to allow him an occasional harmless flirt. It will seldom amount to more than that if you're his proper mate. It will help keep his spirits up. A Twin out of sorts, as you well know, is capable of brewing up a whirlwind of trouble. Better tolerate his flirting—within eyeshot, of course—than lose your cool.

As far as children go, you are both pushovers. One of you will have to learn to fill the role of house disciplinarian, otherwise chaos will reign.

GEMINI WOMAN
CANCER MAN

Chances are you won't hit it off too well with the man born under Cancer, but then Cupid has been known to do some pretty unlikely things. Cancer is a very sensitive man, thin-skinned and occasionally moody. You've got to keep on your toes, and not step on his if you're determined to make a go of the relationship.

The Cancer man may be lacking in many of the qualities you seek in a man, but when it comes to being faithful and being a good provider, he's hard to beat.

It is the perceptive Gemini woman who will not mistake the Crab's quietness for sullenness or his thriftiness for penny-pinching. In some respects he can be like the wise old owl out on a limb; he may look like he's dozing but actually he hasn't missed a thing. Moon Children often possess a well of knowledge about human behavior; they can deliver very helpful advice to those in trouble or in need. Cancer certainly can keep you from making unwise investments in time and especially money. He may not say much, but he's always got his wits about him.

The Crab may not be the match or catch for many a Gemini woman. In fact, he may seem dull to on-the-move Gemini. True to his sign, he can be cranky and crabby when handled the wrong way. He is perhaps more sensitive than he should be.

Geminis are usually as smart as a whip. If you're clever you will never, in any way, convey the idea that you consider your Cancer a little short on brain power. Browbeating is a surefire way of sending the Crab angrily scurrying back to his shell. It's possible all of that lost ground may never be recovered.

The Crab is most comfortable at home. Once settled in for the night or for the weekend, wild horses couldn't drag him away unless those wild horses were dispatched by his mother. The Crab is sometimes a Mama's boy. If his mate does not put her foot down, he will see to it that his mother comes first whenever possible. No self-respecting Gemini would ever allow herself to play second fiddle to her mother-in-law. If she's a tactful Gemini, she may find that slipping into number-one position can be as easy as pie (that legendary apple pie his mother used to make).

If you take enough time to pamper your Cancer man with good cooking and comfort, you'll find that "Mother" turns up less and less—at the front door as well as in conversations.

Cancers make protective, proud, and patient fathers, but they may resent a youngster's bid for freedom.

GEMINI WOMAN
LEO MAN

For the Gemini woman who enjoys being swept off her feet in a romantic whirlwind, Leo is the sign of love. When the Lion puts his mind to romancing, he doesn't stint. It's all wining, dining, and dancing till the wee hours of the morning.

Leo is all heart and knows how to make his woman feel like a woman. The Gemini in constant search of a man she can look up to need go no farther. Leo is ten-feet tall—in spirit if not in stature. He's a man in full control of his faculties, and he also manages to have full control of just about any situation he finds himself in. He's a winner.

The Leo man may not look like Tarzan, but he knows how to roar and beat his chest if he has to. The Gemini woman who has had her fill of weak-kneed men finds in a Leo someone she can at last lean upon. He can support you physically as well as encourage your plans and projects. He's good at giving advice that pays off. Leos are direct. They don't believe in wasting time or effort. They almost never make unwise investments—something a Gemini often does.

Many Leos rise to the top of their profession and through their example prove to be a great inspiration to others.

Although he's a ladies' man, Leo is very particular about his ladies. His standards are high when it comes to love interests. The idealistic and cultivated Gemini should have no trouble keeping her balance on the pedestal the Lion sets her on. Leo believes that romance should be played on a fair give-and-take basis. He won't stand for any monkey business in a love relationship. It's all or nothing.

You'll find him a frank, straight-from-the-shoulder person; he generally says what is on his mind.

The Gemini woman who does decide upon a Leo for a mate must be prepared to stand squarely behind her man. He expects it—and usually deserves it. He's the head of the house and can handle that position without a hitch. He knows how to go about bread-winning and, if he has his way (and most Leos do have their own way), he'll see to it that you'll have all the luxuries you crave and the comforts you need.

It's likely that the romance in your marriage will stay alive. Lions need love like flowers need sunshine. They're ever amorous and generally expect similar attention and affection from their mate. Lions are fond of going out on the town; they love to give parties. You should encounter no difficulties in sharing his interest in this direction.

Leos make strict fathers, generally. You'll have to smooth over your children's roughed-up feelings.

GEMINI WOMAN
VIRGO MAN

The Virgo man is all business—or he may seem so to you. He is usually cool, calm, and collected. He's perhaps too much of a fussbudget to wake up deep romantic interests in a Gemini. Torrid romancing to him is just so much sentimental mush. He can do without it and can make that evident in short order.

He's keen on chastity. If necessary, he can lead a sedentary, sexless life without caring too much about the fun others think he is missing. You may find him a first-class dud. His lack of imagination and dislike for flights of fancy can grate on a Gemini woman's nerves. He is always correct and likes to be handled correctly. Almost everything about him is orderly.

He does have an honest-to-goodness heart, believe it or not. The Gemini who finds herself strangely attracted to his feet-flat-on-the-ground ways will discover that his is a constant heart, not one that goes in for flings or sordid affairs. Virgos take an awfully long time to warm up to someone. A practical man, even in matters of the heart, he wants to know just what kind of a person you are before he takes a chance on love.

The impulsive Gemini had better not make the mistake of kissing her Virgo friend on the street, even if it's only a peck on the cheek. He's not at all demonstrative and hates public displays of affection. Love, according to him, should be kept within the confines of one's home—with the curtains drawn. Once he believes you are on the level with him as far as your love is concerned, you'll see how fast he loses his cool. Virgos are considerate, gentle lovers. He'll spend a long time, though, getting to know you. He'll like you before he loves you.

A Gemini-Virgo romance can be a sometime—or a one-time—thing. If the bottom ever falls out, don't bother to pick up the pieces. Nine times out of ten, he won't care about patching up. He's a once-burnt-twice-shy guy. When he crosses your phone number out of his address book, he's crossing you out of his life—for good.

Neat as a pin, he's thumbs-down on what he considers sloppy housekeeping. An ashtry with just one stubbed-out cigarette in it can be annoying to him, even if it's just two seconds old. Glassware should always sparkle and shine.

If you wind up marrying a Virgo man, keep your kids spic-and-span, at least by the time he gets home from work. Train the children to be kind, respectful, and courteous. He'll expect it.

GEMINI WOMAN
LIBRA MAN

If there's a Libra in your life, you are most likely a very happy woman. Men born under this sign of the Lawgiver have a way with impulsive, intelligent women. You'll always feel at ease in his company; you can always be yourself with him.

Like you, he's given to occasional fits of impulsiveness. His moods can change rapidly. One moment he comes on hard and strong with "I love you", and next moment he's left you like yesterday's mashed potatoes. He'll come back to you, though; don't worry. Libras are like that. Deep down inside he really knows what he wants even though he may not appear to.

You'll appreciate his admiration of beauty and harmony. If you're dressed to the teeth and never looked better in your life, you'll get a ready compliment—and one that's really deserved. Libras don't indulge in idle flattery. If they don't like something, they are tactful enough to remain silent.

Libras will go to great lengths to preserve peace and harmony—even tell a fat lie if necessary. They don't like showdowns or disagreeable confrontations. But the frank Gemini woman is usually impelled to air grievances and get resentments out into the open, even if it comes out all wrong. To Libra, making a clean breast of everything sometimes seems like sheer folly.

You may lose your patience while waiting for your Libra friend to make up his mind. It takes him ages to make a decision. He weighs both sides carefully before committing himself to anything. You seldom dillydally—at least about small things—and so you will find it difficult to see eye-to-eye with a hesitating Libra when it comes to decision-making methods.

All in all, though, he is a kind, gentle, and fair person. He is interested in the "real" truth. He'll try to balance everything out until he has all the correct answers. It is not difficult for him to see both sides of the story.

Libras don't pose or prance to get attention like a Leo might do. They're not show-offs. Generally, they are well-balanced people. Honest, wholesome, and affectionate, they are serious about every love entanglement they have. If he should find that his date is not really suited to him, he will end the relationship in such a tactful manner that no hard feelings will come about.

He never lets money burn holes in his pockets. You don't have to worry about him throwing his money all over the place, though. Most likely he'll spend it all on you—lavishly.

The Libra father can teach youngsters fairness and tolerance in a gentle, patient way. A peace-loving man, he encourages discussion and debate but frowns on physical fighting. He teaches the children how to play by the rules.

GEMINI WOMAN
SCORPIO MAN

Many find the Scorpio's sting a fate worse than death. The Gemini woman quite often is no exception. When his anger breaks loose, you had better clear out of the vicinity.

The average Scorpio man may strike the Gemini woman as being a brute. He'll stick pins into the balloons of your plans and dreams if they don't line up with what he thinks is right. If you do anything to irritate him—just anything—you'll wish you hadn't. He'll give you a sounding out that would make you pack your bags and vow never to go back.

The Scorpio man hates being tied down to home life—and so do you to a certain extent. Instead of wrestling with pots and pans, you'd rather be out and about, devoting plenty of time to your many interests. The Scorpio man would rather be out on the battlefield of life, belting away at whatever he feels is a just and worthy cause, instead of staying home nestled in a comfortable armchair with the evening paper. If you're a Gemini with a strong homemaking streak, don't keep those home fires burning too brightly too long; you may run out of firewood.

As passionate as he is in business and politics, the Scorpio man has plenty of pep and ginger stored away for lovemaking. Most women are easily attracted to him. The Gemini woman is no exception—at least before she is really aware of what she might be getting into. Those who allow a Scorpio to sweep them off their feet soon find that they're dealing with a pepperpot of seething excitement. The Scorpio man is passionate with a capital P, you can be sure of that.

But even while he is providing so much pleasure to his lover, he can deliver a knockout emotional blow. He can wound on a deep level, and you may not know if he really means it. Scorpio is blunt and can be as cutting as a razor blade. An insult can whiz out even more quickly than a compliment.

If you're a Gemini who can keep a stiff upper lip, take it on the chin, turn a deaf ear because you feel you are still under his love spell in spite of everything—lots of luck.

If you have decided to take the bitter with the sweet, prepare yourself for a lot of ups and downs. Chances are you won't have as much time for your own affairs and interests as you'd like. The Scorpio's love of power may cause you to be at his constant beck and call.

Scorpios like fathering large families, but they seldom give youngsters the attention they need.

GEMINI WOMAN
SAGITTARIUS MAN

The Gemini woman who has set her cap for a man born under the sign of Sagittarius may have to apply a lot of strategy before she can get him to say "Will you marry me?" Although some Archers may be marriage-shy, they're not ones to skitter away from romance. A Gemini woman may find a relationship with a Sagittarius—whether a fling or the real thing—a very enjoyable experience.

As a rule, Sagittarius are bright, happy, and healthy people. They have a strong sense of fair play. Often they're a source of inspirations to others. They're full of ideas and drive.

You'll be taken by the Archer's infectious grin and his light-hearted friendly nature. If you do wind up being the woman in his life, you'll find that he's apt to treat you more like a buddy than the love of his life. It's just his way. Sagittarius is often chummy instead of romantic.

You'll admire his broad-mindedness in most matters—including that of the heart. If, while dating you, he claims that he still wants to play the field, he'll expect you to enjoy the same liberty. Once he's promised to love, honor, and obey, however, he does just that. Marriage for him, once he's taken that big step, is very serious business. The Gemini woman with her keen imagination and love of freedom will not be disappointed if she does tie up with an Archer. The Sagittarius man is quick-witted—but not as quick-witted as you sometimes. Generally, men of this sign have a genuine interest in equality. They hate prejudice and injustice.

If he insists on a night out with the boys once a week, he won't scowl if you decide to let him shift for himself in the kitchen once a week while you go out with the girls.

He's not much of a homebody. Quite often he's occupied with far-away places either in his dreams or in reality. He enjoys—just as you do—being on the go or on the move. He's got ants in his pants and refuses to sit still for long stretches at a time. Humdrum routine—especially at home—bores him. At the drop of a hat, he may ask you to pack your traveling bag for a quick jaunt. He'll take great pride in showing you off to his friends. He'll always be a considerate mate; he will never embarrass or disappoint you intentionally.

His friendly, sunshiny nature is capable of attracting many people. Like you, he's very tolerant when it comes to friends, and you'll most likely spend a great deal of time entertaining.

Sagittarius are all thumbs when it comes to little shavers. He'll develop an interest in youngsters when they get older.

GEMINI WOMAN
CAPRICORN MAN

The with-it Gemini woman is likely to find the average Capricorn man a bit of a drag. The man born under the sign of the Goat is often a closed person and difficult to get to know. Even if you do get to know him, you may not find him very interesting.

In romance, Capricorn men are a little on the rusty side. You'll probably have to make all the passes.

You may find his plodding manner irritating, and his conservative, traditional ways maddening. He's not one to take chances on anything. "If it was good enough for my father, it's good enough for me" may be his motto. He follows a way that is tried and true.

Whenever adventure rears its tantalizing head, the Goat will turn the other way; he's just not interested.

He may be just as ambitious as you are—perhaps even more so. But his ways of accomplishing his aims are more subterranean; at least they seem so. He operates from the background a good deal of the time. At a gathering you may never even notice him, but he's there, taking in everything and sizing up everyone, planning his next careful move.

Although Capricorns may be intellectual, it is generally not the kind of intelligence a Gemini appreciates. He may not be as bright or as quick as you are; it may take ages for him to understand a joke.

The Gemini woman who does take up with a man born under this sign must be pretty good in the cheering up department. The Capricorn man in her love life may act as though he's constantly being followed by a cloud of gloom.

The Capricorn is happiest in the comfort and privacy of his own home. The security possible within four walls can make him a happy man. He'll spend as much time as he can at home. If he is loaded down with extra work, he'll bring it home instead of staying at the office.

You'll most likely find yourself frequently confronted by his relatives. Family is very important to the Capricorn—his family, not yours. They had better take an important place in your life, too, if you want to keep your home a happy one.

Although his caution in most matters may drive you up the wall, you'll find his concerned way with money justified most of the time. He is no squanderer. Everything is planned right down to the last red cent. He'll see to it that you never want.

He can be quite a scold when it comes to disciplining children. You'll have to step in and smooth things over when he goes too far.

GEMINI WOMAN
AQUARIUS MAN

You've never known love unless you've known a man born under the sign of Aquarius. The Gemini woman is likely to find an Aquarius dazzling.

As a rule, Aquarius are extremely friendly and open. Of all the signs, they are perhaps the most tolerant. In the thinking department, they are often miles ahead of others.

The Gemini woman will find her Aquarius man intriguing and interesting. She'll also find the relationship a challenging one. Your high respect for intelligence and imagination may be reason enough for you to settle your heart on a Water Bearer. You can learn a lot from him.

Aquarius love everybody—even their worst enemies, sometimes. Through your relationship with an Aquarius you will run into all sorts of people, ranging from near-genius to downright insane—and they're all friends of his.

In the holding-hands phase of your romance, you may find that your Water Bearer friend has cold feet. Aquarius take quite a bit of warming up before they're ready to come across with that first goodnight kiss. More than likely, he'll just want to be your pal in the beginning. For him, that's an important first step in any relationship—love, included. The poetry and flowers stage—if it ever comes—will come much later. Aquarius is all heart. Still, when it comes to tying himself down to one person and for keeps, he may hesitate. He may even try to get out of it if you breathe down his neck too hard.

The Aquarius man is no Valentino and wouldn't want to be. The Gemini woman is likely to be more impressed by his broad-mindedness and high moral standards than by his feeble attempts at romance.

You won't find it difficult to look up to a man born under the sign of the Water Bearer, but you may find the challenge of trying to keep up with him dizzying. He can pierce through the most complicated problem as if it were a matter of simple math. You may find him a little too lofty and high-minded. But don't judge him too harshly if that's the case; he's way ahead of his time—your time, too, most likely.

If you marry this man, he'll stay true to you. He'll certainly admire you for your intelligence and wit. Don't think that, once you're married, he'll keep you chained to the kitchen sink. He'll encourage you to go ahead in your pursuit of knowledge. You'll most likely have a minor tiff with him every now and again but never anything serious.

Kids love him and vice versa. He'll be as tolerant with them as he is with adults.

GEMINI WOMAN
PISCES MAN

The man born under Pisces is a dreamer. Sometimes he's so wrapped up in his dreams that he's difficult to reach. To the average Gemini woman, he may seem a little passive.

He's easygoing most of the time. He seems to take things in his stride. He'll entertain all kinds of views and opinions from just about anyone, nodding or smiling vaguely, giving the impression that he's with them one hundred percent while that may not be the case at all. His attitude may be "why bother" when he is confronted with someone wrong who thinks he's right. The Pisces man will seldom speak his mind if he thinks he'll be rigidly opposed.

The Pisces man is oversensitive at times—he's afraid of getting his feelings hurt. He'll sometimes imagine a personal injury when none's been made. Chances are you'll find this maddening; at times you may feel like giving him a swift kick where it hurts the most. It wouldn't do any good, though. It would just add fuel to the fire of his persecution complex.

One thing you'll admire about Pisces is his concern for people who are sick or troubled. He'll make his shoulder available to anyone in the mood for a good cry. He can listen to one hard-luck story after another without seeming to tire. When his advice is asked, he is capable of coming across with words of wisdom. He often knows what is paining someone before that person is aware of it himself. It's almost intuitive with Pisces, it seems. Still, at the end of the day, this man will want some peace and quiet. If you've got a problem on your mind when he comes home, don't unload it in his lap. If you do, you may find him short-tempered. He's a good listener, but he can only take so much.

Pisces are not aimless although they may seem so at times. The positive Pisces man is often successful in his profession and is likely to wind up rich and influential. Material gain, however, is not a direct goal for a man born under the sign of the Fishes.

The weaker Pisces are usually content to stay put on the level where they find themselves. They won't complain too much if the roof leaks and the fence is in need of repair. They can evade any responsibility if they feel like it.

Because of their seemingly laissez-faire manner, Pisces are immensely popular with children. For tots the Pisces father plays the double role of confidant and playmate. It will never enter his mind to discipline a child, no matter how spoiled or incorrigible that child becomes.

Man—Woman

GEMINI MAN
ARIES WOMAN

The Aries woman is a charmer. When she tugs at your heart, you'll know it. She's a woman in search of a knight in shining armor. She is a very particular person with very high ideals. She won't accept anyone other than the man of her dreams.

The Aries woman never plays around with passion; she means business when it comes to love.

Don't get the idea that she's dewy-eyed. She isn't. In fact, she can be practical and to the point when she wants to be. She's a gal with plenty of drive and ambition. With an Aries woman behind you, you can go far in life. She knows how to help her man get ahead. She's full of wise advice; you only have to ask. In some cases, Aries women have a keen business sense; many of them become successful career women. There is nothing passive or retiring about her. She is equipped with a good brain and she knows how to use it.

An Aries-Gemini union could be something strong, secure, and romantic. If both of you have your sights fixed in the same direction, there is almost nothing you could not accomplish.

The Gemini man will have to give up flirting if he decides to settle for an Aries partner or wife. The Aries woman is proud, and capable of being quite jealous. While you're with her, never cast your eye in another woman's direction. It could spell disaster for your relationship. The Aries woman won't put up with romantic nonsense even if it's done only in fun.

If the Aries woman backs you up in your business affairs, you can be sure of succeeding. However, if she is only interested in advancing her own career and puts her own interests before yours, she can be sure of rocking the boat. It will put a strain on the relationship. The overambitious Aries woman can be a pain in the neck and make you forget you were once in love with her.

The cultivated Aries woman makes a wonderful wife and mother. She has a natural talent for homemaking. With a pot of paint and some wallpaper she can transform the dreariest domicile into an abode of beauty and snug comfort. The perfect hostess—even when friends just happen by—she knows how to make guests feel at home.

You'll admire your Aries, too, because she knows how to stand on her own two feet. Hers is an independent nature. She won't break down and cry when things go wrong. She'll pick herself up and try to patch things up.

Like you she's social-minded. In the wit department, she can run you a close second. She'll love you as long as she can look forward to a good intellectual challenge.

She makes a fine, affectionate mother and will encourage her children to develop a wide range of talents and skills.

GEMINI MAN
TAURUS WOMAN

The woman born under the sign of Taurus may lack a little of the sparkle and bubble you like. The Taurus woman is generally down to earth and never flighty. It's important to her that she keep both feet flat on the ground. She may fail to appreciate your willingness to run here and there, especially if she's under the impression that there's no profit in it.

On the other hand, if you hit it off with a Taurus woman, you won't be disappointed at all in the romance area. She is all woman, and proud of it, too. She can be very devoted and loving once she decides that her relationship with you is no fly-by-night romance. Basically, she's a passionate person. In sex, she's direct and to the point. If she really loves you, she'll let you know that she's yours—and without reservations. Better not flirt with other women once you've committed yourself to her. She can be jealous and possessive.

She'll stick by you through thick and thin. It's almost certain that if the going ever gets rough, she won't go running home to Mother. She can adjust to hard times just as graciously as she can to good times.

Taurus women are, on the whole, even-tempered. They like to be treated with kindness. Pretty things and soft things make them purr like kittens.

With your quick wit and itchy feet, you may find yourself miles ahead of your Taurus woman. At times you are likely to find this distressing. But if you've developed a talent for patience, you won't mind waiting for her to catch up. Never try grabbing her hand and pulling her along at your normal speed; it won't work. It could lead to a fireworks display that would put Independence Day to shame. The Taurus woman doesn't anger readily but when prodded often enough, she's capable of letting loose with a cyclone of ill will. If you treat her correctly, you'll have no cause for complaint.

Taurus loves doing things for her man. She's a whiz in the kitchen and can whip up feasts fit for a king if she thinks they'll be appreciated. She may not fully understand you, but she'll adore you and be faithful if she feels you're worthy of it.

The woman born under Taurus will make a wonderful mother for your children. She knows how to keep her children loved, cuddled, and warm. She may not be too sympathetic toward them when they reach the teenage stage, however. Their changeability might irk her steadfast ways.

GEMINI MAN
GEMINI WOMAN
Although you and your Gemini woman may be as alike as peas in a pod, there will be certain barriers to overcome in order to make your relationship a smooth-running one. Before settling on anything definite, it would be wise for you both to get to know each other as you really are—without the sparkling veneer, the wit, the irresistible charm that Geminis are so well known for. You're both talkers and if you don't understand each other well enough you can have serious arguments. Get to know each other well; learn what it is that makes you tick. Two Geminis without real knowledge of themselves and their relationship can easily wind up behind the eight ball. But two cultivated, positive Geminis can make a love relationship or marriage work.

You are likely to find a romance with another Twin a many-splendored thing. In her you can find the intellectual companionship you crave and so seldom find. A Gemini woman can appreciate your aims and desires because she travels much the same road as you do, intellectually and emotionally. You'll admire her for her liveliness and mental agility. You'll be attracted by her warmth and grace.

While she's on your arm, you'll probably notice that many male eyes are drawn to her; she may even return a gaze or two, but don't let that worry you. Women born under this sign (the men, too) have nothing against a harmless flirtation; they enjoy the attention. If she feels she's already spoken for, she'll never let it get out of hand.

Although she may not be very handy in the kitchen, you'll never go hungry for a filling and tasty meal. She's in as much a hurry as you are most of the time, and won't feel like she's cheating by breaking out the instant mashed potatoes. She may not feel totally at home at the kitchen range, but she can be clever; with a dash of this and a little bit of that, she can make an uninteresting TV dinner taste like a gourmet meal. Then again, there are some Geminis who find complicated recipes a challenge to their intellect. Every meal they prepare turns out to be a tantalizing and mouth-watering surprise.

The Gemini woman loves people as much as you do—all kinds of people. Together you'll throw some very interesting and successful parties. Geminis do well in organizing social affairs. Everyone invited is bound to have the time of their life.

People may have the impression that your Gemini wife is not the best of mothers. But the children themselves seldom have reason to complain. Gemini women get along with their kids well because they, too, possess a childlike quality.

GEMINI MAN
CANCER WOMAN

If you fall in love with a Cancer woman, be prepared for anything. Moon Children are sometimes difficult to understand when it comes to love. In one hour, she can unravel a range of emotions that will leave you dizzy. She'll keep you guessing for sure.

You may find her a little too uncertain and sensitive for your tastes. You'll spend a lot of time encouraging her—helping her to erase her foolish fears. Tell her she's a living doll a dozen times a day and you'll be well loved in return.

Be careful of the jokes you make when in her company. Don't let them revolve around her, her personal interests, or her family. If you do, you'll most likely reduce her to tears. She can't stand being made fun of. It will take bushels of roses and tons of chocolates to get her to emerge from her shell.

In matters of money managing, she may not easily come around to your way of thinking. Geminis rarely let money burn a hole in their pockets. Cancers are just the opposite. You may get the notion that your Cancer sweetheart or mate is a direct descendent of Scrooge. If she has her way, she'll hang onto that first dollar you earned. She's that way not only with money but with everything from bakery string to jelly jars. She's a saver; she never throws anything away, no matter how trivial.

Once she returns your "I love you," you'll have a very loving, self-sacrificing, and devoted friend. Her love for you will never alter. She'll put you high on a pedestal and will do everything— even if it's against your will—to keep you up there.

Cancer women love home life. For them, marriage is an easy step. They're domestic with a capital D. She'll do her best to make your home comfortable and cozy. She feels more at ease home than anywhere else. She is an excellent hostess.

Cancer women make the best mothers of all the signs of the Zodiac. She'll consider every minor complaint of her child a major catastrophe. She's not the kind of mother who will do anything to get the children off her hands. With her, kids come first. If you are lucky, you'll run a close second. You'll perhaps see her as too devoted to the children; you may have a hard time convincing her to untie her apron strongs. When Junior or Sis is ready for that first date, you have to prevent your Cancer wife from going along.

GEMINI MAN
LEO WOMAN

If you can manage a girl who likes to kick up her heels every now and again, then Leo is for you. You'll have to learn to put away jealous fears when you take up with a Lioness. She makes heads turn and tongues wag. You don't have to believe any of what you hear—it's most likely jealous gossip or wishful thinking.

The Leo woman has more than a fair share of grace and glamour. She knows it, and knows how to put it to good use. Needless to say, other women turn green with envy and will try anything to put her out of the running.

If she's captured your heart and fancy, woo her full force if your intention is to win her. Shower her with expensive gifts and promise her the moon—if you're in a position to go that far—then you'll find her resistance weakening. It's not that she's such a difficult cookie. She'll probably fuss over you once she's decided you're the man for her. But she does enjoy a lot of attention. What's more, she feels she's entitled to it. Her mild arrogance, though, is becoming. The Leo woman knows how to transform the crime of excessive pride into a very charming misdemeanor. It sweeps most men right off their feet. Those who do not succumb to her leonine charm are few and far between.

If you've got an important business deal to clinch and you have doubts as to whether or not it will go over well, bring your Leo partner along to the business luncheon or cocktail party. It will be a cinch that you'll have the contract in your pocket before the meeting is over. She won't have to say or do anything, just be there at your side. The grouchiest oil magnate can be transformed into a gushing, obedient schoolboy if there's a Leo woman in the room.

If you're a rich Gemini, you may have to see to it that your Leo mate doesn't get too heavy-handed with the charge accounts and credit cards. When it comes to spending, Leos tend to overdo.

They're even worse than Geminis. If you're a poor Gemini man, you'll have nothing to worry about because a Leo, with her love of luxury, will most likely never give you the time of day, let alone consent to be your wife.

As a mother, she can be both strict and easygoing. She can pal around with her children and still see to it that they know their places. She won't be so apt to spoil them as you will. Still, she'll be a loving and devoted parent.

GEMINI MAN
VIRGO WOMAN

The Virgo woman may be a little too difficult for you to understand at first. Her waters run deep. Even when you think you do know her, don't take any bets on it. She's capable of keeping things hidden in the deep recesses of her womanly soul—things she'll only release when she's sure that you're the man she's been looking for. It may take her some time to come around to this decision. Virgo women are finicky about almost everything; everything has to be letter-perfect before they're satisfied. Many believe that only Virgos can do things correctly.

Nothing offends a Virgo woman more than slovenly dress, sloppy character, or a careless display of affection. Make sure your tie is straight and that your shoes sport a bright shine before you go calling on this lady. Save your off-color jokes for the locker room; she'll have none of that. Take her arm when crossing the street.

Don't rush the romance. Trying to corner her in the back of a cab may be one way of striking out. Never criticize the way she looks. The best policy would be to agree with her as much as possible. Still, you're an impulsive, direct Gemini; all those dos and don'ts you'll have to observe if you want to get to first base with a Virgo may be too much to ask of you. After a few dates, you may come to the conclusion that she just isn't worth all that trouble. However, the Virgo woman is mysterious enough to keep her men running back for more. Chances are you'll be intrigued by her airs and graces.

Lovemaking means a lot to you. You may be disappointed at first in her cool Virgo ways. However, under her glacial facade there lies a hot cauldron of seething excitement. If you're patient and artful in your romantic approach, you'll find that all the caution was well worth the trouble. When Virgos really love, they don't stint. It's all or nothing. Once they're convinced that they love you, they go all the way, tossing all cares to the wind.

One thing a Virgo woman can't stand in love is hypocrisy. They don't give a hoot about what the neighbors might say if their hearts tell them go ahead. They're very concerned with human truths. So if their hearts stumble upon another fancy, they will be true to that new heartthrob and leave you standing in the rain. She's that honest—to her heart, at any rate. But if you are honest about your interest in her, she'll know and she'll respect and reciprocate your interest. Do her wrong once, however, and you can be sure she'll put an end to the relationship for good.

The Virgo mother has high expectations for her children, and she strives to bring out the very best in them. She is both tender and strict, but always devoted. The youngsters sense her unconditional love for them and are quick to respond.

GEMINI MAN
LIBRA WOMAN

Gemini and Libra combine the airy qualities basic to both your zodiacal signs, so there should be an instant rapport between you. A breezy, chatty friendliness could soon lead to love.

You'll find that a woman born under the sign of Libra is worth more than her weight in gold. She's a woman after your own heart.

With her, you'll always come first—make no mistake about that. She'll always support you 100 percent, no matter what you do. When you ask her advice about almost anything, you'll get a very balanced and realistic opinion. She is good at thinking things out and never lets her emotions run away with her when clear logic is called for.

As a homemaker she is hard to beat. She is very concerned with harmony and balance. You can be sure she'll make your house a joy to live in; she'll see to it that the house is tastefully furnished and decorated. A Libra cannot stand filth or disarray—it gives her goose bumps. Anything that does not radiate harmony, in fact, runs against her orderly grain.

She is chock-full of charm and womanly ways. She can sweep just about any man off his feet with one winning smile. When it comes to using her brains, she can outthink almost anyone and, sometimes, with half the effort. She is diplomatic enough, though, never to let this become glaringly apparent. She may even turn the conversation around so that you think you were the one who thought things up. She couldn't care less, really, just as long as you end up doing what is right.

The Libra woman will put you on a high pedestal. You are her man and her idol. She'll leave all the decision making, large or small, up to you. She's not interested in running things and will only offer her assistance if she feels you really need it.

Some find her approach to reason masculine. However, in the areas of love and affection the Libra woman is all woman. She'll shower you with love and kisses during your romance with her. She doesn't believe in holding out. You shouldn't, either, if you want to hang on to her.

She likes to snuggle up to you in front of the fire on chilly autumn nights. She will bring you breakfast in bed Sunday mornings. She'll be very thoughtful about anything that concerns you. If anyone dares suggest you're not the grandest guy in the world, your Libra is bound to defend you. When she makes those marriage vows, she means every word she says.

The Libra woman will be everything you want her to be. As a wife and mother, her mate as well as her children will never lack for anything that could make their lives easier and richer.

The Libra mother is moderate, even-tempered, and balanced. She creates a gracious, refined family life in which the children grow up to be equal partners in terms of responsibility and privilege. The Libra mother knows that youngsters need both guidance and encouragement in an environment that is harmonious.

GEMINI MAN
SCORPIO WOMAN

The Scorpio woman can be a whirlwind of passion—perhaps too much passion to really suit you. When her temper erupts, you'd better lock up the family heirlooms and take cover from flying objects. But when she chooses to be sweet, her magic is sure to put you under the spell of love.

The Scorpio woman can be as hot as a tamale or as cool as a cucumber. But whatever mood she's in, she's in it for real. She does not believe in poses or putting on airs.

The Scorpio woman is often sultry and seductive—her femme fatale charm can pierce the hardest of hearts like a laser ray. She may not look like Mata Hari (quite often Scorpios resemble the tomboy next door) but once she's fixed you with her tantalizing eyes, you're a goner.

Life with the Scorpio woman will not be all smiles and smooth sailing; when prompted, she can unleash a gale of venom. Generally, she'll have the good grace to keep family battles within the walls of your home. When company visits, she's apt to give the impression that married life with you is one great big joyride. It's just one of her ways of expressing her loyalty to you—at least in front of others. She may fight you tooth and nail in the confines of your home. But during an evening out, she'll hang on your arm and have stars in her eyes.

Scorpio woman are good at keeping secrets. She may even keep a few buried from you if she feels like it.

Never cross her up on even the smallest thing. When it comes to revenge, she's an eye-for-eye woman. She's not too keen on forgiveness—especially when she feels she's been wronged. You'd be well-advised not to give her any cause to be jealous, as difficult as that may sound to Gemini ears. When the Scorpio woman sees green, your life will be made far from rosy. Once she's put you in the doghouse, you can be sure you're going to stay there an awfully long time.

You may find life with the Scorpio woman too draining. Although she may be full of spice, she may not be the kind of partner you'd like to spend the rest of your natural life with. You'd prefer someone gentler and not so hot-tempered; someone who can take the highs with the lows and not bellyache; someone who is flexible and understanding. If you've got your sights set on a shapely Scorpion, forget about that angel of your dreams. A woman born under Scorpio can be heavenly, but she can also be the very devil when she chooses.

As a mother, a Scorpio is protective yet encouraging. She will defend her children against any threat or abuse. Although she adores her children, she will not put them on a pedestal. She is devoted to developing their talents. Under her skillful guidance the youngsters learn how to cope with adversity.

GEMINI MAN
SAGITTARIUS WOMAN

In the astrological scheme of things Sagittarius is the true zodiacal mate of Gemini, but also your zodiacal opposite. With your youthful, adventurous streaks the two of you should be able to experience all the variety of life to the full.

You probably have not encountered a more good-natured woman than the one born under the sign of Sagittarius. They're full of bounce and good cheer. Their sunny dispositions seem permanent and can be relied upon even on the rainiest days.

Women Archers are almost never malicious. If ever they seem to be, it is probably due to the fact that they are often a little short on tact. Sagittarius say literally anything that comes into their heads— no matter what the occasion. Sometimes the words that tumble out of their mouths seem downright cutting and cruel. Still, no matter what she says, she means well. The Sagittarius woman is capable of losing some of her friends—and perhaps even some of yours— through a careless slip of the lip.

On the other hand, you appreciate her honesty and good intentions. To you, qualities of this sort play an important part in life. With a little patience and practice, you can probably help cure your Sagittarius of her loose tongue. In most cases, she'll give in to your better judgment and try to follow your advice to the letter.

Chances are, she'll be the outdoors type. Long hikes, fishing trips, and white-water canoeing will appeal to her. She's a busy person; no one could ever call her a slouch. She sets great store in mobility. Like you, she possesses a pair of itchy feet. She won't sit still for a minute if she doesn't have to.

She is great company most of the time and, generally, lots of fun. Even if your buddies drop by for poker and beer, she won't have any trouble fitting in.

On the whole, she is kind and sympathetic. If she feels she's made a mistake, she'll be the first to call your attention to it. She's not afraid to own up to her faults and shortcomings.

You might lose your patience once or twice with her. After she's seen how upset her shortsightedness or tendency to blabber-mouth has made you, she'll do her best to straighten up.

The Sagittarius woman is not the kind who will pry into your business affairs. But she'll always be there, ready to offer advice if you need it. If you come home from a night out with the boys and you tell your Sagittarius wife that the red stains on your collar came from cranberry sauce and not lipstick, she'll believe you. She'll seldom be suspicious; your word will almost always be good enough for her.

The Sagittarius mother is a wonderful and loving friend to her children. She is always a lively playmate and certainly an encouraging guide. She urges youngsters to study and learn, everything from sociology to sports. She wants the children to have a well-rounded education, the best money can buy.

GEMINI MAN
CAPRICORN WOMAN

If you are not a successful business man, or at least on your way to success, it's possible that a Capricorn woman will have no interest in entering your life. Generally, she's a very security-minded female; she'll see to it that she invests her time only in sure things. Men who whittle away their time with one unsuccessful scheme or another seldom attract a Capricorn. Men who are interested in getting somewhere in life and keep their noses close to the grindstone often have a Capricorn woman behind them, helping them to get ahead.

Although the Goat may be a social climber, she is not what you could call cruel or hard-hearted. Beneath that cool, seemingly calculating exterior there's a warm and desirable woman. She happens to think it is just as easy to fall in love with a rich or ambitious man as it is with a poor or lazy one. She's practical.

The Capricorn woman may be interested in rising to the top, but she'll never be aggressive about it. She'll seldom step on someone's feet or nudge competitors away with her elbows. She's quiet about her desires. She sits, waits, and watches. When an opening or opportunity does appear, she'll latch on to it. For an on-the-move Gemini, an ambitious Capricorn wife or partner can be quite an asset. She can probably give you some very good advice about business. When you invite the boss and his wife for dinner, she'll charm them both.

The Capricorn woman is thorough in whatever she does: cooking, cleaning, making a success out of life. Capricorns are excellent hostesses as well as guests. Generally, they are very well-mannered and gracious, no matter what their backgrounds are. They have a built-in sense of what is right. Crude behavior or a careless faux pas can offend them no end.

If you should marry a Goat you need never worry about her going on a wild shopping spree. Capricorns are very careful about every cent that comes into their hands. They understand the value of money better than most women and have no room in their lives for careless spending. If you turn over your paycheck to her at the end of the week, you can be sure that a good part of it will wind up in the bank.

Capricorn women are generally very fond of family—their own, that is. With them, family ties run very deep. Don't make jokes about her relatives—close or distant. She won't stand for it. It would be good for you to check out her family before you decide to get down on bended knee. After your marriage, you'll undoubtedly be seeing lots of them.

The Capricorn mother is very ambitious for her children. She wants them to have every advantage and to benefit from things she perhaps lacked as a child. She will teach the youngsters to be polite and kind, and to honor traditional codes of conduct. A Capricorn mother can be correct to a fault. But through her loving devotion, the children are so thoroughly taught that they have an edge when they are out in the world.

GEMINI MAN
AQUARIUS WOMAN

If you've fallen head over heels for a woman born under the sign of the Water Bearer, you'd better fasten your safety belt. It may take you quite a while to actually discover what this dame is like—and even then, you may have nothing to go on but a string of vague hunches. Aquarius is like a rainbow, full of bright and shining hues; she is like no other woman you've ever known. There is something elusive about her, something delightfully mysterious. You'll never be able to put your finger on it. It's nothing calculated, either. An Aquarius doesn't believe in phony charm.

There will never be a dull moment in your life with this Water Bearer woman; she seems to radiate adventure and magic. She'll most likely be the most open-minded and tolerant woman you've ever met. She has a strong dislike for injustice and prejudice. Narrow-mindedness runs against her grain.

She is very independent by nature and capable of shifting for herself. She may receive many proposals for marriage from all sorts of people without ever really taking them seriously. Marriage is a very big step for her; she wants to be sure she knows what she's getting into. If she thinks it will seriously curb her independence, she'll return the engagement ring—if indeed she's let the romance get that far.

The line between friendship and romance is a fuzzy one for an Aquarius. It's not difficult for her to remain buddy-buddy with someone with whom she's just broken off. She's tolerant, remember? So if you should ever see her on the arm of an ex-lover, don't jump to any hasty conclusions.

She's not a jealous person herself and doesn't expect you to be, either. You'll find her pretty much of a free spirit most of the time. Just when you think you know her inside out, you'll discover that you don't really know her at all.

She's a very sympathetic and warm person; she can be helpful to people in need of assistance and advice.

The Aquarius woman is like a chameleon in some respects; she can fit in anywhere without looking like she doesn't belong.

She'll seldom be suspicious even if she has every right to be. If the man she loves allows himself a little fling, chances are she'll just turn her head the other way and pretend not to notice that the gleam in his eye is not meant for her. That's pretty understanding! Still, a man married to an Aquarius should never press his luck. Her tolerance does have its limits.

The Aquarius mother is generous and seldom refuses her children anything. Being an air sign like your mate, you both might spoil the children with too much of everything. But the Aquarius mother knows how to prepare the youngsters to get along in life. Her tolerant, open-minded attitude will rub off on the children.

GEMINI MAN
PISCES WOMAN

Many a man dreams of a Pisces lover. You're perhaps no exception. She's alluring and exotic yet capable of total commitment to her man. She's full of imagination and emotion, while at the same time being soft, cuddly, and domestic.

She'll let you be the brains of the family; she's contented to play a behind the scenes role in order to help you achieve your goals. The illusion that you are the master of the household is the kind of magic that the Pisces woman is adept at creating.

She can be very ladylike and proper. Your business associates and friends will be dazzled by her warmth and femininity. Although she's a charmer, there is a lot more to her than just a pretty exterior. There is a brain ticking away behind that soft, womanly facade. You may never become aware of it—that is, until you're married to her. It's no cause for alarm because she'll most likely never use it against you, only to help you and possibly set you on a more successful path.

If she feels you're botching up your married life through careless behavior or if she feels you could be earning more money than you do, she'll tell you about it. But any wife would, really. She will never try to usurp your position as head and breadwinner of the family.

No one had better dare say one uncomplimentary word about you in her presence. It's likely to cause her to break into tears. Pisces women are usually very sensitive beings. Their reaction to adversity, frustration, or anger is just a plain, good, old-fashioned cry. They can weep buckets when inclined.

She can do wonders with a house. She is very fond of dramatic and beautiful things. There will always be plenty of fresh-cut flowers around the house. She will choose charming artwork and antiques, if they are affordable. She'll see to it that the house is decorated in a dazzling yet welcoming style.

She'll have an extra special dinner prepared for you when you come home from an important business meeting. Don't dwell on the boring details of the meeting, though. But if you need that grand vision, the big idea, to seal a contract or make a conquest, your Pisces woman is sure to confide a secret that will guarantee your success. She is canny and shrewd with money, and once you are on her wavelength you can manage the intricacies on your own.

Treat her with tenderness and generosity and your relationship will be an enjoyable one. She's most likely fond of chocolates. A bunch of beautiful flowers will never fail to make her eyes light up. See to it that you never forget her birthday or your anniversary. These things are very important to her. If you let them slip your mind, you'll send her into a crying fit that could last a considerable length of time.

If you are patient and kind, you can keep a Pisces woman happy for a lifetime. She, however, is not without her faults. Her sensitivity may get on your nerves after a while. You may even feel that she uses her tears as a method of getting her own way.

The Pisces mother totally believes in her children, and that faith never wavers. Her unconditional love for them makes her a strong, self-sacrificing mother. That means she can deny herself in order to fulfill their needs. She will teach her youngsters the value of service to the community while not letting them lose their individuality.

GEMINI
LUCKY NUMBERS 2009

Lucky numbers and astrology can be linked through the movements of the Moon. Each phase of the thirteen Moon cycles vibrates with a sequence of numbers for your Sign of the Zodiac over the course of the year. Using your lucky numbers is a fun system that connects you with tradition.

New Moon	First Quarter	Full Moon	Last Quarter
Dec. 27 ('08)	Jan. 4	Jan. 10	Jan. 17
8 7 3 5	5 9 1 8	4 8 2 9	8 4 2 8
Jan. 26	Feb. 2	Feb. 9	Feb. 16
9 6 3 9	9 4 7 5	5 4 3 3	8 8 1 8
Feb. 24	March 4	March 10	March 18
5 6 3 7	7 1 8 7	0 6 6 2	4 4 8 2
March 26	April 2	April 9	April 17
0 8 5 9	3 1 0 9	0 8 4 6	6 1 2 8
April 24	May 1	May 9	May 17
2 6 9 7	7 6 5 5	5 1 3 7	8 5 2 5
May 24	May 30	June 7	June 15
0 8 6 5	0 4 4 9	9 2 6 8	4 1 5 8
June 22	June 29	July 7	July 15
5 3 2 9	2 1 6 8	8 3 4 1	8 7 2 5
July 21	July 28	August 5	August 13
3 1 2 8	9 5 7 2	3 9 6 5	1 4 1 1
August 20	August 27	Sept. 4	Sept. 11
1 2 8 4	9 2 6 8	7 4 1 9	8 6 5 6
Sept. 18	Sept. 26	Oct. 4	Oct. 11
6 4 4 9	1 3 7 8	5 2 6 9	3 7 6 5
Oct. 18	Oct. 25	Nov. 2	Nov. 9
5 5 1 3	0 1 2 8	5 9 3 1	1 0 0 7
Nov. 16	Nov. 24	Dec. 2	Dec. 8
7 4 6 1	5 2 8 3	3 6 4 3	4 2 2 7
Dec. 15	Dec. 24	Dec. 31	Jan. 7 ('10)
7 9 4 5	2 4 8 2	2 9 9 7	7 7 3 5

GEMINI
YEARLY FORECAST 2009

*Forecast for 2009 Concerning Business
and Financial Affairs, Job Prospects,
Travel, Health, Romance and Marriage
for Persons Born with the Sun
in the Zodiacal Sign of Gemini.
May 21–June 20*

For those born under the influence of the Sun in the zodiacal sign of Gemini, ruled by Mercury, planet of learning and the intellect, 2009 promises to combine challenges with productivity and the chance to move toward a more fulfilling lifestyle. Although any move made is always your decision, it appears that change for Gemini folk is inevitable. And the most likely place for change to occur is in joint assets and career affairs, possibly involving a partner.

As the year begins, the Sun, Jupiter, Mars, and Pluto are all placed in Capricorn, your solar house of money shared with other people. So the focus is on financial matters relating to business and personal partnerships. For Geminis who usually have little interest in economic activities, there may be a sudden burst of enthusiasm and energy applied here. And joint enterprises should prove most beneficial. You can expect stability in overall fiscal concerns if sensible money management practices are being followed.

From the beginning of the year into October there will be plenty of opportunities to invest monies wisely through the purchase of commercial real estate, home properties, and stocks and bonds. Buying and selling on the stock market can be rewarding as long as you are well acquainted with possible pitfalls. Entering into the world of big business may be on the horizon for many of you. Foreign trade, other transactions with foreign companies, importing, and exporting are all areas for growth.

Pluto, planet of change and transformation, in Capricorn signals ongoing change in shared resources, taxes, and estate affairs. Geminis engaged in an insurance-claim litigation, an inheritance dispute, or a custody battle should experience a win over the next year or so. And 2009 is an excellent year for the debt-ridden Gemini to make a concerted effort to reduce loans, to pay off credit cards, and to finalize mortgages.

Property and divorce settlements should proceed smoothly. For many Geminis, entering into home ownership for the first time can be a thrilling experience. A big surprise, even the possibility of a windfall, may be forthcoming. The fortunes of a partner may rise. Involvement in a business enterprise should see the beginning of increased profit margins. An offer to buy into a professional partnership might be made, which could be the chance of a lifetime. November is a period when responsibility may be more keenly felt and facing up to daily life more challenging. Defer taking on extra obligations at this time unless you are sure that you can keep on top of all duties and the demands of others.

Jupiter, planet of good fortune, changes signs early in January and enters Aquarius, your solar house of travel and education. Jupiter in Aquarius for the rest of the year keeps you in sync with your on-the-go Gemini nature. Being on the move is important to you, and staying in one place for too long can be boring. You are always seeking ways to widen your horizons and to expand your knowledge, mainly by travel, reading, and researching. Throughout 2009 significant journeys are likely to be high on your goals list as you feel the urge to broaden your mind. The doors of opportunity for learning receive a substantial boost this year. You may travel extensively to unusual parts of the world and experience unique adventures.

Jupiter in Aquarius also shines a spotlight on metaphysics, religion, and a variety of belief systems. These could be worth researching now to ascertain whatever topics hold your interest long enough to move on to formal study. Gemini students and research professionals can make giant leaps as your interest in getting to the bottom of mysteries, in flushing out statistics, and in gathering data is enhanced. This is an excellent year to enroll in or return to school either full time or part time. Education will enable you to obtain qualifications that ease your career path. Gemini teachers, trainers, lecturers, and presenters should enjoy an emotionally and financially gratifying year. Authors, journalists, and broadcasters can also expect to generate more income. The highly talented among you could receive recognition, honors, and public acclaim from the fruits of your creativity.

Wherever taskmaster Saturn resides in your solar chart, lessons unfold. Disciplined Saturn resides in the sign of Virgo until the end of October. Saturn in Virgo impacts home life and roots, both past and present. Ties with family, close kin, oldsters, and youngsters are accented. Yet spending quality time with loved ones is well worth any effort and sacrifice. Issues relating to the family play a major role. Decisions about what is desired from your emotional life may be required. Breaking from the control and restrictions placed by parents could find many young Geminis opting for independence, leaving the nest, and setting up your own abode to obtain wanted freedom. Those of you with elderly parents could face heavy obligations. This may mean remodeling your living quarters to house dependent relatives.

At the end of October disciplined Saturn arrives in the sign of Libra, placing a focus on pleasurable pastimes, romantic encounters, creative expression, and children. Saturn resides in Libra through 2011. Over the next two years a hobby that you are passionate about could become a marketable product and then generate a second income. Geminis achieving parenthood for the first time will experience the joy as well as the hard work of a new addition to the household. Others Twins might decide to marry someone in an older age bracket. While Saturn is in Libra, be prudent with your money. Any form of gambling, speculation, or high-risk venture is not recommended. Stick to safe investments in solid stocks, bonds, and real estate.

As rebellious planet Uranus continues to move through Pisces, the occupational sector of your solar chart, there may be a push-and-pull process when it comes to your career and business affairs. Restlessness within your career environment is a challenge that will need to be overcome throughout 2009. As a Gemini, your tolerance for employment duties that are boring or mundane is generally limited. So it is essential to seek work that provides variety and autonomy. Put plenty of diversity into your daily routines to keep boredom to a minimum.

Breakthroughs are likely in career and business affairs, helping to eliminate limitations that may have been holding up progress. Employment prospects should increase as lucrative offers come your way and as the financial circumstances of an employer change. Initiating change in your own working life may be under consideration. You might opt for self-employment, move on to a higher paid job, or reduce the hours you work. Promotion, salary hikes, or a large bonus surely will fatten your bank account this year.

Healthwise, this is a year to maintain a good diet and a regular fitness program. Appointments for dental care, medical checkups, and optometry visits should be made throughout the year to retain a high standard of good health. Gemini people might need to learn and to practice the art of relaxation. Make this an integral part of your daily routine. Continually running on nerves and adrenaline can raise your stress level, so implement daily activities to unwind are implemented. Meditation and yoga can center you and renew your energy and should be included in your overall health and fitness regime. Listen to music and participate in creative pursuits that don't require intense mental activity. Easy intellectual stimulation is actually relaxing for Geminis. Battling with weight gain might not be a worry for many Twins who pursue an active lifestyle that is to your liking. Walking, dancing, and playing sports can keep the pounds down, as can scheduled trips to the gym. Choose the activities that suit your individuality and health needs. Remember always to avoid speed and haste and to opt for safety.

Romantic encounters for Gemini are plentiful when traveling and while socializing with friends and colleagues. Romance is particularly lively during the long period while Venus transits Aries, your solar house of friendships, from February 3 through the first week of June. A romance with a friend could develop into a strong commitment. There should be numerous opportunities for single Twins to engage in intense and passionate liaisons. From the end of October onward while Saturn is in Libra and Mars is in Leo, love affairs could take on a more serious tone. The chances of entering into a permanent union, getting married, or moving in with a lover are on the rise. If relationship problems exist, counseling can be beneficial. It should bring fruitful results for couples who are experiencing a rough patch. For some Geminis, this is the year when you finally realize that a love affair has outlived its purpose and it is time to separate and move on.

To the uninitiated, a retrograde planet seems to stop before apparently moving backward in the zodiac. All planets except the Sun and Moon appear to go through this optical illusion of retreating, which in astrology is called retrograde motion. It is your ruler, informative Mercury, that causes the most chaos when retrograde. Misunderstandings, delays, and confusion are possible. Breakdowns in electronic equipment, communication, and transportation are also possible. Making decisions, signing important paperwork, and purchasing expensive items are not recommended. However, you don't need to hibernate during a Mercury retrograde. Instead, review, rethink, and reconsider situations, choices, and current goals to ensure that you are working toward your main aim. Mercury usually goes retrograde three times a year, but in 2009 Mercury is retrograde four times: January 11–February 1, May 7–30, September 7–29, December 26–January 15, 2010.

The phases of the Moon can be a guide to decision making and appropriate action. Beginning a venture during the New Moon phase can increase the chances of obtaining a fruitful conclusion. Completing a venture during the Full Moon phase can bring the desired end results. People, including yourself, are likely to be cranky and agitated during Full Moon phase. This is the time to steer clear of risky behavior.

Gemini folk will find that 2009 is a year of steady progress, aided by a little bit of financial luck. Now is the time to make a strong commitment to move toward the achievement of your dreams.

GEMINI
DAILY FORECAST

January–December 2009

JANUARY

1. THURSDAY. Empowering. Life will keep you on your toes as
the new year begins. First and foremost, consider what changes are
needed to increase your emotional comfort. Make use of this holiday to record a list of cherished goals and hopes for your future.
Your ruling planet Mercury governs the mind. So you Gemini folk
have a head start when it comes to a quick wit, resourcefulness, and
the ability to communicate in an articulate manner. This morning
Mercury moves into Aquarius, your ninth house, which will aug-
ment your interest in travel, philosophical ideas, and religious beliefs. This is the time to research a desirable vacation destination
and start making plans.

2. FRIDAY. Fortunate. Trends are favorable and some luck prevails
for Gemini. Nine planets are placed at the top of your solar chart, in
the signs of Capricorn, Aquarius, and Pisces. These placements increase your ambition and the desire to be recognized by your peers.
Ideas that you develop and that can extend your social skills will be
of importance. Working in the wider community will appeal. Fortunate Jupiter is in Capricorn, one of your financial houses, and heralds
good news with an insurance settlement, a legacy, or a large bonus or
salary increase promised to your partner. However, serious Saturn is
retrograde in Virgo. So those of you waiting to hear news about the
purchase of property might need to wait a little longer.

3. SATURDAY. Opportune. Domestic and professional matters
could clash, which might lead to the resolution of a conflict. Someone from your past may return, bringing the chance to catch up, to
reminisce, and, for some of you, to move on altogether. Venus,
planet of love and beauty, moves into the placid sign of Pisces, enhancing your career and business success. From now through February 2, Gemini folk will be able to make smart choices regarding

133

various professional options. Something that begins now could be of benefit in the future. So this is the time to consider going back to school to further your education if it aids career advancement. Singles are destined to find love with a colleague or collaborator.

4. SUNDAY. Passionate. Even if you are in the mood to get out and socialize, this is definitely a day to arrange a long stay in bed with a lover and strengthen the ties that bind. Passion and desire are on the rise as affectionate Venus happily links with intense Pluto. Gemini singles will be thrilled by a powerful romantic encounter. Going out with mutual friends should appeal to coupled Geminis. Interacting and communicating can provide the stimulation you need now and will be a lot of fun. A sentimental possession that you thought was lost could be found, which will increase the pleasure of the day. Discussions about joint finances and partnerships should reach a positive conclusion.

5. MONDAY. Creative. Your artistic talents and skills are to the fore. So this is the time to utilize original ideas and inspiration in order to push creative projects forward. Getting along with people is easy for the friendly Gemini. Today, cooperation and the willingness of others to work with you will assist all endeavors. Carrying out plans that involve joint finances should proceed without a hitch. The savvy shopper can make considerable savings at the January sales. At midday the Moon slips into Taurus, your house of solitary activity. That is the signal to take it easy, to slow down, to relax. Plan a restful evening. If the bank balance can be stretched to cover a massage, treat yourself to sheer bliss.

6. TUESDAY. Expansive. Jupiter, planet of abundance, has just moved into Aquarius, opening up new opportunities for travel and education. Any point this year is a great time for Gemini people to take off on a journey of a lifetime, to move abroad for work, or to become a volunteer abroad. Why not start planning now? Your mind is more open to learning, and a variety of topics will appeal even if you have concluded formal education. Whether you enroll in an academic course or a self-improvement program, expanding your knowledge and skills base will be of interest to most Twins. Belief structures, philosophies, and spirituality could be examined in depth.

7. WEDNESDAY. Leisurely. A slow start to the day is likely. If you are not on the job, taking it easy is recommended. This morning your intuitive abilities are enhanced. So you would be wise to trust that your hunches will be on target and will find their mark. In the afternoon the Moon enters your sign of Gemini, which will renew your enthusiasm and energy for whatever personal tasks are on your must-do list. Make good use of time off. Apply effort to hygiene and grooming, perhaps creating a new hairstyle, changing your makeup, or selecting some designer clothes. Keep financial plans to yourself. Someone close could try to turn you to their way of thinking.

8. THURSDAY. Tricky. Several matters to sort out around home base may bring frustration. There could be a snag connected to renovating your home, purchasing property, or signing a lease for an apartment. Such a holdup will be quite disappointing. Gemini writers and others whose work requires mental concentration could find that distractions and interruptions at home make the going tough and slow down progress. Visas, passports, or paperwork needed for travel could cause concern, particularly for those of you who were tardy in filling out forms and applications within the required time frame.

9. FRIDAY. Auspicious. A much better day is promised by present celestial patterns, although you can expect to confront minor restlessness. The golden Sun and unpredictable Uranus combine, generating a burst of excitement and renewed energy to seek amusement outside of your normal routine. The possibility of an unexpected lottery win might arrive for some Geminis. Others may be the benefactor of an inheritance or a large bonus. Be ready to investigate a number of fresh opportunities opening up in the employment field. Those of you who have been working hard to obtain a promotion or a higher position in your company could be richly rewarded now.

10. SATURDAY. Guarded. The key to getting through the day unscathed will be your ability to sidestep financial discussions and disputes. People may offer advice that is not necessarily of value, or you might become offended at their interference. Emotions are heightened, so rising to anger over minor issues is more likely than usual. Tonight's Full Moon in the sign of Cancer focuses attention on money matters. You might need to balance out what you can spend on pleasure and what is required for regular commitments. Geminis who were a little too free with the credit card and bank account during the festive season may be wishing that you had used more restraint if you are now experiencing a shortage of cash.

11. SUNDAY. Significant. If you need advice from someone with more wisdom than you, today is the time to seek guidance, particularly if money is the cause of your unrest. Recognition for past good deeds could be received and honors bestowed. Finding the right balance in your life should be easy now, and steady progress toward cherished aims can be made. Messenger Mercury, your ruling planet, moves into retrograde motion from today until February 1. Mercury retrograde gives you an opportunity to review study projects, to complete assignments, and to confirm upcoming travel arrangements. Clearing away debris can also be a way to relieve the anxiety of pressing issues.

12. MONDAY. Varied. Mixed trends prevail, although influences do lean toward the more positive flow of energy. With Mercury in retreat, Gemini folk will need to realize that your mind may not be as sharp as usual. So remaining focused on one task at a time might be more difficult. Mistakes are more likely to occur now, so make a habit of constantly rechecking your work to lessen the chances of errors causing problems in the future. Delays are also likely to create obstacles. If possible, avoid signing important paperwork or contracts. Authors can use current influences to advantage by editing or rewriting sections of a manuscript before sending it off to a publisher.

13. TUESDAY. Mixed. Lunar influences are not very helpful this morning, advising Gemini to slow down and to keep cool and calm. Drivers heading to work or dropping children off to school should maintain a steady pace and obey the road rules. Steer clear of any neighborhood disputes. Don't try to resolve issues with siblings until later in the day. Planning a trip or a short break can be rewarding, and you should experience success with plans falling easily into place later in the afternoon. Domestic matters might occupy your time this evening. Most of you are likely to prefer the comforts of home rather than heading out into the bright lights.

14. WEDNESDAY. Vigilant. Sloppy research and unconfirmed facts could undermine a special report or school assignment, so make sure you avoid this trap. Those of you who are taking an exam will struggle if you haven't kept on top of studies. Money problems may bring uncomfortable feelings. For some Geminis, resentment that your current remuneration is lower than colleagues performing the same tasks could rise to the surface. Defer plans to approach your boss about any inequities right now. Doing so might put you in the wrong light, hindering rather than helping your cause. It is another evening when it would be wiser to seek hearth and home than to venture out.

15. THURSDAY. Smooth. Domestic or family concerns are likely to be the main priority for many Geminis today. Tasks at home that have been left unfinished will claim attention, and removing any built-up clutter might occupy those of you who are housebound. A calm discussion with adult members of your household could successfully resolve a number of issues. Loved ones will be open to consider your viewpoint as well as to cooperate fully. Those of you employed in a family company or partnership should finalize plans to improve or to extend business dealings, but wait until next month before putting such plans into play.

16. FRIDAY. Comforting. Purchasing a special gift for a child or arranging a themed party for a youngster could keep Gemini parents happily occupied. Your creative juices should be flowing. Although a few obstacles might hinder progress in some areas, your artistic productivity is unlikely to be affected. Use your talents at home. Redecorating and improving the living conditions can be a comfort as well as uplifting to the spirit. Singles should consider playing a sport, dancing, or participating in a favored hobby. Such activity will be a delightful and relaxing mode of self-expression this evening. Share ideas with your lover about an ideal future together.

17. SATURDAY. Bright. Pondering important matters would be the best way to move forward today. Leave ordinary tasks for another day. Enrolling in a casual or formal class featuring a topic that is different from your usual interests will provide the stimulation and variety you need to remain motivated. The urge to be creative could find many Geminis out early shopping for items of beauty and art. With the Moon in Libra, the sign of partnerships, couples should plan to spend quality time together strengthening loving bonds. A concert, the ballet, or the opera will appeal to your musical sensibilities, so make the trip to see your favorite fare.

18. SUNDAY. Productive. Your ruler Mercury cuddles up to fortunate Jupiter today, increasing the chance of Lady Luck smiling your way. Gemini folk legalizing a partnership, attending a reunion, or celebrating a special anniversary can expect a day full of joy and happiness. Vacationers needn't fear that delays will slow your journey down. Those of you taking any type of exam should find that the required information comes instantly to mind. Attending a conference based on a special interest topic can be a pleasant diversion. If you are dragging or a bit down, consider making an appointment with a health practitioner for a checkup.

19. MONDAY. Promising. A number of celestial influences should guarantee that you will be kept on the move for much of the day. The illness of a colleague could increase your workload, which is unlikely to sit well with you, but grumbling will only increase your stress level. Devising and sticking to a schedule could help keep you on track. The Sun enters the humanitarian sign of Aquarius, which will activate your urge to start formal study, to organize a vacation abroad, or to research philosophical and religious topics. Legal transactions should go favorably. However, be vigilant and carefully read through important documents and paperwork.

20. TUESDAY. Lucky. This should be a good day for most of you, with good things just falling into your lap. An air of confidence can put you in line to take advantage of a lucky opportunity. Educational plans should proceed exactly as envisioned. A business or career matter has the potential to increase your income or profits. Gemini travelers, whether on business or a sightseeing trip, can find plenty to keep you pleasantly occupied. Those of you presenting a lecture or public address should have little difficulty choosing the right words to keep your audience enthralled. A dating service may be the right vehicle for singles to meet potential romantic partners.

21. WEDNESDAY. Variable. Unattached Gemini should be circumspect, not too quick to jump to conclusions or to judge a potential love interest. There may be more depth beneath the surface than is apparent. Couples experiencing conflict should take a step back and remember the good times. Focus on the positive behavior of your partner instead of concentrating on the negative points. Entertaining overseas business clients and associates can raise your profile, especially if you add your own creative flair when it is time to engage in leisure pursuits. Today's energy can be used successfully to resolve old issues of concern and to cement stronger ties with a relative.

22. THURSDAY. Supportive. A number of planetary aspects are in force today, notably the Moon sailing through Sagittarius, your partnership house. Best results are foreseen by operating in the spirit of cooperation and compromise. Be prepared for unexpected situations to arise. Be discerning when it comes to taking a risk, as you may be tempted to push the envelope a little too far. A new venture with financial overtones could be worthwhile pursuing more actively as long as you know when to draw the line. Plan to do something different when socializing tonight. Enjoyment can come from participating in diverse activities. However, make sure personal safety is a top priority.

23. FRIDAY. Beneficial. An unexpected meeting on the job could result in a romantic affair developing for those of you single. But move slowly, if it is at all possible for a Gemini to move slowly. Don't be disappointed if the relationship is of short duration. Just enjoy the experience while it lasts. It is time to work on money matters. If you haven't yet made a will, this is a good day to decide how you would divide your worldly possessions among relatives and friends. Check your insurance coverage of treasured items, your tax status, and all assets and liabilities. A sense of security comes from knowing that your personal finances are in good order.

24. SATURDAY. Happy. This should prove to be a very happy and lucky day, although there are some contradictory planetary influences that could trip you up. Your ability to organize is strong, however. Being confined by mundane obligations is unlikely to appeal. Stick to a plan if you have certain tasks to get through. Otherwise, you will scatter your energies too far afield. Repairs and home maintenance should be attended to swiftly to ensure that problems don't grow any larger. Geminis in the process of building a new home should be pleased with current progress. Take a lottery ticket with an in-law or an Aquarius friend, and visualize a win!

25. SUNDAY. Cautious. Repairs around home base are unlikely to proceed smoothly. Take care, Gemini, as you could end up creating more work for yourself and others, possibly greatly increasing the cost of a do-it-yourself project. It might be wiser to bide your time over a financial decision, particularly if close family members and other relatives are involved or have a say in the outcome. Those of you seeking to buy a new home shouldn't rush in, even if you feel that a house or apartment has your name written all over it. A few more days deliberating and viewing other available properties would be beneficial. Singles will happily discover that a secret admirer is no longer secret.

26. MONDAY. Positive. A great day seems assured for Gemini folk as a New Moon culminates in the sign of Aquarius. A lucky break could arrive in the shape of an overseas business contract, a posting abroad, or the finalization of a legal settlement in your favor. Students seeking to enter a particular course should use current influences to make your application now. Exam takers can expect to do better than envisioned. Entering a competition or purchasing a raffle ticket whose major prize is an overseas vacation could result in a win, with you jetting off to exotic destinations at no cost to you. Projects that are begun during the next two weeks have a very good chance of success.

27. TUESDAY. Favorable. A sharp mind and a quick wit are two blessings bestowed on Gemini folk at most times, and today you receive an extra boost of this energy thanks to your ruler. Intellectual Mercury merges with feisty Mars, enhancing your mental dexterity and communicative ability. This is great if you are participating in a debate, speaking in public, writing, or doing work of an intricate nature. Editing a manuscript and sending off a completed novel will go smoothly. One downside of today's fiery energy is that you may become irritated by people who are not as quick on the uptake as you. Be patient, as there are not many who can keep up with you when it comes to mental agility.

28. WEDNESDAY. Good. A lively day dawns again for Gemini. However, it isn't the best day to make decisions that may have long-lasting repercussions. Those of you who have been working extremely hard and need time off for a vacation could find plenty of last-minute package deals available and affordable. Just find one to suit your budget. Take the time to do the research, and you should be pleased with your efforts once you are lounging in the sunshine of a grand resort or sightseeing in historical capitals of the world. Business and career affairs are to the fore, giving a boost to your efforts to improve profits and prospects.

29. THURSDAY. Measured. Lunar influences are absent until midday, when they then will help Gemini carry out normal daily activities without too many obstacles slowing down progress. Later in the day family and business responsibilities are likely to clash, causing dissension at home base. A restless attitude could be disruptive. So make an effort to add diversity to what might be a boring routine. Some of you might be struggling to juggle all your current obligations. If so, it is time to employ outside help or to organize a chore roster designed for all household members to pull their weight. Singles should enjoy a pleasant flirtation while out socializing this evening.

30. FRIDAY. Busy. Gemini folk who have a crowded schedule should get started early. Your ability to focus on career and business activities will be stronger during the morning hours. When the Moon moves into Aries at mid-morning, your energy is likely to increase but so is the urge to be free and to be out and about. Your mind could be working overtime. So many of you will be thinking about and trying to devise ways to improve business profits or a salary package. This evening is a perfect time to gather with friends who are guaranteed to provide mental stimulation. Catch up on all the gossip, have a few laughs, and unwind after a busy workweek.

31. SATURDAY. Revitalizing. On this leisure day there shouldn't be too many tasks to deal with. Combining efforts with a group of buddies to fund-raise or to volunteer services to your local community will be an empowering exercise. Gemini folk taking off on a bus trip or a cruise should have an enjoyable vacation with a diverse group of people. If you are the tour leader, you can expect a mainly trouble-free journey. Listening to motivational speakers may inspire you to reassess personal and financial goals and to implement ways to move toward realizing cherished desires. Attending a high-school reunion, a baptism, or a wedding can be an uplifting social experience.

FEBRUARY

1. SUNDAY. Fair. You could be inclined to a lazy start this morning, with energy picking up as the day progresses. A luxurious bath, a healthy breakfast, a crossword puzzle, and an electronic game will provide a kick start to the day. Mercury, planet of the mind and your life ruler, moves forward now in the sign of Capricorn. Bright ideas and schemes should begin to flow readily into your thought processes. A desired travel or educational goal could start coming together, and delays with important documents should slowly disappear. Time spent with your honey this evening can make for pleasant memories.

2. MONDAY. Slow. Even though it is the first day of the new working week, celestial influences are urging Gemini to take it slowly and quietly today. The Moon is in Taurus, your house of seclusion. If possible, take a low-key role in the day's proceedings. Watch what is happening on the job from behind the scenes. There could be a number of hidden dealings or secrets that you are not being made aware of, so be on guard. Don't begin new tasks now. Instead, apply energy and effort into finishing old projects that have been hanging around too long. Those of you seeking special funding or influential backing could make advances.

3. TUESDAY. Intense. Hidden matters could again be of concern. Dealing with a sensitive or secretive woman requires tact and discretion, something that some Geminis don't have in abundance. Graceful Venus, planet of love and beauty, glides into the action sign of Aries. Venus here will enhance the quality of organized gatherings, group events, and socializing with friends. Mixing business with pleasure is advised. Income from your profession can increase. Advancement can be swift and profitable. Friends may play an important role in your life, offering more support and assistance. Singles could find that a platonic relationship begins to develop into a romantic affair.

4. WEDNESDAY. Eventful. The day ahead should be busy and active as the Moon slides through your own sign. Still, you will need to guard against scattering your time and attention over a number of different activities. The unattached Gemini can enjoy the attentions of a dating partner if you go out tonight. But play it cool. Passion will increase for Twins of all ages over the next few days as lovely Venus clashes with intense Pluto. Steer clear of situations that could arouse jealousy or suspicion. Apply effort into making love, not war, because romantic emotions can border on the extreme.

5. THURSDAY. Troublesome. The cosmos continues to shake Gemini foundations. There are a number of celestial influences that are creating change and chaos. Your mood and enthusiasm should be high, but do remain focused to avert going off on odd tangents. Warrior Mars is on the move, lighting up Aquarius and your ninth house. Mars here encourages you to broaden your horizons and to widen your contact network. Challenges could appear from many different fronts as structured Saturn confronts erratic Uranus. Juggling family demands and employment commitments can be a difficult dilemma to resolve.

6. FRIDAY. Emotional. Before down the Moon enters the sign of Cancer, raising everyone's emotions and sensitivities. If you feel overwhelmed by too many obligations, chores, or people's demands, include plenty of rest breaks in your daily routine in order to retain your motivation. Pause, take deep breaths, and apply self-nurturing techniques. Give tender loving care to yourself and to loved ones. With intensity and passion enhanced, the talented Gemini can make progress by tapping into your huge reservoir of inspired ideas to create and produce viable plans. Shoppers should go easy on spending even though it provides emotional comfort under current planetary influences.

7. SATURDAY. Fulfilling. If household spending is on today's agenda, keep the purse strings tight and stick to the domestic essentials. This is another day when you will be tempted to splash out on impulse buying, particularly in the later hours. Your organizing ability and flair for handicrafts are strong now. So with the right materials you could turn old furniture into a home feature. Financial constraints might limit your plans for socializing, especially on expensive leisure pursuits. Think outside the box to come up with affordable recreational activities. Diversity will be the key to pleasing yourself.

8. SUNDAY. Sensitive. Romantic vibes are swirling, urging partnered Gemini to snuggle with a lover a little longer than usual this morning. Vim and vitality, qualities most Twins are never short of, may be a little lower right now. If you have a multitude of chores to do, get cracking early rather than later in the day. Things could become hectic, so pace your activities to reduce the likelihood of running out of steam halfway through the tasks. There could be a lot of traffic and action around home base, with siblings or in-laws popping in and out. Keep communication light and friendly. Avoid controversial topics or any discussions that would stir up people's emotions.

9. MONDAY. Volatile. Old elements can now be eliminated to make way for new ones. Today a lunar eclipse takes place while the Moon becomes full in the sign of Leo. This is an important period of Gemini. An eclipse can bring about personal changes. For some of you, this can mean going off in a new and different direction. Pent-up feelings are natural now, and you might become excitable and dramatic. Take care that you are not the target of someone's frustration and angst. Traveling on the highways could be a challenge, with road rage more prevalent as stress rises and anger simmers. Enjoy an evening alone at home away from the volatile emotions of people who push your buttons.

10. TUESDAY. Variable. Wherever you plan to spend the day, take care. Tension from yesterday's eclipsed Full Moon continues to linger on. Family or domestic concerns might be in the picture. Cleaning and organizing at home base will be therapeutic for Geminis who are not governed by a set routine or the clock. If there are issues that need to be confronted, it is not really a day conducive to airing grievances or problems. By doing so, you may create an even larger divide between you and loved ones. Those of you self-employed may happily discover that working from home saves time and energy, and productive results come from your labors.

11. WEDNESDAY. Challenging. Negotiating may be necessary today if you are being pulled between the opposing demands of your personal life and your professional life. Gemini folk continue to confront the issues of balancing employment obligations with family responsibilities. These challenges may cause conflict with either a superior or a loved one. Keep a grip on your temper, endeavor to find an equitable resolution, and remember that an assertive attitude usually works better than a display of aggression. Exhibit your culinary skills this evening. Create a scrumptious home-cooked meal that all the family can tuck into and enjoy.

12. THURSDAY. Varied. Although the lovely Libra Moon helps to ease tensions and stress, cosmic trends are not overtly helpful today. However, inspiration and imagination are enhanced so you should allocate time to pursue a favored creative activity or sport that would add variety to your day. Geminis who don't want to waste time in the kitchen could choose to visit a friend noted for their cooking expertise. Alternatively, take loved ones out to a local restaurant, and chill out by gossiping and relaxing in a casual atmosphere. Romance is bound to be on your agenda. Right now it will be easier to reach a deeper connection and understanding with an intimate partner.

13. FRIDAY. Comforting. There is not a lot happening to upset your equilibrium even though it is Friday the Thirteenth. On this working day, make an early start and jump into action. An eagerness to get along with everyone who crosses your path can assist employment efforts. Dealing with people in person rather than through memo or mail will bring the best results. Geminis planning to celebrate Valentine's Day in style should finalize details now to ensure that everything is in place to make tomorrow's celebration memorable. A weekend retreat might appeal as a venue to reestablish loving bonds in long-term relationships and to strengthen rapport in budding affairs.

14. SATURDAY. Helpful. No matter how hard it might be, curb your tongue this morning or suffer the consequences. Arranging consultations for your health can be helpful now. Avoid eating on the run whether this is your usual style or not. Geminis currently in a committed romantic union should refrain from discussing joint finances. Talking about shared money matters could spark disagreements, which might spoil the enjoyment of the special Valentine's Day activity you so carefully planned. Quality time with a partner is assured if you create the right ambience. Light the candles, play soft music, and draw your lover out.

15. SUNDAY. Idealistic. Your ruler Mercury going direct has just moved forward into Aquarius, your house of foreign connections. You could find that contact with people from overseas is renewed. Academic and educational plans that were put on hold for whatever reason might again be under consideration. An unusual encounter with someone from another country could bring a thrill of anticipation for the currently single Gemini. Enjoy the ecstasy and pleasure, but take those rose-colored glasses off. Expectations of a new relationship moving ahead the way you envision might be dashed. Language difficulties could mar a social occasion.

16. MONDAY. Fortunate. Employment duties and health conditions could occupy your mind under today's Scorpio Moon. You may encounter a touchy individual this morning, especially on the job. Or you could find that the pressure is increased due to the illness of a colleague. Lady Luck is beaming your way because Venus, planet of love and money, happily links up with jolly Jupiter. This duo in tandem increases the chances of fortunate occurrences and incidents. Retain the smile on your face, and blessings are bound to keep coming. Tonight, as the Moon drifts toward your Sagittarius house of partnership, your interest and attention will shift to your partner and the others in your life.

17. TUESDAY. Profitable. Take advantage of today's positive trends. Relationship activities should progress well. Those of you in a business partnership can expect the working environment to be harmonious. Gemini folk catering to the public should experience successful outcomes. Shop owners and retailers in general will see rising sales. Abundant Jupiter is again spreading luck and good cheer by merging with energetic Mars. Twins in sports and in the military can expect to make notable advances. Legal proceedings should be settled amicably. Socializing with people from different cultures can be delightful and informative.

18. WEDNESDAY. Upbeat. Positive trends continue to open the door of opportunity for those born under the sign of the Twins. Cooperation in intimate and in business partnerships remains at the top of your list of priorities. You are bound to apply more effort into making this a period of harmony and happiness. Use tact when dealing with difficult clients, as their purchases could make a big difference in growing your bottom line right now. The Sun, life force of the zodiac, today enters the sign of Pisces, your sector of profession. The Pisces Sun will encourage your focus on career and business over the next four weeks.

19. THURSDAY. Supportive. Productivity can increase because your confidence and enthusiasm are high. However, your physical stamina might not match your optimism. Too much work could sap your energy, so you will need to keep your fingers out of too many pies today. Gemini in a new business partnership should set forth the guidelines so that everyone is aware of individual responsibilities. Doing so will reduce the chances of future problems occurring. A favorable time now exists to apply cost-cutting measures to your household budget. Eat healthful meals, rather than junk food, and shop for nutritional items on sale at local markets.

20. FRIDAY. Agitating. Minor restlessness could have many of you on edge today. Variety is the spice of life, especially for Gemini. So make sure you add diversity to your routine to ease the boredom of tedious, mundane activities. Joint finances are of concern, so you should be aware of exactly what money is coming in and what money must go out. Put extra funds aside each payday so that you have a small nest egg to call upon if unexpected bills arrive. Be shrewd if a friend asks to borrow a hefty sum of money, as it may be some time before repayment is made. Lend the least amount possible to ensure that your bank account is not uncomfortably depleted.

21. SATURDAY. Encouraging. Go with the flow of the day. Join in with the fun and frivolities of people in close proximity. Opportunities should be plentiful, and your Gemini ability to persuade others to your way of thinking is strong. Weekend workers on the job early can expect to be rewarded. Real estate agents should be happy with the size of the commission check for a profitable sale. Home buyers could find just what you are looking for. If you have property to sell, you could find a buyer and have a contract in force today. Any type of detective or investigative work can benefit now. The progress of students doing research or special assignments could surpass all expectations.

22. SUNDAY. Satisfactory. Geminis could face a dilemma today, particularly if a decision requiring a lot of thought needs to be made. People with strong philosophical beliefs might try to influence your choices and sway you to their way of thinking. Mixing with folk from other cultures is encouraged now. Do the relevant research on traveling overseas. You will expand your knowledge base and broaden your horizons. Vacationers should include sightseeing trips to the seats of government in the countries visited. Romantic vibes are enhanced. If you are unattached and seeking companionship, be wary. Make sure you mingle with eligible singles.

23. MONDAY. Thoughtful. Pondering your options could consume spare time. Returning to study may be one direction you are considering. Another decision may be to pursue either voluntary or paid employment overseas. The opportunity to tender for a foreign contract would be a welcome boost to small business owners, generating a renewal of enthusiasm and energy. Although Gemini is generally a skilled conversationalist, there are times when you may say too much and put your foot in it. Right now is one of those times. Be careful what you say. People can be easily offended by thoughtless remarks. Making promises that you might not be able to honor is also a folly to avoid.

24. TUESDAY. Lively. Excellent celestial trends prevail. Informative Mercury, your ruler, cuddles up to Jupiter, planet of good luck and wealth. Negotiations with VIPs, lawyers, and professors should bring desired results. The energy to begin new career or business projects is enhanced. Tonight's Pisces new Moon increases your inspiration and imagination. Authors and journalists should begin editing current work or begin writing a new opus within the next two weeks while cosmic influences are supportive. Anticipate a positive change in a relationship with an authority figure or someone you respect. This development could prove advantageous at some point in the future.

25. WEDNESDAY. Fulfilling. Whatever Gemini wants, Gemini can get today. Mercury, your life ruler, happily engages with Venus, planet of money and romance. This planetary aspect enables you to attract people and situations that will aid your endeavors. If you need a lawyer, trust your instincts but choose someone who specializes in the area of law that meets your requirements. Chasing long-term career goals becomes more important as your ambitions are fueled now. You are urged to let your talent for communication be the vehicle to generate more income. You can write articles for publication. You can motivate people by speaking in public. You can teach a special skill.

26. THURSDAY. Diverse. Most of you are likely to look back at the end of this day with fondness. Positive changes are making a difference to your quality of life. Geminis who have been working hard without due recognition from a boss or a teacher should receive a boost to the ego now. Talks with business promoters and agents can be beneficial. It is also a good time to network with friends and associates. You are capable of achieving a tremendous amount as long as your focus remains strong. Later in the day a need to be free and to assert your independence could find you shaking off ties and taking off to explore new territory and diverse experiences.

27. FRIDAY. Erratic. Scattered energy can be your enemy today, Gemini. You could be pulled in a number of different directions, making it difficult to accomplish the bundle of work in your basket. Make sure personal possessions are kept under lock and key. Secure doors and windows against intruders before leaving home. You should be in tune with your network of friends, so try to schedule a couple of social interludes over the weekend to catch up and have a few laughs. Boundless energy can have you considering unusual means to generate more income and to achieve cherished desires. Improving your education could be at the top of your list.

28. SATURDAY. Guarded. It is another day to guard your valuables. Gemini travelers should beware pickpockets and con artists. Handling frustrating situations will test your patience and resolve. Attending a family get-together might be more of a duty than a pleasure. It would be wise to defer visiting in-laws and testy relatives, as arguments could create tension and spoil the occasion. If expert advice is required, this is not the day to seek it. Someone could unintentionally steer you down the garden path. Take care if you have advertised household products for sale or are seeking a new roommate. Ask a neighbor or friend to come over rather than be alone with strangers.

MARCH

1. SUNDAY. Informative. Even though you are one of the movers and shakers of the zodiac, today is a day to take things at an even pace and to tidy up loose ends. Minor delays could block progress with do-it-yourself projects. Creative and spiritual pursuits could find favor with many Gemini individuals. If there is a New Age fair in your locality, browsing the tables and stalls will be enlightening and profitable. Those of you conducting workshops or presenting seminars can hold audience attention without any problems. Students researching the Internet or closeted in the library should find the data needed to enhance an assignment.

2. MONDAY. Quiet. The stars continue to encourage Gemini folk to move slowly. If you cannot enjoy peaceful solace, at least step back and observe what is going on around you. Don't let people push you into action. Otherwise, errors could be made through inattention to detail or constant distractions. Be prepared for difficult communications with foreign connections. Legal issues could test your patience and resolve. Behind-the-scenes financial negotiations can be completed as long as any risk has been removed. Organizing a charity fund-raiser might bite into leisure time, but the ensuing emotional rewards should more than compensate for time spent away from home.

3. TUESDAY. Lively. A welcome boost to self-esteem and confidence should be felt now as the Moon zips through your sign of Gemini. The challenges of the past few days are likely to recede, and you can move forward with renewed determination. With energy on the rise, you are ready to talk to whoever can assist and support your endeavors. Prepare for the future by reviewing your aspirations and plans. This could pave the way to an exciting new personal contact or the beginning of an enterprising venture. Venus still in the energetic sign of Aries accentuates your urge to socialize in large gatherings, with hobby groups, and with special friends.

4. WEDNESDAY. Encouraging. Gemini folk are alert, agile, and ready to take on whatever challenges are presented. Most of you should be feeling pretty good about yourself and your life. If you need to impress others, wear a stylish outfit to stand out in the crowd. Bright and unique ideas that come to mind should be recorded for future reference. Support will come from friends and acquaintances who hold views similar to yours. So mix and mingle, making good use of these strong connections. Persuading people that your opinions hold merit should be a breeze. Be confident that you can sell yourself and the products and services you represent.

5. THURSDAY. Confusing. Beware overzealous feelings when it comes to aspirations and ideas. Although it doesn't hurt to engage in daydreaming and idealistic thinking from time to time, right now you need to keep your feet firmly planted on the ground. It is essential to discern what is and what isn't achievable, at least in the short term. Protracted financial negotiations could be keeping your mind locked into the fantasy realm, hindering your ability to look at where you can generate more income or cut expenditure. Frustration over issues that are not fully understood may cause angst. Creative and leisure pursuits will give you some relief.

6. FRIDAY. Wary. An innovative wealth creation idea may be worth a second look, but bide your time with all financial matters this morning. If you have been doing the hard slog and working diligently on the job, don't be too surprised if you receive a call advising you of a pay increase. Venus, planet of the good life, moves retrograde in Aries from today until April 11. An opportunity to review past romantic decisions arises now. For some Geminis, an ex partner from whom you have been separated for some time could make overtures to renew the love affair. Initiate discussions that can help resolve an outstanding matter with a friend or an associate.

7. SATURDAY. Variable. Lunar energy is more helpful through the morning rather than later in the day. Plans can be implemented, errands run, and people contacted, with positive results the likely outcome. Speaking your views clearly and concisely would be the best approach to avoid misunderstandings, particularly on the job or with someone in authority. Excitable people are likely to cross your path. Some encounters may even cause raised emotions and upsets. Discussions with siblings or neighbors could lead to a forceful exchange if you become entangled in their dramatics, so steer clear. Geminis who must attend special celebration or event this evening should make allowances for traffic delays.

8. SUNDAY. Mixed. A bevy of planetary influences will be in play today. Notably, your life ruler Mercury zips into Pisces, your tenth house of professional matters. Mercury here emphasizes business and career negotiations and discussions. The vital Sun and restrictive Saturn are in conflict, which might convey some gloomy thoughts. Don't allow progress to be hindered. Instead, keep busy and remember that this influence is short-lived. It is a good day to get with relatives and friends to discuss everyone's current complaints as well as what is happening in the wider community. Once worries are offloaded, a feeling of lightness is bound to arrive.

9. MONDAY. Useful. Do errands and chores that require plenty of movement first thing this morning, as later on domestic concerns will move into the frame. Activities and interests that affect family life may need more attention to ensure that everything is in order. Twins who have had enough criticism leveled your way could find that just ignoring whatever is said will do the trick. By using this method, arguments are avoided and energy is not expended on petty matters. Enjoy a quiet evening at home playing games with youngsters or cuddling on the couch with your favorite companion.

10. TUESDAY. Complex. Contradictory influences rule the day. Positive stars beam on Gemini together with a rising emotionality brought on by the approaching Full Moon in the earthy sign of Virgo. Things could become highly charged, but urgent responsibilities shouldn't be neglected. Tonight's Full Moon augurs opportunity to wind something up, finalize an agreement, and remove deadwood from your life and replace it with the fresh and new. Problems related to balancing career and personal life could multiply, calling for you to sort out your priorities. An interview for employment could go well, and a long-held dream may become a reality. An adult child might leave the nest, arousing feelings of sadness tinged with happiness.

11. WEDNESDAY. Opportune. The planets are on your side, and life should definitely be looking up. As your professional and business affairs continue to gain impetus, your current optimism is justified and will guarantee further progress. Take time to examine long-term goals, think about where you want to be by the end of the year. Once you establish your priorities, realistic plans can be kept ticking over to increase the possibility of aims coming to fruition. Money spent on minor repairs and maintenance around the home environment will be worthwhile, as your investment increases in value with each improvement made. In romance, don't be reticent in making the first move.

12. THURSDAY. Eventful. A hectic pace is likely today if you have places to go and people to see. Under current influences Gemini mobility is a positive trait leading to positive outcomes. But restlessness could be keenly felt, so add variety to your daily routines in order to maintain enthusiasm. Concentrate on important matters rather than wasting time on trivial issues. Don't give up on a good idea. It might just take time and patience for that idea to be implemented. The creative talents of Twins will shine now. Those of you who appreciate the fine arts can experience a delightful visit to a gallery, ballet, or musical event.

13. FRIDAY. Lucky. Take advantage of the day's positive vibes, and forget old supersuspicions about the date. Today is more likely to be lucky for some of you. It is an excellent period for Gemini individuals to enter competitions and to purchase lottery tickets. Try out a new social venue. It could become a great meeting place for singles seeking romantic interludes and eligible partners. An unexpected visitor may keep youngsters occupied while you carry out important chores. An educational game will amuse as well as teach, so have relevant fare on hand for children of all ages. Being surrounded by loved ones is a perfect way to unwind after a busy week.

14. SATURDAY. Varied. Health concerns, either yours or someone close to you, could bring a change of plans this morning. Staying active should be natural to those born under the mobile sign of Gemini. But if regular exercise is not part of your daily regime, you may need a lifestyle change. Start to include a fitness program into your day-by-day routine. Take care when handling valuables in order to prevent breakages. Repairs will be costly. And some items are irreplaceable. Auditions and rehearsals should proceed smoothly. A successful career on stage or on screen may begin for some Geminis now.

15. SUNDAY. Motivating. Dynamic Mars has just entered Pisces, your solar tenth sector, increasing your urge to push forward with career and business goals. Your desires and ambitions become stronger, and your enthusiasm to strive toward personal aims is unlikely to waver. You will be more inclined to assist others. Performing a good deed may bring an introduction to a potential mate. The challenge for Geminis while Mars visits Pisces until April 22 will be to remember that physical resources might be lower and you might attempt tasks that are physically impossible. Lots of self-nurturing and a good diet will be beneficial throughout this period.

16. MONDAY. Manageable. Early morning trends are unhelpful for negotiating partnership concerns and dealing with customer complaints. However, the negative vibes should disappear by mid-morning. Strive for cooperation with colleagues and clients, as it will reduce the likelihood of dissension lingering. Gemini folk can act as mediators. Your ability to state both sides of a case in a clear and concise manner allows logic to rule the day. Persuade a friend or a partner to go running with you so that you get your daily exercise and fulfill your fitness goals. A romantic relationship will benefit from open and honest discussion of any issues that are causing problems or anxiety.

17. TUESDAY. Productive. Those of you who are involved in retail sales should find that business is brisk and profits are on the rise. Gemini booksellers and travel agents are also likely to have a busy, prosperous day. Staff or team meetings planned for today will provide valuable feedback so that managers can implement the helpful suggestions across the board. If you are one half of a couple, suggest taking a romantic walk with your partner. It can clear the air in a positive way to resolve relationship discord. This tactic could have the double advantage of allaying fears that discord is insurmountable and of strengthening ties and mutual understanding.

18. WEDNESDAY. Low-spirited. Your life ruler Mercury sets the tone of the day by challenging serious Saturn and linking happily with jolly Jupiter. Pessimistic Twins could succumb to gloomy thoughts. But Geminis who tend to be positive should get through the day relatively unscathed. Communication problems, delays, and misunderstandings could increase your frustration. Dealings with people in authority may be fraught with difficulties. Defer major decision making, as your mental agility may be slowed down and your judgment skewed. Silence at home is golden when to avert conflict over the pull between business and family obligations.

19. THURSDAY. Promising. Although a tendency toward doom-and-gloom thoughts may persist, an increased burst of power provides loads of energy for you to perform tasks on your current to-do list. Your persistence is enhanced when assertive Mars links up with forceful Pluto, giving your career and joint finances a big boost.

Recognition and a possible pay raise could mark this day as one of the best so far this year. Some Twins may be thrust into the limelight for services rendered. Gemini folk seeking a personal loan, overdraft protection, or a home mortgage should have the application approved. Now you can follow through on a number of precious goals.

20. FRIDAY. Vibrant. The astrological new year begins splendidly for Gemini. Today the Sun enters the sign of Aries, heralding a new cycle. It is the arrival of the spring equinox when the hours of night and day are equal. A burst of energy encourages you to open new doors. Look for and receive opportunities to move ahead. Rely on the friends and associates who can help you to reach long-term goals and cherished wishes. Social life should increase. Meeting unusual people puts extra excitement into your life. Involvement with a humanitarian group or organization would be an excellent service to others as well as a source of comfort to all. This is the time to join up.

21. SATURDAY. Unpredictable. Your ruler Mercury and erratic Uranus stir up unsettled feelings over the next few days, arousing restlessness and a nervous disposition. Keeping on the move and doing lots of different things will maintain some productivity. But trying to focus may be difficult. Attempt one task at a time to prevent scattering your energy. Happily, Gemini inspiration and insight are enhanced. Writers should find that words fly off the page now. Those of you who are presenting a training course or a seminar should receive due appreciation from your audience. As your mental interests begin to change, you will be seeking a new creative pastime or leisure pursuit.

22. SUNDAY. Diverse. A range of cosmic energy prevails, charging up today's atmosphere. A novel idea will generate a burst of energy and enthusiasm. Focused discussion and relevant input can send plans surging forward. Seriously consider enrolling in a new course that furthers your education if this is the way to maximize your chances of gainful employment. Singles could meet a potential love interest in the classroom. Teaming up to study will have a twofold benefit. Romance can be pleasant as long as you remove the rose-colored glasses and avoid putting the one you desire on a pedestal.

23. MONDAY. Hopeful. This is an excellent period to plan or to prepare for an overseas vacation. Applying for a passport, purchasing new luggage, and shopping for clothes for the journey should have you bursting with excited anticipation. Geminis already on a trip will find plenty of curiosities and souvenirs to give to the folks back home. An innovative business scheme should flourish if meetings with the legal people clear all obstacles and challenges. Don't inadvertently divulge a secret, your own and especially any entrusted to you by others. Arrangements for an upcoming social event may be running over budget, so immediate cost-cutting measures should be implemented.

24. TUESDAY. Easygoing. Be content with this average day, which you can use to advantage. You have a chance to catch up on employment and business tasks without obstacles standing in your way. Keep busy at work. Headway can be made when a surge of energy arrives this morning. Consider implementing new methods of performing routine tasks. Figure out how to reduce the time it takes to do them. Relationships with colleagues should show signs of improvement, with recent tension or friction easing off. Joining a hobby group tonight will help you to unwind.

25. WEDNESDAY. Fine. An enticing and unexpected proposition might set the tone for the day. Romantic vibes are enhanced, and love could bloom for the solo Gemini. A group event will be lively, leading to a promising encounter. So make sure socializing is on the agenda over the next couple of days. Slow down the process of implementing a special plan. There may be a dozen things that require organization before your project sees the light of day. Mercury, your life ruler and messenger planet, visits Aries from now until April 9. Mercury here activates your friendship circle, group affiliations, and hopes and wishes.

26. THURSDAY. Auspicious. Blessings are conveyed by the cosmos today. A fresh New Moon in the active sign of Aries emphasizes your solar sector of social undertakings and cherished aims. Exciting trade contracts signed now promise higher income for the Gemini business operator. Ventures begun now have an excellent chance of a successful result. Prepare for changes in your social life. A friend could move on to greener pastures. The way to achieve a special aim will become clear as your ambition, drive, and motivation soar skyward. Donate realistically when it comes to humanitarian and philanthropic pursuits.

27. FRIDAY. Beneficial. A bevy of celestial influences will be in force over the day. Creative talents of Gemini individuals are enhanced. Take the lead within a group environment when it comes to innovative and artistic endeavors. Lovely Venus meets up with the Sun, attracting support from friends and associates. Take action to turn dreams into reality. But if money is involved, accept wise counsel from experienced others when it comes to matters of financial security. This may be an area of concern now. Stability within your primary relationship is also important. So steps to strengthen loving bonds should be implemented over the weekend.

28. SATURDAY. Constructive. Creative ideas and plans will be taking shape. Some of you may be about to move forward with a project that shows real promise of financial and emotional rewards coming your way. Give an elderly relative a call or drop into their nursing home for a visit. It will brighten their life to know that you are thinking of them. Tact and diplomacy could be called for this evening when socializing with influential friends and colleagues. The saying that familiarity breeds contempt may apply here. So behave if you are in line for promotion or pay increase.

29. SUNDAY. Good. It is never easy for those born under the sign of Gemini to slow down and relax. The Moon is drifting through Taurus, your solar sector of solitude and personal limitations. The Taurus Moon is signaling you to rest, relax, and recharge your batteries whether they are run-down or not. Indulge in favorite foods, discuss world affairs with knowledgeable others, read, or stay in bed for an hour longer than usual. Nurturing yourself provides time to look at your life and see if there are areas where change can be implemented to maximize emotional fulfillment and satisfaction. Being privy to a secret could work to your advantage

30. MONDAY. Fair. A sluggish start to the day vanishes once the Moon zooms into your sign this morning. Then the tempo picks up and it could be go, go, go for the energetic among you. Beware of becoming overly opinionated or argumentative. Geminis inclined to chat should prepare to listen also. Otherwise, in your bid to express opinions and views to whoever is in close proximity, you could miss out on hearing important news. This is an excellent period to make decisions, sign contracts, and generally put your goals into action. Spending time and money on personal grooming should also be on your agenda. You and others are bound to be very pleased with the results.

31. TUESDAY. Uncertain. Leave important family discussions or decisions until this evening when the universe will be more supportive. Arguments and tension could arise on the job unless a concerted effort to remain cool and collected is applied. Compromise and cooperation with colleagues can pave the way to a harmonious working environment. Be mindful of personal safety, and especially watch where you are walking. Take what you hear with a grain of salt, as minor deceptive forces are in play. A renovation project may be costing more than the budget allows. Make sure you obtain firm estimates from tradespeople you might hire to complete the work.

APRIL

1. WEDNESDAY. Chancy. Personal aims and ambitions are likely to occupy your mind as the new day and new month begin. Later on today financial matters could take precedence, but your urge to splurge dominates. The Sun remains in Aries, your house of friends, so the desire to party and have a good time could see you over-indulging and overspending. Be clear about what belongs to you and what belongs to others. Geminis with something to sell should beware of overestimating the value of the product for sale. Making promises that are unrealistic and overscheduling your time are two traps to avoid if you can.

2. THURSDAY. Calm. Focusing on the basic issues of personal saving and spending would be productive today. Heeding the wise words of an elder can help you clear up money worries. Your ruler Mercury is creating friction with structured Saturn. So even if you have preset plans, these are likely to change. Confirm arrangements before going out, as travel delays may mean you cannot meet people when or where you are expected. Enjoying an evening out after a long day on the job will revitalize your spirits. Even a leisurely walk to a nearby restaurant for a quiet meal by yourself or with a companion would do the trick.

3. FRIDAY. Intense. Gemini home owners might need to borrow money for unexpected repairs or renovations. Even though this could be problematic in the short term, using funds to improve your property should be worthwhile and will make for future gains. Harmonious Venus challenges intense Pluto, exposing both the hidden passion and conflict in romantic relationships. Sexual tension, dramatic events, or money problems could arise over the next few days, requiring focus and attention to bring about satisfactory resolutions. Regardless of what unfolds, refuse to be drawn into power plays and emotional manipulation initiated by others. The weekend promises excitement and change.

4. SATURDAY. Varied. Mixed fortunes are in store for Gemini folk today. Communicative Mercury combines happily with Jupiter, which will enhance your good judgment and positive thinking. Decisions involving education, travel, and long-term goals can be made with more confidence that your choices will be the right ones. But Saturn, planet of limitations, may spoil the party for some of you. Saturn in opposition to dynamic Mars can deplete your physical energy and slow down your enthusiasm and drive. If you have big plans for tonight, take it easy through the day and schedule an afternoon nap to ensure you have plenty of vitality in reserve to enjoy socializing.

5. SUNDAY. Low-key. It is another day when your physical resources could be in short supply. Do the urgent duties first just in case you run out of steam by midday. As a Gemini you are an expert in the art of communication. But it would be wise to steer clear of controversial topics this morning in order to avoid possible unpleasant incidents. Pluto, the planet of transformation, is moving retrograde through Capricorn from now until September 11. Dig deep and search for answers on hidden matters, death, rebirth, and the joint resources of people close to you. These issues should be brought to the surface and examined.

6. MONDAY. Improving. The dawn of a new working week could find some of you a little restless and not ready to settle down to routine tasks. The thought of breaking free from a daily regime may be exciting but impractical. Endeavor to work this energy off effectively by keeping on the move. The Moon in practical Virgo does help to improve Gemini organizational skills. Cleaning, cooking, and general housework should appeal to those of you at home. Filing and rearranging your working environment will be useful to boost job productivity. Meditating together with a gentle exercise program will be beneficial for relaxation and unwinding.

7. TUESDAY. Perceptive. Gemini imagination and sensitivity are enhanced today as alert Mercury harmonizes with inspirational Neptune. Your mental focus may not be as sharp as usual, so this energy is better applied to creative and artistic projects. Writing prose and lyrics for music can be a joyful experience, and your compositions will send a powerful message to potential listeners. Flowers gifted to a loved one will speak volumes, especially to someone ill and in need of cheering up. Your intuition, spiritual insight, and psychic awareness are high now. So this is an excellent period to use meditation and visualization as ways to aid the creation of your own reality.

8. WEDNESDAY. Vexing. Although the Moon is gliding through Libra, your house of play, lunar aspects to other planets are not very helpful. Mild agitation and frustrating occurrences can slow down progress and productivity. Joint finances could be the cause of disputes this morning. Unless money matters are pressing and must be addressed with a significant other, postpone discussions for a few days. If you are hosting a dinner, keep the menu simple, inexpensive, and devoid of foods that could cause allergic reactions among guests. Social life is unlikely to be swinging tonight. So save money and remain at home instead. Aim for an early night.

9. THURSDAY. Significant. Take care under today's Full Moon in the sign of Libra, which could bring clashes among friends over money and social pursuits. The Full Moon phase urges Geminis to complete outstanding projects. An important step regarding a child's future should be taken now. A long-range goal might come to fruition. Defusing built-up emotions in your love life will require diplomacy and patience, so don't jump the gun and do something you will regret. Your life ruler Mercury enters Taurus, your house of sorrows, secrets, and solitary activity. With Mercury in Taurus, secret strategies to move ahead can be devised. And confidential negotiations can go forward.

10. FRIDAY. Lucky. Although sensitive emotions may persist, it should be an action-packed day. The Sun and Jupiter increase the chances of Lady Luck smiling your way. Buy a lottery ticket, plan an overseas vacation, enroll in a language course. Being more absorbed than usual in your own world of thoughts, fantasies, and dreams is very helpful to the authors, and designers among you. Geminis attending an interview or audition have a head start on your competitors. And students given a number of tricky questions to answer are unlikely to be tripped up. The resumption of talks and negotiations with someone in authority should spell future financial gains.

11. SATURDAY. Persuasive. Gemini concentration and focus are very strong today. Your life ruler Mercury happily connects to powerful Pluto. And retrograde Venus slips back into Pisces. If there is a need to lay things on the line, to speak up, don't hold back. Confidently state your views and be heard. Writers, teachers, and those of you involved in any sort of intellectual work should experience a positive period. Ideas flow because of your ability to express thoughts succinctly. Buying, selling, and negotiating deals can proceed smoothly as your powers of persuasion reach a peak. Go easy on the food and alcohol you consume this evening. Be kind to your digestive system.

12. SUNDAY. Enjoyable. Current planetary energy assists Geminis who need to get to the bottom of a mystery or to do some research. Many of you will be putting your nose to the grindstone in order to complete various tasks even though it is supposed to be a day of rest. Schedule some time to examine health issues. Pay special attention to signals from your body. Parents could find that an outing designed for youngsters turns out to as exciting for you as it is for them. So have fun and rediscover your inner child. Make the evening a child-free zone. Put the kids to bed early, then bond and relax with your significant other.

13. MONDAY. Agitating. Minor restlessness can slow down progress. Arguments might create conflicts, and coworkers or members of the public could be more demanding than usual. Don't let the mask of composure slip, Gemini. Remain calm, and to the best of your ability do whatever tasks need to be done. Energy expended on running around or trying to please everyone is a waste of time, and you are unlikely to accomplish too much anyway. Check your car's battery, tires, and gas gauge before driving too far from home to lessen the chance of a breakdown. It is not the day to press people into signing contracts or making agreements.

14. TUESDAY. Uncertain. Mixed planetary trends advise caution, particularly when it comes to business as well as intimate relationships. Partners are bound to make their presence keenly felt. Important issues should be discussed during the morning hours or later in the afternoon in order to reduce the possibility of conflict. Resolution of an ongoing legal matter appears likely, although not everything will fall in your favor. You may need to settle for less than was anticipated at the outset. Radical views are likely to be challenged now. So make sure you have supporting evidence to back up your claims.

15. WEDNESDAY. Cautious. Lunar influences impart a financial theme to the day. Straightening out records, obtaining competitive quotes for home or vehicle insurance, and trading on the stock market could claim your time and attention. A spiritual atmosphere also prevails. Use your imagination to overcome barriers and blocks with creative and artistic enterprises. Beware impulsive action and rash behavior on the job site. Anger toward coworkers or clients might be hard to restrain, and unreasonable eruptions would prove embarrassing. Slow down if you are in charge of mechanical equipment. Be especially careful handling electrical items.

16. THURSDAY. Chancy. A financial or business proposition might be too risky to accept right now. It would be wiser to think about it and review your options before coming to a definite decision. Gemini folk have the ability to get things done with efficiency. However, your efforts may be challenged by people who think they know better than you do. It will be difficult to overlook critical comments, but doing so will prevent tension from arising. An informal meeting with a business client or collaborator could turn into something more romantic. If that happens, it would be in your best interest to keep the liaison quiet for the time being.

17. FRIDAY. Promising. With several planetary patterns forming in the sky, this is a day when problems large and small can be more easily resolved. A practical approach works to your advantage. Press ahead with a project that has been delayed or placed in the too-hard basket. Travel opportunities could arise. So those in need of a vacation should jump at the chance to take off. Venus stops backtracking and now goes forward in Pisces, your sector of vocation. Venus here promises higher profit for business owners and increased pay for employees. Learning something new is always a pleasure to the inquisitive Gemini, so listen intently to wise and knowledgeable folk.

18. SATURDAY. Unsteady. Up-and-down influences are likely to shadow your every move today. Relatives may be unreasonable, so finding a solution to meet everyone's expectations is unlikely. Communications might be fraught with difficulty. Getting through to the right person to assist with a query can be much harder than usual.

You need a breath of fresh air. The wide open spaces will appeal to those of you keen on adventure and exploration. Gemini students, researchers, and readers will profit from quiet time for concentration. Head to the library or surf the web in order to locate information needed to complete an assignment.

19. SUNDAY. Fair. Don't place too much faith in rumors circulating today. If you are in any way affected by the gossip, do your own research to confirm or deny innuendoes before taking action. The Sun joins your ruler Mercury in Taurus, your twelfth sector. The Taurus Sun encourages you to utilize creative and artistic talents. Gemini individuals may have more than your fair share of unfinished tasks, impending visits to sick relatives or friends in the hospital, and personal problems to resolve. But over the next month your body will send signals to slow down and treat yourself to an extra dose of nurturing. This is a time to remember the three rules: rest, relax, and recharge.

20. MONDAY. Slow. If you have vacation time coming, consider taking a couple of days off now in order to restore your vitality. Making decisions might be difficult, and family issues may demand more of your time and energy. Having the final say in what you do today is unlikely, and you may need to defer to loved ones' wishes in order to maintain harmonious vibes. You could become caught up in routine responsibilities involving your employment or just the general run of life's situations. An older family member may require attention. Although the matter might be fraught with heavy emotion, dealing with it sooner rather than later is advised.

21. TUESDAY. Fruitful. If discussions and negotiations regarding business and professional concerns are on today's agenda, resolutions should be in your favor. When a project plan successfully comes together, a promotion or pay increase will put more money in your wallet. Affectionate Venus and passionate Mars merge, arousing lust as well as love. Finding romance on the job is highly likely for Gemini. Social life should be fruitful. At a party you could meet someone with whom you click, and mutual feelings lead to a new relationship. Creative tendencies on the rise augur a little fame and fortune.

22. WEDNESDAY. Demanding. The pressure could feel overwhelming today. Ask close friends or colleagues for assistance so that you can cope with everything on your plate. Seeing only the big picture might be to your detriment if important finer points are overlooked in the process. Be on guard in ongoing negotiations, and make sure that everyone fully understands the facts that you are presenting. For Gemini with humanitarian inclinations, Mars now moving into Aries will heighten your inclination to become involved in charitable activities. And with Moon in Aries today, sexual vibes are high. So use your imagination to increase the zest in a romantic relationship.

23. THURSDAY. Mixed. Be wary of friends' inflated ideas and grandiose promises. Someone is likely to let you down. Even you could be prone to overly optimistic thinking today. At the very least you should fully verify important information. You also need to consider the long-term repercussions before signing documents and contracts. Your influence over others will be more powerful as your leadership qualities are enhanced. Expect a raise, bonus, or large advance payment. Some Geminis might gain financially through a game of chance. Add soothing lotions to your bath, have a massage, or take a yoga class to aid relaxation.

24. FRIDAY. Lively. On this very busy day in the heavens, things could become extremely hectic. To reduce being stressed or overwhelmed by constant demands, draw up a list of urgent tasks and then pace your activities. Venus moves forward into Aries, your sector of contacts, which will open up opportunities to make new friends and allies who can advance your goals. Over the next few days your ruler informative Mercury duels with nebulous Neptune, posing confusing and deceptive influences. Your imagination will be stimulated, so separating fact from fiction is essential. Late tonight a New Moon in Taurus advise Gemini to reflect, retool, and strategize.

25. SATURDAY. Deceptive. Today is all about Geminis needing to restore flagging energy. Deceptive trends are also being conveyed by the universe, so make sure you are alert and not caught out. If something looks too good to be true, it probably is just that. Think twice before signing important paperwork and entering into verbal agreements. Communications must be clear and concise. A lapse in concentration when passing on messages could result in misunderstandings, errors, or mix-ups. Artistic and spiritual activities will appeal as a relaxing form of leisure pursuit. Try to discover different methods of tapping into your creative side.

26. SUNDAY. Gratifying. Playing a key role in helping someone out of a difficult situation will make your day. Your energy and your mood should lift later this afternoon when the Moon enters your sign of Gemini. Mingling with friends or family members becomes more appealing. Over the next several days Mars and Pluto are in conflict, which can pose a potentially accident-prone period if you are careless. So take extra precautions with personal safety. Intense power struggles might occur, and it is recommended that you steer clear of danger zones. Discussions over a seemingly minor problem could reveal a larger issue that needs to be addressed.

27. MONDAY. Manageable. Today the intensity level should drop a bit, and you will probably be grateful for this quieter interlude. Safety is again the number one priority. Those of you seeking a mortgage or home equity loan should check with several different financial institutions before deciding which creditor would best suit your needs. A sense of humor will save the day if you have to put up with sarcastic comments or needling criticism. Youngsters could create some mischief around the home environment. But with practical thinking and logic, any problems should be resolved swiftly.

28. TUESDAY. Eventful. A busy and diverse day requires your unwavering attention in a number of areas. Gemini energy and health levels swing upward now. Take advantage by implementing positive personal changes in your life. Give your self-image a boost. Splurging on yourself would be in order, particularly if it has been a while since you invested time and money in your appearance. Don't feel guilty about upstyling your clothes, accessories, cosmetics, hairstyle. Just do it, then feel confident about the new you. Avert a potential problem by refusing to loan a large sum of money to a friend or associate.

29. WEDNESDAY. Reassuring. Financial remuneration for all your hard work should come your way, helping you move the bank balance out of the red and into the black. A refund or settlement check long delayed should finally arrive. A continued need to avoid volatile people and situations exists. Beware vacation packages offered via Internet competitions. Some contests are scams, taking money up front from you with no guarantees that you will get what you were promised. When shopping, compare prices and examine merchandise for defects. The vibes are good for moving a new romance forward.

30. THURSDAY. Diverse. A nervous restlessness pervades to-day's atmosphere. There may be unexpected or unforeseen occur-rences, which arouse unsettled feelings. Release pent-up energy through a physical activity or exercise regime. The pace of everyday life is about to pick up and you will feel like things are beginning to make progress. Your life ruler Mercury zips into your sign and your solar first house of self. Mercury here puts you Gemini people in the limelight. Prepare for increased popularity and a surge of social invitations. Surprising news could spark exciting plans. A tantaliz-ing opportunity to do something nice for the one you love the most will arise.

MAY

1. FRIDAY. Scattered. A busy day dawns as the new month begins and the working week draws to a close. Juggling priorities will be essential if you must complete an important project. Remain fo-cused and consolidate your efforts rather than scattering your en-ergies and trying to be in two places at once. There is a need to be honest with those you love, so avoid making promises that you might not be able to keep. Gemini creative talents are in evidence. You may be in the spotlight, as congratulations for a job well done arrives from peers or someone in authority. With sexual passions currently aroused, you will thoroughly enjoy a romantic flirtation.

2. SATURDAY. Intense. Love and lust arrive just in time to spice up weekend pursuits. The more open to change you are, the more you will gain from today's challenging aspect between loving Venus and passionate Pluto. The playing out of this heavenly drama can impact both your financial life and your romantic life. The potential for power plays, jealous taunts, and money mismanagement exists. If your relationship is bordering on the rocky side instead of the stable side, then this may be a time when a break can be made. Gemini singles could discover romantic sparks flying between you and a friend, with both of you willing to move the friendship a lot further.

3. SUNDAY. Structured. Become more organized around home base so that everyday tasks and routines run like clockwork. Draw up a chores roster, including the youngest to the eldest, so that everyone has set responsibilities. Gemini home buyers should investigate the cost of house and land packages now to gauge how far finances can be stretched. Home owners should assess necessary renovations and repairs, then get estimates on potential costs. Those of you lucky enough to have a garden should get it ready for outdoor dining. Indulge a fascination for cooking. Why not invite a few friends over to sample your recipes?

4. MONDAY. Manageable. Be careful that you don't blow things out of proportion or make mountains out of molehills. Personal activities could be neglected because you are so busy climbing the ladder of success. Pause to and review where you are going. Question if your emotional life is completely fulfilled. If the answer is no, then make the needed adjustments to maximize your satisfaction and contentment. Gemini's traveling overseas should be prepared to encounter difficulties at borders. Those of you with creative talents should display your products at local markets and street fairs.

5. TUESDAY. Rewarding. Working diligently behind the scenes now is the way to accomplish set tasks and routine obligations. The key to choosing the right path is to be true to yourself. Keep your options open, as there will be many chances to venture into new directions that can be adventurous, challenging, and interesting. Attending an event, you might be introduced to someone who appeals to your romantic side. However, take care that an infatuation with a colleague doesn't get out of hand. Go out of your way to be generous with your time and attention. An interest in the arts could lead you to render important services that will be gratefully acknowledged.

6. WEDNESDAY. Lively. Remaining busy can be a positive for Gemini folk who prefer to be on the move and to keep your mind occupied. Make sure you tackle problems and tricky situations as they arise. Right now you may have an inclination to put things off or file them in the too-hard basket. Try to add variety to your day. Staying chained to your desk or production line can increase the likelihood of errors occurring when tedium sets in. Spending time with children forges a closer bond and also helps you relax and forget about daily cares. Mixing business with pleasure can bring gains. Dinner with a potential client or a local politician can lead to profitable dealings down the road.

7. THURSDAY. Tricky. Proceed gingerly on this tricky day. Illusory trends are in play now, so try not to be deceived by notions

that are not realistic. The absence of someone who is crucial to negotiations or discussions could delay ongoing proceedings, creating
confusion and angst. The winged messenger Mercury, your ruler,
begins going retrograde in your sign of Gemini, advising you to
take care when imparting important information and data. Difficulty in communicating thoughts and ideas either orally or in written form could be experienced by some Twins. This is not the best
time to sign binding agreements or legal documents.

8. FRIDAY. Guarded. Be careful when asserting yourself today. A
buildup of emotions can spill over into discord and arguments as
the Moon comes to the full in the sign of Scorpio by midnight tonight. The lunar influence could create extra stress on the job or
with health conditions. Clashes with authority figures are also more
likely. A lack of confidence in your mental abilities may be displayed negatively by a bombastic or overopinionated approach. Secret love affairs could be enticing. However, you will need to go
into any romantic liaison with your eyes open to possible pitfalls.
Think twice before volunteering information that could be twisted
to your detriment.

9. SATURDAY. Spirited. Being a free spirit will be the preference
of many Geminis under today's Full Moon. You will not take
kindly to limitations, as they will grate on your nerves. The good
news is that a break from routine arrives, adding a dash of variety
to your day. Those of you who are working should refuse to allow
peers to distract or push their obligations your way. If this does
happen, take action rather than letting resentment fester. Patience
is required in full measure if you are responsible for training a new
person. Remember, not everyone is as quick on the uptake as you
are. A sensitive partner could require more understanding on your
part, so be aware of what is happening around you.

10. SUNDAY. Promising. New financial strategies implemented
over the next two weeks could pay off, with handsome profits coming your way almost immediately. Social activities are to the fore.
Spending time with loved ones may appeal as the main source of
entertainment today. Don't assume the worst if you hear something
that appears to be detrimental about your significant other. Wait
for an explanation or follow through with your own investigations
before jumping to conclusions. Cultivating romance in your life can
be as simple as lighting scented candles, dimming the lights, playing
soft music to aid easy companionship and intimacy.

11. MONDAY. Lethargic. Physical resources are likely to be at low ebb today, so make sure you pace all your activities. Relationships could cause slight problems for many of you. Unfortunately, the people close to you may be difficult to please. Working alone on an individual task would be the best tactic to avoid annoyances and interruptions. Interesting ideas could come from friends. Socialize with folks who are happy-go-lucky so you can get plenty of laughs and a few good tips. Obtain more than one estimate before moving ahead with a home improvement plan. Otherwise, you may be in for a shock when presented with the bill.

12. TUESDAY. Constructive. Communications with loved ones may be strained today. You may be inclined to come up with ideas that peers refuse to consider in a serious manner. Don't become upset or try to change their minds. Instead, focus your energies on productive possibilities. Find a creative outlet that allows you to be innovative. You are bound to be proved right in the long run. If you are trying to sell a number of old treasures via the newspaper or the Internet, handle the responses in a fair and honest way. Evaluate the true worth of goods for sale without exaggerating. A business proposition could put extra dollars in your pocket.

13. WEDNESDAY. Fine. A financial theme pervades the atmosphere. Buying selling, trading, and extending credit facilities should progress smoothly. Good news regarding a long-term financial opportunity or a property refinance could be received and a home mortgage approved. Shopping bargains can be found if your search is expanded to include closing-down sales, secondhand stores, and outlets that specialize in overstocked items. This evening your ruler Mercury, moving retrograde, ships back into the sign of Taurus and your twelfth house. Beware becoming so wrapped up in making it onto the rich list that you overlook the flaws in some of your ideas.

14. THURSDAY. Temperate. Restraint is keyword for today. Joint finances, investments, or a legacy could create upsets between family members unless every effort to diffuse conflict is made. Some Geminis may be in an extravagant mood, finding it difficult to avoid the temptation to splurge on luxury items. Curb bad habits, and use restraint when it comes to spending big on your credit cards. It might not be the most auspicious period to socialize with clients and customers, so try to limit contact to business only. Emotional satisfaction can come through helping others move through their troubles and worries. Make your affection known to your sweetheart, and you can expect something memorable in return.

15. FRIDAY. Agitating. Keep a low profile today, as a variety of agitations may arrive to upset your equilibrium. Conduct an in-depth research of possible vacation spots and weekend retreats so that when you visit you will know what services are available to guests. Act on plans to further your education and your career advancement. Adding a new language to your repertoire will increase your value to a prospective employer and will enable you to find work abroad. Don't be too eager to spend money on trivialities, especially if the bank account is running low. Interactions with older people or relatives might be a test of Gemini patience and tolerance.

16. SATURDAY. Restless. Routine activities are unlikely to appeal this leisure day. You would probably like nothing better than to take off to sights unseen and explore the wonders of the world. A mini vacation or even a scenic drive may quench your desire to break free. Enjoyment can be doubled by persuading a friend or lover to accompany you on an adventure. Geminis required to be on the job should find ways to free the mind of restrictions so that you can fantasize about the destinations you most want to visit. Adopt a flexible and tolerant manner, which will helps you to get along with most people you encounter. Although you probably do possess answers to tricky questions, avoid a know-it-all attitude.

17. SUNDAY. Deceptive. With the amount of rushing around you may have been doing lately, an extra long stay in bed would be in order this morning. A confusing atmosphere prevails, with a touch of deception, so watch whom you trust and where you venture. It is not the time to make major decisions or to place all of your eggs in one basket. Mental activities are not favored, as your concentration and focus may be limited. Beware propositions that appear too good to be true. Watch out for con artists and pickpockets. Geminis purchasing so-called brand-name goods from street markets should be discerning. Otherwise, you might be the victim of a scam.

18. MONDAY. Variable. It is a day for the Twins to be self-indulgent, to rest and recharge run-down batteries. Cooperation will be required to advance an important project, so let it be the more the merrier. Some of you may try to juggle too many tasks at the one time, which might result in several errors occurring. Keep affirming in daily mediations exactly what you want to bring into your life now. Romantic difficulties may arise if you and a partner have very different approaches to expressing love and affection. Aim to finish domestic duties early this evening, put your feet up, and relax.

19. TUESDAY. Fortunate. The celestial patterns that are forming now promise to bring happiness and some luck. Your intuition remains strong, and it can guide you toward new opportunities and ventures. Listen to those sudden flashes of inspiration. Decisions that affect your professional position and status can be made now. This is not a day to beat around the bush. Being upfront and honest can increase your good fortune. Review your approach to handling employment tasks and processes. Being organized and efficient in business and career will enable you to spend more quality time with loved ones and close companions.

20. WEDNESDAY. Auspicious. Happy Birthday! The Sun enters into your own sign this afternoon, signaling a monthlong period for all Gemini people to stand out from the crowd and shine. Your energy and popularity are on the rise, and personal interests are likely to claim your attention over the next month. Early today, however, will not be such a peaceful time. With your ruler Mercury in conflict with deceptive Neptune, you should be wary of signing contracts, entering into agreements, or making life-changing decisions. Your judgment may be a bit cloudy. Disappointment may be inevitable if you expect too much from people.

21. THURSDAY. Innovative. In a very inventive frame of mind, you could come up with a number of brilliant ideas and plans. A high buzz of activity is evident, energizing your day and helping to make life easier. A surge of optimism can be very helpful for completing projects that haven't progressed as quickly as you envisioned or are complicated to decipher. Rearranging your daily routine, beginning a new enterprise, or participating in a team event can be successful now. Geminis seeking amusement this evening should try an unfamiliar venue. Introducing diversity to your social life will increase your chances of meeting new and exciting people.

22. FRIDAY. Mixed. Although your mental faculties are sharp, it is a day when your mind may be willing but your body refuses to cooperate. You probably will be more content to think rather than take action. A preoccupation with your own thoughts and reflections can be productive if you figure out the steps needed to move forward on goals and aims. Backstage business moves can be made, and a personal touch will make a lot of difference to a creative venture. Shop carefully to avoid overpaying or making silly decisions that prove costly in the long term. Social life might be subject to change, and friends might let you down at the last minute.

23. SATURDAY. Dreamy. A few quiet and lazy moments just doing your own thing will not go astray today as the Moon sails through Taurus, your house of solitude and private concerns. You might find that daydreams occupy much of your thoughts. This can be very relaxing for the Gemini who finds it hard to relax the mind, but not so good for those of you with deadlines to meet or a boss to please. Someone in authority might not be as rational as you are and should be avoided if they are prone to pushing your buttons. It may be past time to tie up loose ends, complete outstanding tasks, or attend to pending projects.

24. SUNDAY. Vital. Gemini folk have extra vim and vitality now, and you surely will put this energy to good use. Today's New Moon in your own sign of Gemini heralds the beginning of a personal new year, giving you the opportunity to embark on fresh adventures and challenges. Make plans for the future, as these should be more fruitful than envisioned. Now is the time to meet with people who can assist your endeavors. It is also an excellent time to begin an important project or venture. Plan a shopping trip to update your wardrobe. Make appointments for a massage, a new hairstyle, and a consultation with a beauty therapist.

25. MONDAY. Renewing. Don't deny yourself today. Make a few changes to your grooming that will enhance your appearance and the image you want to project. Gemini charisma and popularity are on the rise, so prepare for a deluge of invitations. Time spent catching up with personal matters can be productive. Dreams regarding a special relationship might begin to take shape. Fresh and exciting ideas will come thick and fast as your imagination and inspiration move into high gear. If you are single, romance might present a pleasant surprise. If you are partnered, add a little spice to your love life.

26. TUESDAY. Vigorous. Make sure personal documents are in order. Dynamic Mars is combining with Uranus, Jupiter, and

Neptune, which urges an expansion of your horizons and your knowledge. Your tolerance of the faults and weaknesses of other people will be appreciated, so display a more flexible attitude. Heightened optimism and vitality are giving you the confidence to surge ahead with new business moves, to seek a promotion, and to make positive changes in your lifestyle. Aim to socialize this evening to relax and to release any stress. Dancing to your heart's content and letting the music wash over you will soothe your soul.

27. WEDNESDAY. Bright. Review your goals to ensure that current aims continue to resonate with personal values. Put your finances in order, especially personal or domestic expenses. It is a good day to establish a household budget. Don't let emotion interfere with moneymaking deals. Otherwise, your judgment will be clouded. Abundant Jupiter and imaginative Neptune meet together, which enhances your creative talents and expertise. This is an excellent period to organize the vacation of a lifetime, to write inspired verse, or to take part in a special celebration or reunion. Congratulations to Geminis celebrating an anniversary or wedding over the next few days. Look forward to a wonderful and joyful experience.

28. THURSDAY. Active. A busy day is foreseen for the Twins as the Moon slides through dramatic Leo. Many errands, phone calls, and letters requiring action or a response can keep you on the move. Be punctual for meetings and appointments. Otherwise, you might experience some sort of financial loss or the wrath of one higher up the ladder than you. At midnight inspirational Neptune starts a retrograde through Aquarius, your travel sector. This retrograde may cause delays with passport or visa applications, problems obtaining vacation leave, or a risk of Gemini tourists being deceived by the unscrupulous.

29. FRIDAY. Steady. Travel related to work should prove to be pleasurable, particularly if you move at a steady pace and refuse to be rushed. Completing duties on the job could be made more efficient if you devise a few time-saving improvements. Purchasing upgraded computer software may be the answer for some of you. If you are experiencing problems with circulation, ask your health practitioner about an appropriate exercise and fitness regime. At work or at play beware of bragging or trying to foist your opinions on close companions. Make sure idle chatter doesn't develop into nasty gossip.

30. SATURDAY. Comforting. This is a good day for improving home comforts and living conditions. Make it a sharing process. If you are in the throes of packing and relocating, things should proceed reasonably well and without too many obstacles. Your life ruler Mercury tonight turns direct to begin the forward march through the sign of Taurus. If you have been waiting for news of a confidential or financial nature, word could be forthcoming now. If you have doubted your intuition, put misgivings aside and listen to inner messages and feelings. Your home could be the place you most want to be tonight, so take a break from socializing and stay in.

31. SUNDAY. Fair. Keep busy this morning to reduce the possibility of gloomy or depressive thoughts arising. Fortunately, this influence is temporary and should be gone by early evening. Action-oriented Mars moves into Taurus, your house of institutions and confidential matters. Mars here will stir up private responsibilities that are waiting to be taken care of. From now until July 11 can be a period when you work best alone or at least not in close conjunction with others. If you undertake menial tasks, frequent rest breaks are needed to keep motivation at a premium. Repressed energies should be healthfully expressed through sport or physical labor.

JUNE

1. MONDAY. Interesting. Variety is the spice of life, especially for Gemini. Changes initiated at home could add diversity and interest to daily routines. A certain amount of discord in your relationships might be caused by your own attitude. There is always a way to create a win-win situation, to reduce arguments and tension, particularly when family members are involved. Give the gift of a compliment or a nice word to someone special. Even though you should be on the job, social activities could pull you away. Some of you will choose to relax at home with your made. Singles may be out looking for love and affection.

2. TUESDAY. Bountiful. Social life is about to take off as Venus happily makes contact with Uranus, Neptune, and Jupiter. Good fortune is also likely to come your way. As your creative imagination is stimulated, this can be an excellent time to display innate talents to the full. Restraint is necessary if you are inclined to overindulge in food and drink. Doing so could lead to an expanding

waistline and lost time on the job. Planning for a wedding party or
a graduation ceremony can make good progress. Tonight is made
for relaxation and pleasure. Do not push yourself or get involved in
activities that require excessive expenditure of energy.

3. WEDNESDAY. Pleasurable. Inspiring comments about a venture
that is nearing completion should enthrall you. Cooperating
with people at home or on the job can bring a successful outcome.
Gemini parents of young children should give honest answers to
their questions even these are strange or hard to respond to. Art
exhibits and gallery openings will be enjoyable activities. Those of
you shopping may be urged to visit secondhand stores and antiques
dealers. Don't miss the chance to explore, as you might make a major
discovery. Look forward to a sizzling evening with your significant
other that will feel just like old times.

4. THURSDAY. Spirited. Energy is on the rise as dynamic Mars
blissfully links up with passionate Pluto over the next few days. An
opportunity that allows for more on-the-job training could appear
and should be taken advantage of. Keep busy on tasks that you
like and do well. Staying on top of your responsibilities will lessen
stress and pressure. The desire to improve employment conditions
could push some of you to the limit and beyond if care is not applied.
Consider a new diet and fitness program if you have been lax
about your health lately or if nervous energy increases your urge to
be on the move.

5. FRIDAY. Helpful. A sobering tone to the day settles as the Sun
and Saturn engage in conflict. However, your logic and insight
should be very strong. Recognize the need for structure and discipline
without allowing this to totally take control of your activity.
Health and hygiene could again be to the fore. Joining a gym or
hosting an exercise group in your home could be a fun way to remain
fit and healthy. An adult child could leave the nest against
your advice. Someone from the past may reenter your life. Financial
matters should go fairly smoothly, particularly if legal documents
and important paperwork are all in order.

6. SATURDAY. Demanding. On this highly energized day business
and intimate partnership concerns are in focus. Dealing with a
competitive situation could be disconcerting, and now is not the
time to take people for granted. Venus moves into Taurus, your
twelfth house, accentuating your confidential affairs from now until

July 5. You might have a tendency to withdraw from social activity and to spend more time on private pursuits. Personal and romantic relationships may be kept under wraps. Gemini singles should be discerning in romantic encounters, as falling in love with someone unsuitable or who is not free could set you up for future problems.

7. SUNDAY. Touchy. Today could prove to be a little overwhelming when emotional sensitivities begin to rise higher than usual. Tension could be cut with a knife, and interaction with close companions becomes fraught with difficulties. A standoff with a personal or professional partner may increase stress levels all around. For some Geminis this may be the end of the road for a rocky relationship. The Full Moon in your opposite sign of Sagittarius increases your need for freedom, bringing something to an end either of its own accord or through your intervention. Couples in committed unions can expect the relationship to be put to the test over the next two weeks.

8. MONDAY. Bright. Although highly charged emotions from yesterday's Full Moon still linger, today brings a much improved atmosphere with love and lust pervading the air. Committed partnerships can blossom under the pleasant link between affectionate Venus and intense Pluto. Love at first sight might also occur under this influence, urging Gemini singles to place yourselves in situations where you can meet an eligible partner. A strong emphasis falls on your financial concerns. There is a chance that a family home or landholdings will provide the extra funds to give your bank balance a much needed boost. A big tax break could also be the source of fresh resources.

9. TUESDAY. Mystifying. Messenger Mercury, your ruler, is busy making contact with excitable Uranus and deceptive Neptune. Defer signing legal documents, especially travel contracts. Restless tendencies may be evident. Some Gemini folk will probably be working on automatic pilot, carrying out normal routines in a dream state. Have your notebook handy to record the unusual ideas and inventive plans that are likely to flow thick and fast. Keep track of meetings and messages, as memory lapses are foreseen under today's influences. If you have overspent on the credit cards, instigating a few economies would be in order.

10. WEDNESDAY. Chancy. Your ruler sets the tone for the events of the day. This morning Mercury duels with abundant Jupiter, increasing your optimism and overconfidence to such an extent that some of you could feel that you are indestructible and invincible. Take a second look at financial investments, be knowledgeable in any negotiations, and avoid wasting your resources. Overbearing individuals are likely to cause annoyance, so make sure that your tendency to exaggerate or boast is contained. Delivering on past promises could prove difficult. Be careful when handling fragile possessions.

11. THURSDAY. Diverse. Stick to your principles but at the same time respect the belief systems of others. If you follow this procedure, you can maintain friendships with people who have a totally different perspective from you. Meeting new people and exploring cultural differences can appeal to the inquisitive Gemini now, and doing so will make your life seem more adventurous and fun. Students should ease off the socializing and spend more time preparing for an important exam. Love could arrive through a study course or an online chat room, but make sure the person's claims are genuine before you become too involved.

12. FRIDAY. Good. Communication from overseas could smooth the pathway to a new career or business opportunity. Some of you may need to look at ways to reinvigorate your energy. The ideal stress release for busy Geminis would be to take off on a weekend retreat with a lover or to arrange time out every day to be outdoors communing with nature. Religious and spiritual topics could appeal and may encourage a closer examination and even formal study. A bothersome trend might make it difficult to avoid conflict later in the day. Misunderstandings may creep into a financial issue, so double-check facts before taking any action.

13. SATURDAY. Inspiring. Today's planetary influences suggest a slow and thoughtful day. Gemini travelers should refrain from eating food displayed in the open and drink bottled water to reduce the risk of stomach upsets. Wondering about many of the unanswered questions in the universe could see you spending hours online researching topics of interest. If furthering your education is a priority, this is a good time to look into training courses and seminars that can help your advance. Tonight your ruler Mercury enters your sign, and the tempo picks up. Choose stimulating entertainment and companions to match your mood.

14. SUNDAY. Rewarding. Professional and career matters are accentuated even though it might be a day off for you. Self-employed and home-based Gemini workers could make good progress as long as you don't spend all day at the task. Your talents can be used to assist others. Helping the needy at your community center or local charitable organization can be an emotionally gratifying experience. Creative Gemini folk might also consider tutoring children or teenagers to express in an artistic manner. Your social charm remains high, so attracting romantic attention should be easy for the friendly Twins.

15. MONDAY. Vibrant. Your ruler Mercury joined to the Sun in your sign of Gemini is spiraling many of you into the spotlight. Social activities are likely to increase, and your presence will be welcome at many activities and outings. This is the time to forge ahead with ideas, plans, and schemes. Let people know how simply brilliant you really are and what you have to offer. Giant Jupiter is now reversing through Aquarius, your house of travel and education. Jupiter retrograde gives you an opportunity to rethink previous decisions made in these areas. If you are considering long-distance travel, make sure that all visa and passport applications are sent in early to avoid delays.

16. TUESDAY. Exciting. Many Gemini folk will be in the limelight again, so take advantage to move your cause and plans forward. The Moon begins transiting Aries today, firing up your enthusiasm and energy. Over the next couple of days the Sun makes aspects to other planets, which will convey possible good fortune, a restless attitude, and enhanced creative urges. These influences can incline you to take on too many chores and to make promises that you may have difficulty honoring. An authority figure or a senior associate could display an inflated sense of self-importance, but keep your annoyance hidden.

17. WEDNESDAY. Promising. A restless attitude can be used positively if imagination and intuition are allowed to take the lead. This day will certainly not be dull, but there is a need for intellectual Gemini folk to translate thoughts into action. Past hard work could pay off as long as your opinions about your boss or supervisor pulling their weight are kept strictly to yourself. The people in charge as well as your peers are likely to notice your increased self-confidence and capacity to take control when colleagues are dithering. Pressures in the love department because of a significant other could create angst this evening.

18. THURSDAY. Opportune. Another lucky day dawns for Geminis who are alert enough to recognize opportunities when presented. A fierce determination and sheer desire to do your own thing can bring successful outcomes. Seeking creative ways to generate more cash is time well spent now. As the hours pass, you might hope in vain for things to proceed at a more leisurely pace. Your body might not instantly respond to signals from your brain. So be content to do routine chores that don't demand too much effort and attention. Take advantage of quiet time to finish tasks that have been languishing on the back burner, waiting for someone to complete them.

19. FRIDAY. Quiet. Take time to rest and review your thoughts and actions. Work behind the scenes, observe what others are doing. Someone may offer some type of backing or support. Geminis who have little choice but to work with others should not display an obstinate approach. Bullheadedness may be evident as today the Moon glides through stubborn Taurus. If there are many demands on you now, it would be wise to highlight upcoming appointments and meetings so as not to miss them. Dream about future goals and how these can be implemented to assure long-term security and stability.

20. SATURDAY. Changeable. More time than may have been allowed could be required in order to complete a task set down for the weekend. Energy might be in short supply through the morning hours. At noon your vim and vitality will slowly begin to pick up as the Moon flits into your sign. Consider relaunching some of your pet projects that have been sidelined. If they are now no longer of value, put them out of mind and move on to fresh ventures. Social activities look set to sparkle. If you have a special function to attend later in the day, it will be an excellent time to make an impression, even a grand entrance.

21. SUNDAY. Important. The Sun is now residing in Cancer, your solar second house of money and possessions. The accent is on your financial arrangements. Over the next four weeks you should focus your attention on values, priorities, and restructuring of funds to improve and enhance security. Over the next few days love planet Venus is smiling on your love life. Single Gemini folk may be more eager to seek interactions that lead to romance. Those of you in couples will want to share more happy times with your partner, maybe even a second honeymoon. Relaxation music is a balm if you are straining under daily pressures.

22. MONDAY. Constructive. Several cosmic patterns are forming in the heavens today. Notable is the dawning of a bright New Moon in Cancer, which will positively affect your financial affairs. Past promises could finally be honored. If you have been expecting news of a pay increase, promotion, or financial settlement, today could be your lucky day. With your sound business judgment, confidently make decisions. There is a good chance of financial gains coming your way. Adjustments to an intimate partnership will enable you to progress to a more fulfilling phase. Strong desires arising now need expression and release. Artistic pursuits are one way to achieve this.

23. TUESDAY. Unsettling. Prepare for a much more intense day than yesterday. Avoid becoming stressed about money matters that are beyond your control. The Sun opposes giant Jupiter, posing a possible clash of egos, temper tantrums, and conflicting viewpoints. Financial discussions with a business partner or a love partner could produce angry words, an atmosphere of tension, and upset daily routines. Be vigilant and restrained. Going over the top or making promises that have little chance of ever seeing the light of day might be the cause of later regret. Geminis who wield a great deal of power must resist a temptation to lord it over others.

24. WEDNESDAY. Improving. Moneywise it might be time for an overhaul of sorts. Future financial security may be a concern. If a shared budget is one of the causes of household problems, seek ways to cut expenditures all around. Less stress and more positive outcomes are likely if errands are performed around midday. Communication on many levels should begin to improve, but do be careful later in the day. Tact and diplomacy will then be needed to avert possible conflict. Keep an ear out for key information that can help further your aims. A yearning to gain more knowledge may be satisfied by enrolling in some short and interesting courses.

25. THURSDAY. Variable. There should be a pleasing result with a debt or some other financial matter that has carried on for too long. Information may be harder to gather, and you might need to go on a fishing expedition to get to the bottom of something. Eventually, you should obtain answers to all of your questions. Responsibilities could be overwhelming, and the way to avoid frustration is by organizing plans right down to the most intricate details. Later in the day you might notice some tension in the air. So adopt a low profile and you will escape a major confrontation. Exchanging unpleasant words with someone special would put a damper on the evening's proceedings.

26. FRIDAY. Relaxing. Tolerance will be needed with people who disagree with your ideas and plans. Perhaps taking time to listen to their views would be worthwhile as they could come up with a number of interesting alternatives. Make sure the fridge and pantry are well stocked to serve guests arriving over the weekend. You will want to live up to your reputation for being a most hospitable host. But don't go overboard with the housework and get stressed out. Relax, chat with loved ones, and catch up on their daily happenings. Social activities outside the home will not seem particularly inviting.

27. SATURDAY. Productive. Today's celestial patterns trigger activity around the domestic environment. The Moon is gliding through the sign of perfectionist Virgo, your solar sector of home and family. Geminis who are moving house would be wise to call in the professionals. This will ensure that your treasured possessions are packed and shipped to their new home in the same condition as when they left. This is a great time to improve the comfort and efficiency of your home-based office; which in turn will increase your productivity. The best way to deal with a family problem is to talk things through with all members of the household. Many minds working together can come up with a number of solutions.

28. SUNDAY. Prickly. Some of you may be prone to a hypersensitive attitude today. Refuse to let critical remarks upset you or spoil your enjoyment of the day. A major clean around home base, removing clutter and items in disrepair, can be tiring but emotionally fulfilling once the job is completed. Seize the chance to show off a special talent or skill. Impress others with your creative expertise and ingenuity. You may find an outlet to display your wares. Recent worries should begin to fade, with life taking on a more balanced flavor. There is plenty going on behind the scenes now, but be patient. It might be a while before you are told what is happening.

29. MONDAY. Difficult. The cosmos is not playing on your side right now when it comes to money and love. Over the next few days fair Venus makes contact with foggy Neptune, spreading confusion and disappointment to affairs of the heart. Logic and reason might go out the window, warning you against making important choices that involve finances and affectionate ties. If your expectations are not being met by your current lover, it might be time to move on and look for someone who has goals and values similar to yours. Children's expenses could make a large dent in the budget, and it will take some discipline to halt unnecessary spending.

30. TUESDAY. Varied. Mixed trends exist today. Opportunities can be found if you try hard enough. Finding enjoyment in life can be easier than envisioned. Begin by writing out a list of all the things you would like to do and that would give you joy. Then make sure you take time out every now and then for some self-indulging. Your love life could heat up a little now, with a number of surprises coming your way. Committed unions may experience a new lease on life. Resist the urge to go on a shopping spree. Gemini vacationers should set a limit for daily spending to make sure your funds will last from start to finish.

JULY

1. WEDNESDAY. Deceptive. Erratic planet Uranus begins to move retrograde through Pisces, your solar sector of career and business. Keep tabs on what you spend while shopping, as you may be prone to excess and blowing the budget. Today has a romantic overview, and time should be given to this area of your life. You need to be realistic when it comes to affairs of the heart, especially if your relationship is shaky. Emotional deception is probable for some Twins. You may be the victim of untruths told by a lover, a spouse, or a child. Geminis socializing this evening should be protective of your health and well-being. Overindulging could find you feeling a little unwell around bedtime.

2. THURSDAY. Improving. There is a strong accent on health and fitness. Progress can be made by implementing a new diet or by adding a few moves to your daily exercise regime. Remember to keep you water intake up as well. Gemini employees should follow orders given by a boss or other authority figure, even if you suffer inconvenience by doing so. If you are eager to change jobs, an employment opportunity suggested by a friend could be worth investigating. With Uranus retrograde in Pisces until December 1, it is important to review your work processes and procedures. Regularly maintain business equipment to avert faults or breakdowns and the inevitable costly repairs.

3. FRIDAY. Active. Partnerships may be a focus today. Rekindling the flame with your beloved should not be too difficult. Gemini singles can expect unusual experiences when it comes to romantic encounters. If a legal matter has been worrying you, deal with it quickly to ease the stress. Putting it off will only increase your anxiety. Your ruler, witty Mercury, zips into Cancer, one of your money houses, and will highlight personal values and financial matters. Future security could be a key, so this is the time to firm up objectives and to make plans. Start performing private activities; stop making excuses that you are too busy elsewhere.

4. SATURDAY. Sociable. Enjoy spending this important holiday with family members and special friends. Your nearest and dearest may need extra love and attention. Don't fret about the little things that may never grow to consequence. Instead, remain focused on the bigger picture. And don't bring up any controversial topic that would cause friction and upsets with a loved one or partner, especially if it involves joint finances and assets. Plan a strategy for following up an insurance settlement or an inheritance. Make sure you have excellent legal counsel if a divorce or property split is in the offing.

5. SUNDAY. Enchanting. Prepare to receive plenty of love and appreciation from today until July 31. Before dawn lovely Venus slips into your sign of Gemini and your first house of self and personal interests. This is an excellent period to spend time and money on personal grooming and appearance. Hair, nails, teeth, and skin will prosper from loving attentiveness, and so will your self-confidence. Those of you contemplating minor cosmetic procedures should be pleased with the prices quoted before you decide. Current influences could prompt long-term commitments from Gemini lovebirds. Singles should attract a lot more romantic interest now. And your creative juices will flow freely.

6. MONDAY. Thorny. Some impediments are likely to cross your path today. Cranky Mars is in conflict with excessive Jupiter and foggy Neptune, warning that honesty is definitely the best policy. If you or others try to cover something up, you are bound to become unstuck. Don't let anyone talk you into doing things that may impact unfavorably on your public image or your finances at a later time. If you are in involved in organizing a charitable event, take extra care, particularly if your responsibilities include handling funds. Gemini treasurers of voluntary groups should see that the account books are up-to-date and in good order.

7. TUESDAY. Poignant. A slightly troublesome day looms for Gemini. Avoid overreacting or making mountains out of molehills. Consider your options as each issue arises so that the best decision can be made on an individual basis. You could be more emotionally wrought up under the eclipsed Full Moon in the sign of Capricorn. This Full Moon lights up the part of your solar horoscope that includes your financial houses of personal income, Cancer, and of joint resources, Capricorn. Balancing the budget and sorting out who owes what among those with whom you share expenses could be a hassle. A change in financial circumstances, possibly through making the final payment of a loan, can be expected.

8. WEDNESDAY. Important. Finances and assets shared with other people may be of primary importance to you now. Check that your insurance coverage is adequate in case of theft or accidental breakage, that your will is up-to-date and in a safe place, and that any issues relating to a legacy have been appropriately addressed. Loan officers could look kindly on your request for a mortgage or increased credit line. Interstate and international travel can broaden your horizons and expand your knowledge. But if you cannot afford a vacation now, do research and learn more about your interests. Launch your own website to showcase your talents.

9. THURSDAY. Advantageous. Sensible solutions to financial issues affecting the home environment can come easily now as the Sun joins happily with structured Saturn. Foreign links may feature strongly. Gemini individuals will find that time and energy spent entertaining and working side by side with folk from overseas can be hugely profitable. Learn what they do differently, share ideas, and provide feedback. In this way everyone grows, and a bond of friendship is created. Cultural events featuring music can be an uplifting experience. Creative pastimes will relax as well as teach and inspire.

10. FRIDAY. Liberating. Talents are unlocked, creative inspiration will flow. You should be bursting with unique ideas. A supportive atmosphere prevails now and over the next few days when it comes to finances. It will help you get ahead with your outstanding bills and personal loans. Travel plans should proceed without any problems. If you are flying long distance to see someone you love, a happy time can be expected. Finding out what your lover is thinking will be easy if you serve dinner by candlelight and soft music in the background. Intimate conversation should lead to issues being resolved to suit both of you.

11. SATURDAY. Calm. An ability to study quietly, to focus on complicated or detailed work, and to think clearly about serious issues is enhanced now. Gemini students can make major inroads on research required for a special assignment as well as on writing up the results. Expect top marks if you are taking an exam. Those of you with leisure time to spare should get some mild recreation outdoors while you contemplate what areas of life need more attention. Shopping to give the home environment a lift will appeal. If you are handy at do-it-yourself projects, start a few renovations around your living quarters.

12. SUNDAY. Energetic. You should have plenty of physical vitality on hand to tackle any energetic activity today. Assertive Mars has joined graceful Venus in your sign and your house of self, which will up the tempo of your life and your physical resources until August 25. With a heightened ambition to succeed, your efforts applied to various aims can be successful. Minor accidents and injuries are also likely to mount unless you take a cautious approach to personal safely. Walk, don't run, in areas where you could have a mishap. Keep an eye out for hidden obstacles. Drive within the speed limit and obey the road rules. Plan to spend more private time with your significant other.

13. MONDAY. Promising. Overall conditions should continue to improve as you begin to experience the surge of power sent by Mars in your sign. Don't let impulse or heated emotions cause issues with someone who is important in your life. A flurry of business and career communications will revolve around negotiating higher earnings and generating more profit. Geminis who have been working hard on the job should see the deserved benefits coming to you now. A reckless and more daring side of your personality could be on display, and you are ready for an adventure or two. A hiking trip will bring plenty of excitement.

14. TUESDAY. Invigorating. Imaginative friends will turn you on to a fresh creative scheme that you can run with. A mentor can offer wise advice on your future career direction. If a long-term friendship is suffering from neglect, work hard to restore easy companionship and warmth. A promotion or job offer may be a dream come true, but prepare for delays or some adjustment to your goals. Burning the midnight oil over the past few weeks could begin to take a toll, so now you should give both your body and your brain a rest for a few days. Start this evening by relaxing with a good book or a compliant lover.

15. WEDNESDAY. Interesting. A bevy of celestial influences will make for an eventful day ahead. Higher energy can enable many Gemini individuals to take a leadership role within a group or organization. New friends could come through club affiliations, and getting along with people should be easier. Your ruler Mercury is causing friction with Jupiter and Neptune, which can create an unrealistic and overoptimistic approach to money matters. This is not the time to enter into financial agreements or to make decisions that might affect your long-term security and stability. A complicated business situation will test your patience and resolve.

16. THURSDAY. Vexing. Under current stubborn and fidgety celestial patterns, a gentle approach should be taken to everything you do today. Even though you may have an urge to comple a number of tasks, your energy could be depleted and you may even feel a little unwell. Don't wait around for others to pick up the slack. Buckle down to clean your slate. A past romance may be on your mind and an ex-lover could return to the scene, perhaps only to seek closure rather than to reestablish an intimate link. The evening can bring contemplation and quiet companionship as you go about your regular duties.

17. FRIDAY. Inspiring. Lots of hustle and bustle is happening in the heavens today, so prepare for action. If you are tired of the same old routines, add some excitement and pleasure to your life. But guard against excess and overconfidence, and especially be protective of your health and well-being. Mercury, your life ruler, visits dramatic Leo, which will accentuate a desire for pleasure and good times. Communication, already your forte, will take on a more creative flair. Gemini writers and orators will excel at your craft now. Sightseeing trips, a weekend jaunt, and partying at a new location will appeal to the fun-loving among you.

18. SATURDAY. Renewing. Gemini strength and vitality return in full measure now. With the Moon in your own sign, it is an ideal day to catch up with friends and acquaintances who make you feel good. Invitations to various social events attest to your popularity. People could go out of their way to impress you, so acknowledge the compliments. Do not overlook any helpful hints that would ease your path to success. Take advantage of all influential support and encouragement to give yourself a push. Business and pleasure are a happy mix, and could lead to a move up the career ladder.

19. SUNDAY. Tricky. Challenging influences from your ruler Mercury to serious Saturn could increase the pressure around home base today. Be careful making decisions that would affect your home life, as your thinking may be more negative than need be. Although words should come easily, problems dealing with elders may be difficult to talk about. Join forces with a sibling or another relative around vacation plans. This can be a pleasant diversion now and ultimately productive for the future. Use this leisure day to get out and about in the great outdoors. Head to the beach, a park, or the countryside to free your mind and refresh your body.

20. MONDAY. Bright. A sharp mind and a quick wit are innate characteristics of Gemini, and today these traits are even stronger. Your ability to take the initiative and to act quickly can assist all efforts undertaken now. Original ideas to increase income and to bolster the family budget can be implemented under current supportive stars. Tasks that require intense concentration and attention to detail can be successfully carried out. Shoppers should write a list of goods required before venturing to the mall or supermarket. Seek bargains and don't let emotional responses govern your decisions. Otherwise, you might spend far more than you intended or can afford.

21. TUESDAY. Guarded. Home owners should take it easy in the process of renovating and refurbishing living quarters. Costs are likely to escalate, or tradespeople may fail to show up for appointments. There is a solar eclipse during this evening's New Moon in Cancer. So it would be wise to defer purchasing a home, signing a contract to lease, or making an agreement to build. Venus, planet of love and money, is in dispute with restrictive Saturn, which might create delays and dramas. Next week would be a better time to implement financial plans. Romantic prospects for singles could be far and few, and committed relationships may be somewhat cooler than usual.

22. WEDNESDAY. Lively. Give people the opportunity to speak out, and you will be very impressed with their thoughtful suggestions. This is not a favorable period to lend money or possessions to a sibling or a neighbor. There is a chance that things will not be returned and money will not be repaid. Business operators should be a little wary about providing credit now. Try to limit the number of slow payers on your account books. At midday the Sun moves into sociable Leo, so you can expect a lot more chatter and extended family gatherings over the next four weeks. Visits to and from relatives, sightseeing ventures, and weekend trips are likely to take priority on your social calendar.

23. THURSDAY. Trying. There may be some minor trouble in the workplace over petty issues or problems arising from gossip and innuendo. Cranky employees or an employer could also cause tension, and it will fall on you to inject some humor into the atmosphere to calm things down. Some of you may command a great deal of power now. But you will need to use that power in a positive manner, as coming on too forcefully might undermine your reputation for being friendly and approachable. Restlessness could limit productivity, so curb any impulsive behavior that would impact on future stability and security. Hammering a point home is fine as long as you know when to stop.

24. FRIDAY. Pressured. Some of you may feel that you are languishing in unfulfilling employment. If so, consider a residential move to get a better job or to further your educational qualifications. Steer clear of a male family member who has a habit of putting you down. Even if such a slight occurs in a subtle manner, holding your temper may be extremely difficult. Find a way to work alone because you are in no mood to suffer fools gladly. A major project could appear overwhelming. But if it is broken down and tackled in smaller chunks rather than all at once, you will have the necessary time and energy to complete it.

25. SATURDAY. Unsettling. It may be harder to juggle two situations at once. The time has come to make a decision and address the problem, the sooner the better. Keep an eye on your current financial status so that you are aware of exactly where you stand. An unexpected bill could throw the budget or bank balance into disarray. Be very wary of signing any contracts or financial paperwork unless you have had legal advice and have made sure you have thoroughly read all the fine print. Delays in communication or with transport could result in not meeting someone as arranged.

26. SUNDAY. Pleasing. Moderation is the key to remaining healthy, wealthy, and wise, as the saying goes. With lovable Venus happily linking to abundant Jupiter, it can be extremely difficult to keep indulgences in check now. Restrict the amount of alcohol you consumed, maintain a sensible diet, and leave the credit cards at home when shopping. Although you may win a few dollars on a game of chance, it would be in your best interest to steer clear of casinos and the racetrack, especially if gambling is becoming a habit. Leisure time would be better spent with loved ones and children, participating in favored pastimes that all the family can enjoy.

27. MONDAY. Artistic. Displaying your creative abilities can earn you praise from your peers and could also generate extra money for you. Social events held at home should be successful and enjoyable for all who attend. Some activities scheduled elsewhere might be canceled, so check early in the day to make sure you are not left stranded. If you have been considering upgrading your car or computer, you stand to pay an affordable price now for secondhand goods as well as for new items. Sitting down and listening to a child's problem will make a big difference as to how the youngster perceives an issue and intends to deal with it.

28. TUESDAY. Comforting. Your inner interior designer is in top form, waiting to get out in order to make improvements to your lifestyle. Many Gemini folk should be brimming with new ideas for storage solutions, color schemes, and room layouts to enhance the living quarters. You may be packing and organizing a move to a new location. Or you may be interviewing prospective housemates to take up shared residence. Loving trends arise now. So treat your lover to a delightful occasion on which special feelings and romantic desires can be confirmed. Singles seeking companionship should find plenty of romantic attention coming your way now, some of it entirely unexpected.

29. WEDNESDAY. Reassuring. This is a favorable day to reflect on employment, health, and domestic conditions. Review all these before starting to implement improvements that would enhance the quality of your life. A number of annoyances could hinder progress and slow you down, but perseverance and tenacity will win the day. Consider organizing a weekend away with your mate so you can enjoy a romantic escape and renew the magic once shared more regularly. Make up your mind about something that must be resolved, wound up, or permanently addressed. Once this is done, you can turn your attention to matters of importance coming up.

30. THURSDAY. Collaborative. The day begins with daily duties being the focus of attention before your concentration moves to personal and business partnerships. The opposing forces of Mercury and Jupiter will enhance your imagination and inspiration, but may pose a lack of sharp logic and sound judgment. Moderation is again the key to preventing any losses, as you may be tempted to go to extremes. Beware an extravagant streak and the inclination to bite off more than you can chew. A winning opportunity may be offered, but you should check if the timing is right. Socializing with live-wire companions will keep your mood upbeat.

31. FRIDAY. Unpredictable. Tricky cosmic patterns are taking shape today. Separating what is real and what is not can be difficult now, as your ruler Mercury is in conflict with both Neptune and Uranus. Upsetting influences and disruptions may prevent you from staying on top of your workload. Find a way to limit possible distractions. Venus, planet of love and money, moves into Cancer, your personal money house, tonight. Venus here will attract more income your way over the next few weeks. Help can come through family and friends. Much of your time could be spent entertaining others. Steer clear of controversial topics, or arguments might spoil an otherwise lovely occasion.

AUGUST

1. SATURDAY. Challenging. A desire for fun and action is strong as the new month begins. Being tired of the same old routines could find you organizing a trip away or visiting new social venues to expand your immediate environment. Sophisticated Venus confronts intense Pluto, advising Gemini folk to steer clear of romantic interests that are not sincere or that involve a third party. Personal and joint money matters will not be straightforward over the next few days, warning you against trying to settle a property dispute or custody battle. Challenges are likely to arrive in connection with professional partnerships. Business concerns could face increased struggle from competitors.

2. SUNDAY. Helpful. Issues of power and control could arise for committed couples. Lovers in a developing relationship should beware jealous and possessive tendencies. Partners may be helpful in finding avenues to exhibit the products of your creative talents if you are willing to display your flair to the general public. Chatty Mercury slips into Virgo, helping to coordinate things around home base. Bright ideas involving real estate and property matters can be implemented. Inspirations for Geminis seeking to revitalize living conditions should be forthcoming. Social activities that involve the whole family will go well, with lots of communication and talk to brighten the occasions.

3. MONDAY. Good. Keep a gauge on financial matters, particularly the amount of money currently slipping through the hands of a partner. Gemini business owners need to know where you stand with debtors and creditors. Make sure your account books are up-to-date and that you have the resources to cover monthly bills. Consider trying your hand at writing verse. Keep a journal so that you can reexamine thoughts and inspirations at a later time. Your powers of speech and of persuasion are enhanced, helping those of you employed in sales. Research work and in-depth investigation will also benefit.

4. TUESDAY. Empowering. Gemini verbal and written skills remain accentuated, and further study can commence. Enroll in an internship or special training course to add to your knowledge. Logical thinking should continue to impress people. Your high level of confidence can make meetings and negotiations proceed smoothly. Public speaking, interviews, and media appearances are favored. Endeavor to keep mood swings under control in order to avoid petty arguments with family members and close companions. This is a time to share. More can be achieved by working with a partner or within a team environment than by going it alone.

5. WEDNESDAY. Variable. Gemini vacationers may meet some very interesting fellow travelers and also discover areas of interest to explore in depth. If you have a knack for detective work, researching an assignment or conducting an audit will be a perfect way to express this talent. A strained and sensitive atmosphere is likely this evening as the eclipsed Moon comes to the full in the erratic sign of Aquarius. You might discover during the next two weeks that not everything is black and white and that there are many shades of gray. A problem may not be easy to solve, but getting angry when it is not swiftly put to bed is a waste of time and emotional energy.

6. THURSDAY. Mixed. Unpredictable influences still prevail, encouraging some Geminis to rebel with or without a cause. You may be more than happy to move out of your comfort zone to perform a special chore or to make a point. Dreaming of getting away from it all could occupy your mind as you drift off into your own world. If an overseas journey is calling you, booking travel arrangements or setting off to the desired destination should proceed smoothly with the likelihood of a wonderful vacation to look forward to. Sudden incidents could demand a choice, which may cause confusion as to what direction you should follow. Take the time to consider all options before moving ahead.

7. FRIDAY. Tempering. Money can be made if you make wise choices. Right now you need to check your bank balance and save receipts. Geminis on a business expense account should not take too many liberties, or the company accountant might complain. Self-indulgent tendencies are in evidence, but try to be strong to resist the temptation of the ponies, fattening food, and the shopping malls. If you are running late to book a summer vacation, the special package deals may now be very limited and more costly than envisioned. Home owners, on the other hand, are likely to locate lots of good buys to enhance living quarters.

8. SATURDAY. Accomplished. You may find that something has ended and now you can move on. On this leisure day you may be busy with tasks left over from the workweek. Taking it easy might be more appealing, but it would be wise to catch up on the backlog this morning so you can have a restful afternoon. Relationships with males or authority figures could be unpleasant because egos will clash. Your ability to express yourself clearly and concisely should be in full force. This helps the romantic Gemini tell a significant other how much you care and appreciate loving support. Keep quiet about any secrets you uncover. Exposing them now could cause trouble.

9. SUNDAY. Circumspect. Find useful amusements rather than gambling or shopping for expensive items if you are trying to save. Otherwise, you may forget about an upcoming obligation and waste money on trivial things. Gemini is prone to thinking at a faster rate than other individuals, so be patient if you are working with a colleague this afternoon. You could become rather agitated, even losing your cool, which will result in hurt feelings. The attention-seeking antics of a friend or a family member could irritate you, possibly prompting an emotional outburst at an inconvenient time. Vigorous chores such as gardening, housework, and home repairs will constructively tap your energy.

10. MONDAY. Restrictive. Because you are a free-spirited Gemini, working under constraints is not an acceptable option. For this reason today might not be to your liking, especially if you are tied down in a mundane or boring activity. Short-fused Mars is in an unfriendly alliance with restrictive Saturn, reducing your vim, vitality, and enthusiasm. Someone in the family could be very defensive, making it hard to discuss issues of importance. Other household members are likely to contribute nothing but irritation. Membership in a prestigious group could mean escalating fees, which you cannot afford. You may have to decline or come up with another option.

11. TUESDAY. Accommodating. Today appears to be much easier for Gemini folk. Concentrating on future goals and priorities will boost your confidence and make you feel good about your life. A lovely surprise could eventuate, and a message from a friend may the culmination of a lovely day. The possibility of reconnecting with someone special from your past could be on your mind. If getting together is not feasible, at least you have pleasant memories to mark that eventful time. Once you walk out the office door, forget about work. Invite friends to share your hospitality. Entertaining at home may be more convenient than going out visiting.

12. WEDNESDAY. Constructive. It is a day to relax. Take a break from the work pressures and the social obligations that make up so much of your daily life. If you have sick days owing or time off the job, catch up on domestic or personal pursuits. There may be a number of uncompleted projects that you would like to tackle and bring to a close. Delving into the past and dealing with unresolved emotions might require the help of a professional counselor. Don't try to figure out everything on your own. Volunteering your services to a hospice or meals on wheels organization can be a way to gain new skills and to receive emotional satisfaction.

13. THURSDAY. Lucky. Greet the day with a smile. Blessings are bestowed on Gemini now, and good fortune abounds. Just about any activity you undertake shows a great chance of a successful conclusion. With your initiative enhanced, don't hesitate to gear up for action. Get out and get in touch with people who can provide support. Drawing on your experiences and leading by example will aid progress. Your reputation can be boosted by making financial or physical contributions to a worthy cause. Partaking in a fund-raising event will be enjoyable. Be a little careful about promoting yourself. You don't want to make a negative impression.

14. FRIDAY. Active. By the time most of you get out of bed this morning, the Moon will be flitting through your sign of the Twins. During the next couple of days you can attract what you want and hold on to it as well. You should have plenty of energy to burn. The quickest way to move through sticky problems and dilemmas is to keep on the move, resolving each issue as it arises. Confronting issues of power and control with a personal or business partnership could be difficult unless egos are kept in check and compromises that suit both parties are found. Pay attention to personal grooming and appearance. Dress to impress now.

15. SATURDAY. Fulfilling. Today's message is for you to think about finding the right goals and aims in order for your enthusiasm and personal drive to remain high. Don't waste time or energy on unrealistic hopes. Instead, lay the foundations for a more fulfilling future. Pay attention to detail, and things should fall easier into place. Get active today. Breathe new life into yourself by participating in pursuits that help revitalize both your physical body and your emotional being. Refuse to take to heart any critical comments made by siblings or other relatives. Focus on developing specialized skills and talents. Planned amusement this evening should be a lot of fun.

16. SUNDAY. Unsettling. A sense of discontent may pervade the home atmosphere today. Problems with a will or an insurance policy could emerge and demand solution. Trying to locate important paperwork relevant to your claim may be frustrating and time consuming. Your taste for the good life could override your better judgment, which might be to your detriment. There is a need to protect your finances. So keep spending to a minimum to ensure that you have enough ready cash to last until next payday. Social activities might not bring the excitement you had hoped for, but they can be a pleasant escape from the confines of home base for a few hours.

17. MONDAY. Diverse. There are many planetary patterns operating on this eventful day. Prepare to shine, to take the lead, to utilize creative skills, and also to be deceived. Today many Gemini folk can naturally assume a leadership role and show how things should be done. Be aware, though, that not everyone will appreciate your efforts. Be mindful of major bills that will arrive in the coming weeks. Stash some money away for a rainy day. Your powers of concentration are strong, which gives you an opportunity to make progress on a creative endeavor already in the pipeline. A colleague may be tempted to take credit for your efforts and innovative ideas, so act shrewdly to prevent this from happening.

18. TUESDAY. Tricky. Explosive conditions are in force today, which can make for a very unsettling atmosphere. Make sure you are not exaggerating a situation or boasting about your effectiveness. Controlling your temper and handling issues in a rational manner will be essential even for Geminis who are not prone to erupting without provocation. Choose gentle exercise and amusements. Defer activities that could cause an accident or a mishap, such as any kind of extreme sports or driving beyond the speed zone. Rediscovering creative pastimes that you haven't pursued for a long time could bring joy. Start using those dormant talents and skills once again.

19. WEDNESDAY. Fair. Restless urges continue to create unrest today. Watch where you are going and pay attention to the signals around you. Move slowly, take notice of major and minor details, and handle machinery and electrical appliances with care. Either send them out for repair or discard those with faulty power cords. Venus is positively affecting your finances, helping to bring stability and a sensible approach to spending habits. Gemini singles could begin a serious love affair that has the potential to be long enduring and fulfilling. Those of you already committed can renew your vows and strengthen loving ties. You can successfully harness your creative energies now to produce a work of art.

20. THURSDAY. Trying. Promising more than can be delivered is a failing that many Gemini folk possess. Be mindful of this trait today, and know what your limitations and boundaries are. Refrain from taking on tasks and responsibilities that belong to others. You may be unduly worried over a property matter or a delay to a home building project. Try not to get upset by the situation. Frustration will not move things along any quicker but will only add negatively to your stress level. The job will be completed, though perhaps not to your timetable. Your intuition could be a little faulty right now, so postpone decisions and choices until things are clearer in your mind.

21. FRIDAY. Demanding. Give yourself a bit of a break today. Mental overload arrives in full force, and your ability to focus and concentrate is likely to be fraught with difficulties. For many Gemini individuals, your mind may be up in the clouds or on anything other than the job at hand. The discovery that a family member hasn't been totally honest could have you reeling. Worse, you realize how naive you can be. No matter how tiny your living quarters are, improvements can be made that add to the overall sense of style and comfort. Flowering plants, framed photographs, carefully placed souvenirs all create areas of interest in a harmonious ambience.

22. SATURDAY. Happy. Gemini charm and sociability are high as you greet the weekend. Romance should be on the agenda so that you make the most of current cosmic trends. With a number of invitations to choose from today, select the most exciting social activity offered. You will have a great time mixing and mingling with friends and family. Be sympathetic toward a lover or child, even if you have to deal yet again with an ongoing problem from the past. Say the right words and provide emotional support. This evening the Sun enters Virgo, your solar sector of home, family, and near environment.

23. SUNDAY. Supportive. With the Sun settled in Virgo until September 22, home and family life will be to the fore. With the advent of this new cycle, changes and improvements can be made to your living quarters and domestic arrangements. Clearing away clutter and removing items no longer in use can be easier to do, especially for Geminis who are inclined to hoard things. What is broken can be discarded in favor of more modern articles. Strengthening family bonds can come through special gatherings of relatives. Entertain loved ones in the comfort of your own home. Today your leadership qualities are heightened, and where you go others will follow.

24. MONDAY. Rewarding. A happy and lucky day is on the cards. Although there are a couple of obstacles to halt the peaceful flow of events, the Moon floating through balanced Libra until the afternoon will ease tension and increase harmony. Your ability to reach a compromise and to gain cooperation is in evidence, whether you are on the campus or on the job. The talented Gemini is in a strong position to move forward and to make gains. Your artistic creations and innovative ideas can be put forward to the people who count. Romance, affection, and good times are the gifts of the current cosmic trends. Many of you can reach a deeper level of commitment with a significant other now.

25. TUESDAY. Reassuring. You may wish to seek alternative health remedies as the Moon today sails through Scorpio, your zone of health and service to others. Massage and yoga are effective centering techniques, great for Geminis who are prone to scatter energies all over the place. Now is the time you can try to kick unhealthy habits and to improve your overall well-being. At midday dynamic Mars visits Cancer, your zone of finances. Mars here magnifies your motivation to generate more money and assets, especially if there is a small cut in income or in profits. This afternoon your ruler Mercury enters Libra, your zone of pleasure, leisure, and treasure, and remains there until mid-September.

26. WEDNESDAY. Forceful. An intense day is sent by the universe as powerful Pluto makes a couple of difficult planetary connections. Beware workaholic tendencies. Gemini women who work late into the night should take extra safety precautions when leaving your place of employment. An accident-prone period exists, warning against taking silly risks over the coming days. The tempo of your social life is apt to pick up now that your ruler, talkative Mercury, is visiting sociable Libra and sophisticated Venus slips into outgoing Leo. Expect a wealth of invitations to come across the airwaves to you. Such popularity could pose a dilemma as you dither over which parties to attend and which to skip.

27. THURSDAY. Productive. Dedicating time and energy to the demands of loved ones may have you running ragged today. Issues around home base and problems with employment could come to a head and will need to be resolved. Venus, the planet of love, beauty, and the good life, has settled into Leo, your sector of communication and short travels, and will reside in Leo until September 20. Frustrated writers and artists will find it helpful to join a specialized hobby group. This way you can get feedback and see if your ability to paint, write, or perform other creative pursuits is sustained. Enrolling in a short course will appeal if you want to refresh your skills.

28. FRIDAY. Spirited. Now is the time to make the most of your creative talents and expertise. Romance writers could make good headway. If you have a few songs or poems tucked away in your mind, begin penning these masterpieces. Those of you who dance in a competitive arena may win an award. Gemini folk attending business meetings, job interviews, or auditions can experience success. Romantic vibes are strong. This is the perfect time to tell someone you care or otherwise express your love and affection. Here also is an opportunity to get things out into the open and clear the air if that is needed. Remember to listen as much as you talk.

29. SATURDAY. Beneficial. Progress can be swift when your communicative abilities are combined with sensible planning and practical expertise. With financial institutions constantly changing the way money agreements are structured, it might be time to review and revamp your credit and savings accounts, loans, mortgages, and other debts. Check that you are still receiving a good deal on all of these. Compare rates and penalties before you make a decision and choose. Astute Gemini folk might be interested in making money from the stock market. Taking a course outlining investment techniques could get you started on the path to financial freedom.

30. SUNDAY. Carefree. Life could keep you on your toes even though the pace might be a little slower now. If you know that someone needs comforting or a shoulder to cry on, this is the time to extend sympathy and support. If you are in the early stages of a love affair, today is all about moving closer together to cement the bond. Lavishing attention on your house or condo can work to advantage as you have the energy and motivation to fix, upgrade, and upstyle. All this will add value to the property. Social functions may take up all of your leisure time. So think about curling a few invitations to give yourself space for private affairs.

31. MONDAY. Promising. Buying, selling, or trading may be on your mind. Pick your targets carefully, and money can be made. Doing things on the spur of the moment doesn't always work, but this shouldn't be the case today. With a sensible approach on display, your ability to problem solve on the run is enhanced and can help you move through the daily list of chores and responsibilities.

This is another day when you may encounter someone who needs a helping hand. Don't fret that you might not know what to say or do to provide comfort. Instinctively, the way to offer assistance will appear. Browse the local bookshop and pick up a couple of good reads.

SEPTEMBER

1. TUESDAY. Slow. There might not be much zip to the beginning of this new month, but at least things won't be difficult for most. Clear-cut answers are unlikely to be available today, and news from overseas may not be what you hoped to hear. Sit tight if you have been experiencing emotional turmoil, as the outcome should begin to swing in your favor soon. Lack of motivation in a teenager will arouse 60th anger and guilt. But it would be wise to keep quiet until you are in calmer frame of mind. Take your time with anything related to a legal matter. Rushing in to sign paperwork or to make a final decision could result in the wrong choice.

2. WEDNESDAY. Easygoing. If any zodiac sign can go with the flow and take a flexible approach, you can, Gemini. Do this today, and things will proceed smoothly. Expanding your horizons may be on your mind. Your tolerance for everyday occurrences could be very limited. A wish to take flight caused by a fidgety attitude could make life a little difficult. A quiet word with someone should solve a couple of your problems and lead to more lucrative outcomes. Generosity can come in a number of different forms, not just financial support. So if you can give service or some other form of assistance without breaking the bank, this would be a charitable act.

3. THURSDAY. Complicated. Gemini intellect is sharp as your ruler Mercury challenges Mars today. Beware a sarcastic and quick tongue. Otherwise, you are bound to upset those you care about. Wait until there is solid information before placing all your financial eggs in one basket. The love and romance zone of your solar chart is about to get a bit of a shake-up now. Singles might not be able to think straight after a romantic interlude, so postpone important decisions for the future until things are clearer in your mind. A radical employment move by a sibling may come as a complete surprise, and supporting their choice could create some inner doubts.

4. FRIDAY. Eventful. Daily schedules are likely to undergo many alterations, so keep your cool. Make sure you can tell the difference between the real and the rosy. Family life might not be the quiet haven you desire if employment duties are taking priority. The Full Moon in the complex sign of Pisces can bring changes to the domestic environment. Someone may leave the nest, or another may move in. It is time for a cleansing. So let go of anything that may be holding you back. Remove physical clutter as well as emotional muddles that need resolving. Your sympathetic and compassionate side may be revealed now. Helping others will bring spiritual gratification.

5. SATURDAY. Variable. A vexing beginning to the day is likely. Some of your responsibilities could be overwhelming. If you are not required to work or be anywhere special, take the time to rest, especially if a heavy social night is planned. Geminis on the job are impressive, displaying a high level of expertise, friendliness, and willingness to go the extra mile for clients or coworkers. Don't be too outrageous espousing ideas and schemes. You could go over the top. Even if money is flowing in nicely, a conservative approach to spending would be wise. Be cautious shopping, especially if you are in only-the-best-will-do mode.

6. SUNDAY. Unsettling. If you are of two minds about joining a prestigious organization, get some feedback from members of the group to ensure that their values coincide with yours. Be ready to dish out tea and sympathy and a shoulder to cry on for a friend who may be facing a turbulent time in a love relationship or other tricky alliance. Just before midnight your ruler Mercury goes into retrograde motion in the sign of Libra, so don't be surprised if communication goes haywire during the next three weeks. Misunderstandings with children, being stood up by a lover or new date, mix-ups with social venues, and delays with just about everything else can be expected.

7. MONDAY. Positive. A fresh workweek poses new opportunities. You may feel more physical energy surfacing as the day progresses, although the energy is likely to tamper off by day's end. Staff and team meetings should provide productive feedback, a spirit of cooperation, and a willingness to move ahead with any given duties at hand. Making arrangements online for an international business trip or a family vacation could save time and money. But you will need to lock yourself away for an hour or two to accomplish the task. With Mercury now in retrograde motion, double-check all paperwork. Handle a treasured collection carefully, as accidental breakages might occur.

8. TUESDAY. Calm. The Moon in Taurus, your twelfth house, signals Gemini to slow down. Slot in frequent rest breaks. Don't attempt strenuous tasks that require lots of time to complete. Backing away from a new romance would be wise if possessive and manipulative influences are beginning to appear. If this is the case, it might not be long before you also have to deal with issues around power and control. Don't settle for the first thing you find while shopping. A desirable item could be overpriced or contain hidden defects. Something that was once regretted will now be accepted, and you can move on.

9. WEDNESDAY. Mixed. It might take some effort to regain your concentration and discipline for everyday responsibilities this morning. Tackle heavy tasks around midday. That is when you should experience a burst of energy to combat any lingering lack of vitality. Although it is in your nature to trust others, you do need to beware a gullible attitude. If something smells off, it probably is. So take a good look before making a move. The revelation of a secret or a breaking scandal could send the rumor mill into overdrive among friends and colleagues, warning Gemini people to avoid getting caught up in all the hype. If you have any type of food allergy, watch what you eat.

10. THURSDAY. Bright. You should be at your best today, as the Gemini Moon recharges your energy and self-confidence. Relax if you have someone special to meet. You are bound to make a great first impression. Implementing a special plan now can guarantee a good measure of success. Resisting the impulse to splurge may be difficult if household and personal spending is on the agenda. Keep tabs on the purse strings and stick to essential purchases. Something you were looking forward to or hoping to happen could come to a standstill. Don't fret about this. Over time, things should work out in the way you envisioned.

11. FRIDAY. Moderate. Even though laziness is not a typical Gemini trait, current celestial trends may incline you toward taking the easy way out now. Something you are anxious to get off the ground might not have moved very far forward. It is bubbling away in the background, almost ready to advance once Pluto goes direct later today. Have a serious talk with the builder or contractor if property renovations or home maintenance work seem to be proceeding too slowly. Consider a mini makeover if you are tired of your current appearance. An upstyled wardrobe and a little more physical activity could be the answer to relieve stress.

12. SATURDAY. Strategic. Powerful planet Pluto is now marching forward in Capricorn, your house of shared income and joint assets. Delays on property and communal settlements should soon let up, and divorce proceedings could move to completion. Income and outgo may be mismatched. So it would be in your best interest to consider reining in your spending habits and implementing a savings scheme to ensure future financial security. Your urge to help others becomes more prominent now. You can apply special skills and expertise to a project in which you might make a difference to the lives of others. Seek professional advice if self-treatment isn't helping a health issue.

13. SUNDAY. Varied. A day of mixed trends is ahead for Gemini folk, posing scattered energies, mix-ups, and confusing communications. Fortunately, by mid-morning, things begin to improve. Increased motivation and drive will kick in. Check bank statements for mistakes that could leave you out of pocket. Count the change given back to you when making purchases. A special mission should succeed, although you may be working harder than imagined on your day off. Additional expenses for travel and vacation are possible. Students living away from home could experience problems relating to housing. An early night is advised to escape family squabbles.

14. MONDAY. Fruitful. Money is again to the fore, but beware the tendency to think too big. Have in hand the relevant shopping receipts and other paperwork if you applying for refunds, exchanges, or credit. A generous and caring attitude from someone close could help you to improve your financial situation. The decisions you make this week can open up new possibilities. Weighing the pros and cons could be exhausting, but this is a good time to force the issue on something you might have been considering for a long time. A creative activity can be a great form of stress release. Part-time writers and students with assignments to complete should make good progress now.

15. TUESDAY. Foggy. Love and money are not a good combination now. If there are important decisions to be made, wait until things become clearer. You may be misled, accidentally or deliberately, as lover Venus confronts poseur Neptune. This is a time when Gemini folk should try extremely hard to remain practical and logical. If you are in a romantic relationship, disappointment might be the outcome if you place your partner on a pedestal. Ultimately, he or she will fall off. Leave the credit cards at home if you are on a shoestring budget. Your tendency to purchase whatever takes your fancy without thought of the consequences is higher than usual.

16. WEDNESDAY. Revealing. Sheer determination can enable you to overcome most obstacles confronted now. You know exactly what you want, but you must dig deep to find the right words in some of your discussions. Don't be afraid to ask for a favor today. The worst that can happen is the answer will be no. However, there is a very good chance that your request will be granted. Something you have wanted to know for a while might be revealed now. A snippet of information that you discover could open a new door to opportunities. Geminis living away from family may need to take steps to lessen homesickness. There are various ways you can keep in touch.

17. THURSDAY. Erratic. Expect the unexpected is the theme of the day. For many Geminis this is the sort of atmosphere that you prefer anyway. Routine and boring are words that are not usually included in your vocabulary. Nervous agitation could result in an accident if care is not taken. Obsessive or finicky people probably will cause irritation for you. Go slow when you meet up with these types, particularly if your attention to detail doesn't match their high standard. It could be too easy for misunderstandings or conflict to occur over trivial matters. Tonight your ruler Mercury, which is in retrograde motion, slips back into the sign of Virgo, your sector of home environment.

18. FRIDAY. Powerful. Mixed emotions are likely to be experienced throughout the day. Domestic matters and the home environment will be accentuated for the next two weeks. Past family customs could be discussed, recorded, or acted upon to preserve ongoing traditions. Today's Virgo New Moon is an excellent occasion for change, new beginnings, and fresh starts. The Gemini home owner and those of you wishing to become one can find particular benefit now. This is a fine time to plan renovations and also to expand your real estate portfolio. Contemplate what is needed to redesign a home or to design a new one, and then to build it. Things should come together without problems.

19. SATURDAY. Inspiring. Arrangements for a special celebration could keep you busy for much of the day. If the event is for tonight, put your feet up for an hour or so to maintain enough energy to enjoy the evening. This is the time to clean your slate, remove clutter, and tidy up. Venus, purveyor of love and money, happily connects with intense Pluto over the coming week. Gemini folk will embrace the love and affection coming your way. A fortuitous financial development can put money in your pocket and have you smiling all the way to the bank. A social outing may be more of a duty than a pleasure, but your attendance will bring joy to older folk and family friends.

20. SUNDAY. Happy. There are some pleasant planetary influences today that should ensure a sociable and romantic atmosphere. Passion and desire remain strong. Spending time with a lover will help to cement loyal ties. You and your love partner could finally realize how each of you is viewing a problem that has been causing discontent, then begin to make headway in resolving the issue. This morning Venus moves into Virgo, your sector of home and family for a visit of over three weeks. So entertaining friends, family, and colleagues from the comfort of your own home will appeal. Beware an extravagant approach to decor if you are making changes to your living quarters.

21. MONDAY. Hectic. A pet could keep you busy today. You might go searching for an escaped cat or dog, be visiting the vet, or making boarding arrangements for an upcoming journey. Healthwise, pace yourself wisely to avoid burnout. If your mind goes into overdrive, put the focus on becoming more active, especially if you have gained weight. It might be time to enroll in a yoga or exercise class to increase vim, vitality, and fitness. Don't take a frustrating domestic situation to heart. Display patience and calmness, and your aims set down for the day can be achieved. A family expense could cut into the household budget, leaving the bank account short of funds.

22. TUESDAY. Encouraging. A practical atmosphere pervades the day. Remain positive. Make sure you don't give way to maudlin sentimentality or a doom-and-gloom attitude. A solution to a costly venture or long enduring project could be found now, bringing relief for all those who took part in the exercise. A journey that was put on hold due to cost might now seem more affordable. The Sun is now shining in Libra, your house of pleasure, fun, and romantic partners, until October 23. Gemini popularity is likely to rise. Recreational and creative activities are to the fore, so this is your chance to display charm and social skills to the max.

23. WEDNESDAY. Tricky. A difficult day is likely. There are a number of hard planetary aspects beaming down on the heads of Gemini. Restless trends are evident. So be sure not to take impulsive risks that could result in injury or other consequences that will be regretted. A task that had seemed so easy in the beginning could now become complicated, and you might begin to have second thoughts about the whole situation. A casual remark on the job could convey a flash of inspiration that will be of assistance in solving a tough problem. Steer clear of a boss or other authority figure who is inclined to press your buttons. A volatile reaction is possible if you are pushed to the limit.

24. THURSDAY. Unpredictable. Gemini activity remains strong. Although the lunar influence is good, obstacles are still around ready to trip you up. Continue to keep a distance from people who are prone to argue without any real cause. Don't let a persuasive talker push you into making an expensive acquisition. Make your own decision. Think twice before signing on the dotted line, particularly if you have to invest a lot of money. And don't even think about borrowing it. Listen to the comments and complaints of associates and customers. Be prepared with the right words and solutions to settle any grievances.

25. FRIDAY. Favorable. If you open up a little and show a friendly disposition, getting along with cranky and hard-to-please customers and clients can be much easier today. Even small talk about the weather could do the trick. This is a favorable period to investigate possible new avenues to place investment capital that can bring good returns. Review all financial matters, but don't sign leases, contracts, or important documents until after your ruler Mercury moves forward on Tuesday. Consider pooling resources with friends to cut down on expenses. Early evening is an auspicious period to collect money or possessions that people owe you.

26. SATURDAY. Productive. Evaluate projects before making a commitment and getting involved. Expectations of how much time you have available for ventures other than work and family matters might be too high. A financial arrangement with another could come to a head and will need to be clarified. Once this is addressed, more understanding comes. Include a number of pleasant leisure activities in your day to keep yourself active and to aid relaxation. Buy a lottery ticket, as luck is on your side. Your creative imagination is stimulated, so this is an excellent period to express your talent in a constructive way. A fun change of scenery will bring excitement to social life.

27. SUNDAY. Smooth. Business partnerships and creative collaborations might occupy most of your time this morning. As far as joint ventures are concerned, money could be a sore point and cause arguments. Watch the body language, especially if you are meeting with a male who holds a position of power. Perhaps adding humor to the conversation will temper everyone's attitude. For some of you, a change in residence may be the focus of discussion. Getting all the family together to celebrate a special function could be problematic, but will be worthwhile once all the plans have been agreed upon and put into play.

28. MONDAY. Successful. Excellent results from an exam or assignment will put a wide smile on the face of Gemini students. Students can also make gains throughout the day, although research work and study might be disrupted this evening. If someone close is reaching a milestone, being there to assist and to celebrate will generate happiness all around. Those of you with a special deadline to meet should have little difficulty in reaching that predetermined goal. Take charge when others are dithering. If you have a vacation itinerary to plan, you can make headway and complete all arrangements in half the time it would take others.

29. TUESDAY. Gratifying. Some agitating forces are evident today, but things are picking up for Gemini. Early this morning irresistible Mercury, your ruler, begins trekking forward after three weeks of retrograde motion. Delays on a home mortgage, a sales agreement, or building works should be resolved. Steady progress should begin. Students presenting a paper should please your teacher or lecturer. A legal issue will most probably come to a successful conclusion. The business operator should hear good news from overseas, with a chance of increased profits that can put you on the road to financial success. A sporting event could appeal tonight.

30. WEDNESDAY. Stable. Challenges are likely to appear on the horizon, but you can push through any obstacles encountered. A competitive spirit is the encouragement you need to move ahead on an educational goal that provides good career chances. Take advantage of opportunities to socialize with the higher-ups who can give you a boost up the career ladder. Getting a pleasure trip off the ground should be easier to accomplish now, so you have something to look forward to. Settle your finances before going too far with house hunting or making major changes to living conditions. Your ideas may be bigger than your bank balance.

OCTOBER

1. THURSDAY. Lively. Chatty, sociable, and alert might describe many Gemini individuals on this eventful day. Beware being taken in by the persuasive words of others. Although your mind is sharp, avoid making snap decisions. Be very clear in all forms of communications, as there is a strong chance of misunderstandings occurring. Idealism and ambition combine, encouraging you to work harder to achieve career and business goals. Something that was considered a lost cause should begin to move forward. Don't rush to judgment about a long-distance relationship. Instead, deliberate and then decide.

2. FRIDAY. Helpful. Effort applied on the job could be repaid in full. Take action to advance career and business matters. Achieving a cherished personal goal can bring happy surprises. Expect to face conflict between work and family life if your private aims clash with the demands of loved ones and your profession. Just make sure not to get so worked up that you become mentally drained and end up not being able to function at top-notch capacity. You can be very persuasive today, particularly when it comes to business. Use this ability to your advantage during critical negotiations and transactions.

3. SATURDAY. Complicated. The stars are not aligned so favorably today. There are a few minor issues to contend with. This is no time to trust to luck or to hope for the best, particularly when it comes to the accomplishment of a cherished aim or the smooth sailing of a social occasion. Self-employed Geminis should endeavor to cut down on the number of hours you work over the weekend. You will feel better by relaxing with family and friends. Tricky situations could arise in group dynamics, and a shared activity is unlikely to proceed as planned. Be very wary of proposals put forward by a friend if money is involved. Refrain from lending money or valuable possessions despite urgent pleas.

4. SUNDAY. Complex. Energetic planetary patterns are in force, which means you will have an active day. Both your mind and your tongue may be very sharp. But you might not know whether you are coming or going while your life ruler Mercury plays havoc with your mental activity. Your reputation can be enhanced by making contributions to a worthy cause. But make sure you don't become a martyr or allow others to take your generosity for granted. The Aries Full Moon adds sensitivity to today's mix, heightening the emotions within a romantic relationship or friendship connection. Tact is not always a strong Gemini characteristic. So tread gently wherever you go and whatever you say.

5. MONDAY. Challenging. Restlessness may persist and continue to disrupt your thoughts and activities on this changeable day. Endeavor to move outside your normal routines. Take an opportunity to explore the unusual, to participate in new things. There is the possibility of a separation or at least a significant change within a relationship. Something comes to a close. Don't be sad. Remember, everything does happen for a reason so that you can learn and grow. As day turns into night, treat your body with care and respect. Limit heavy physical activities as soon as your stamina begins to wane. Plan to spend an hour or so on relaxing pursuits and opt for an early night.

6. TUESDAY. Revealing. The lunar influence could create underlying tension, which would have a negative impact on your general well-being. There is a chance that health issues will demand attention, which might mean a visit to a hospital or a clinic for tests. Research into spiritual and occult interests can be fulfilling. Such quiet study will help to calm you down if you are running on nerves and adrenaline. Don't attempt labor-intensive tasks now. Your energy may be at a low level and you are bound to run out of oomph very quickly. Factors that have been hidden or submerged could be exposed and will need to be addressed.

7. WEDNESDAY. Eventful. The early hours are inclined toward confusion and uncertainty, which warns against major decision making. Wait awhile before making decisive moves. Traffic conditions could be hazardous, and clashes with drivers and commuters quite likely. The tempo picks up nicely as the day progresses and as lunar trends become supportive. Confidential financial deals and transactions should proceed extremely well, so get a prompt start on money matters. Collectors and dealers in secondhand goods are apt to find value in old items and what some people consider junk. Keep an eye out for bargains and goods that are being donated or given away for free.

8. THURSDAY. Satisfying. Logical and practical solutions for anything to do with home and family emerge today. Gemini folk are able to totally concentrate and focus on the issues that arise. An analytical mindset is enhanced as your ruler Mercury merges with disciplined Saturn. This planetary conjunction encourages you to make internal or external changes in order to restructure your home and family life. Remodeling the living quarters to enhance your own space or to build an office can aid in this renewal. Spending money shouldn't present a problem. Right now your eye for quality and nose for a bargain price will lead you to find excellent things.

9. FRIDAY. Unpredictable. Think twice before making a leap of faith. If you are heading off to work or somewhere else important, dress to impress. On the other hand, if you are shopping, do not splash cash around just to make an impression. Spend wisely using affordable guidelines. There is murky confusion surrounding both love and money. This isn't the time to ask the boss for a pay raise or to ask a lover for a significant gift. Geminis in a developing romance or just starting dating should be wary, as there is little comfort in current planetary influences. Jumping into a love affair today can lead to heartache and pain tomorrow.

10. SATURDAY. Opportune. The stars are pretty much on your side today. Overnight your ruler Mercury settled into Libra, your zone of leisure and creative expression. The typical Gemini generally has a laid-back approach allowing most things to just go with the flow. Right now luck is likely to play a large part in what happens. You can be the star in your own show. Winning the support of another is easier. If you need a special favor, your request should be viewed in a positive light. Make your own special luck by taking advantage of current good fortune. However, don't jump to conclusions or make mountains out of molehills or take people for granted.

11. SUNDAY. Fair. Clashes of opinion are very likely to create discord now. Steer clear of controversial topics, especially religion and politics. Listen to the preaching of others but with a discerning ear. Don't get caught up in any sales hype. E-mail is a great way to communicate. But sometimes the message can be read differently from the way you meant it, so be careful if using this media today. If you are entertaining at home, everyone should have a great time. You can revel in the company and lively chatter of special guests. Just make sure that catering doesn't include too many expensive items.

12. MONDAY. Positive. A pleasant atmosphere arrives, encouraging Geminis to put on a friendly and cheery face wherever you are going to be. Current stars indicate that your mind will be working overtime, so most chores will not be too much to grasp. With dynamic Mars forming a helpful link to serious Saturn, wise investments could pay off in future dividends. Real estate is one area where many of you can make gains. Those of you in the fields of building and renovating various types of homes are likely to experience a boost in profits. The joy of receiving is matched only by sharing gifts with loved ones, and the chance to do this is high right now.

13. TUESDAY. Fortunate. Love and money come to the fore as gracious Venus merges with serious Saturn and harmonizes with dynamic Mars. Permanent commitment, possibly leading to marriage and children, will be very much in line with your thinking today. For some of you, a romantic encounter of the physical kind will be desired. Talented Gemini can apply determination and expertise into bringing innate talent to public notice. Interior designers and landscapers involved in enhancing people's home and property can expect lucrative new contracts. Be careful not to make too many pressing appointments and overschedule your agenda.

14. WEDNESDAY. Advantageous. Gregarious Jupiter has now moved forward in Aquarius, your sector of education and travel. This could free up situations that have been delayed, perhaps having to do with vacation or with study to gain a particular qualification. Gemini students waiting to hear news of a scholarship or exchange program should be informed of decisions made in this regard now. Don't expect much peace and quiet or time for yourself around the house. Lively conversations at the dinner table will be par for the course. Stocking up in preparation for home entertaining may be a priority.

15. THURSDAY. Tricky. Protect yourself and your own needs today. Love planet Venus has moved into Libra, one of the signs Venus rules. Venus here joins mischievous Mercury in Libra and challenges the might of intense Pluto in Capricorn. Take care with your actions and communications. Jealousy and possessiveness can make this a negative time if emotions are ignited. Gemini singles should be extremely careful in any potential romantic encounter or scenario. The experience may not be to your liking. Instead of affection, power and control might dominate the relationship with a partner.

16. FRIDAY. Invigorating. A myriad of celestial influences greets you today, enhancing your desire to be recognized in your own right. In a lovely conjunction, the golden light of the Sun shines on inspirational Neptune. Those of you involved in any facet of music and theater can make good progress developing your talents and expertise. Enrolling in a course that teaches special techniques associated with the arts can be beneficial now. Short-fused Mars slips into Leo, your sector of relatives and neighbors, warning Gemini to proceed carefully in all discussions. The chance of conflict with people in close proximity is high. Practice yoga and deep breathing to reduce anger issues.

17. SATURDAY. Easygoing. A quieter day in most areas of your life is promised by the heavens. Issues involving money, love, or children could prove vexing. The key to a successful day is to deal with problems as they come to your attention. A social function should make for a happy time. Your friendly and cheery disposition ensures that everyone will have a good time. Younger Gemini folk seeking to purchase a first car or cycle should find exactly what you are looking for, but first ask someone older and wiser for advice first. If you are prone to speeding, better slow down to avoid fines and mishaps.

18. SUNDAY. Interesting. There might be some tension in the air throughout the day. It would be in your best interest to avoid confrontations with neighbors and angry siblings. Arguments are bound to arise, possibly causing upsets and distress. Good news does arrive for the currently single Gemini as a New Moon culminates in Libra, your house of pleasure, passion, romance, love affairs, and children. During the next two weeks the chance to encounter the perfect partner is high. Get out mixing and mingling. An accomplishment of a child could surpass all expectations, bringing a smile to parents. A special invitation will let you celebrate long and hard.

19. MONDAY. Stressful. It doesn't appear to be an easy day for relating to others. An argumentative and controlling approach should be avoided. Otherwise, friction is likely to endure for the whole day. Your changeable moods can make it awkward for you to settle down to anything in particular. You might also disrupt the people around you who have duties to perform. Take care in matters of a confidential nature. There is a chance you could accidentally slip up and reveal things that should have been kept to yourself. Talking out of turn could also trigger the wrath of a partner or close friend.

20. TUESDAY. Gratifying. Higher education, religious topics, and community activities are to the fore. The Twins will be stimulated with lots of talk, ideas, and schemes. This is a great time to brainstorm and troubleshoot in any area involving communication. Formulate a strategy on how to reach goals and gain financial benefits in the quickest manner. Intense discussions with a supportive partner will also reveal tactics that can help you succeed sooner than planned. Geminis seeking a new job should create an eye-catching resume that will interest prospective employers. Visit your local astrologer, who could provide in-depth answers to various questions.

21. WEDNESDAY. Surprising. A sense of balance and moderation toward everything is needed today. Be alert for the deceptive influences surrounding you due to the agitation between sexy Venus and misleading Neptune. A romantic affair could take a surprising twist when a past lover comes back on the scene. This may not be a good thing, Gemini, so move slowly and give the matter serious consideration before making a major move. Be watchful while shopping with friends. You may be a bad influence on one another by buying lots of stuff that none of you need or can afford. Check the receipts and guard your wallet when making purchases.

22. THURSDAY. Varied. Current cosmic influences help Gemini folk to move ahead with challenging and difficult tasks. Good results are the likely outcome. Nervous anxiety can cause a few issues around midday. But if you stay grounded and refuse to scatter your energy, accomplishment will be your reward. Something that didn't work out in the past might reappear. If effort is applied, you should have more success with this venture now. Your ability to talk convincingly to clients and the general public is a great asset in business and in all sales fields. Your inquiring mind can be utilized productively by researching philosophical topics of interest.

23. FRIDAY. Constructive. Today the Sun moves into Scorpio, the sector of the Gemini horoscope that governs health, job conditions, and the people you work with. There may be times over the next month when working alone rather than with others will be more to your liking. Those of you unemployed now can make good progress finding suitable work. There is an increased chance of promotion or pay increases for many hardworking Twins. Visitors may invade your space, and someone may need your sympathetic ear to unload their burdens and issues. Listen to investment advice. A financial tip could bring gains over the next few months.

24. SATURDAY. Promising. An intelligent focus on financial assets and resources can ensure long-term economic stability. Change can be profitable now as the Moon moves through Capricorn, your sector of shared assets. With intense mental activity, you can make progress on any work that requires in-depth investigation and research. Complex problems can be analyzed, and the astute Gemini will come up with a sound evaluation. Potential home owners who have made an offer on a house could receive good news, and you may be on your way to moving in. Creative inspiration is on the rise, encouraged by listening to music and poetry.

25. SUNDAY. Enjoyable. Gemini vim and vitality remain at a high peak. Shoppers could find loads of bargains at weekend markets and specialty stores holding special sales. Hearing about an inheritance inspires happiness along with poignant memories of former times and how quickly life moves by. Catering to the emotional needs of a mate shouldn't cause too many problems. If you have joint assets to dispose of, this chore can move forward without conflict. Your creative imagination is peaking. Use leisure hours for composing lyrics and music, playing an instrument, knitting, painting, sculpting. Record your memories in a journal for later generations to enjoy.

26. MONDAY. Slow. There isn't a lot occurring in the cosmos today. Attending to the usual activities and routine tasks will make your workload decrease rather than become unmanageable. If a legal matter is pending, take time out to organize the paperwork. Then everything that can help your cause will be in order. An older relative could provide assistance or guidance on a special project. Listen keenly to what those wiser than you have to say. Love is in the air now, urging the solo Gemini to be on the lookout for a special attraction that has your heart pumping. Explore new interests rather than going over old ground.

27. TUESDAY. Active. Expect an easy day when most things should proceed without too much effort on your part. Study for an upcoming exam could be a serious consideration now. Doing well can move your employment aspirations forward. So hitting the books earlier will mean that you retain the important information and probably ace the test. Write down interesting concepts and ideas in a structured manner before presenting them to a boss or teacher. Make a solid case. An award or honor could take you by surprise. Something you read might change your mind on an issue. Remember, actions speak louder than words.

28. WEDNESDAY. Reassuring. Today's cosmic activity creates interesting scenarios for the Twins. Your partner should be very agreeable to whatever you present. This is an excellent time to propose or to accept a marriage proposal. There should be plenty of choices available for the busy Gemini single seeking love or companionship. If you search online, make sure you know who you are dealing with and that you are not being conned. Assistance or support could appear at a crucial point. Eliminating stress can be as easy as delegating routine tasks. Planetary influences make this period great for a group tour or travel with special friends.

29. THURSDAY. Supportive. Your ruler Mercury is now visiting Scorpio, your zone of health and employment conditions. Mercury here provides chances to improve issues currently being experienced in either of these areas. Many individuals in the sign of the Twins are apt to take good health for granted. Throughout the next four weeks focus on proper care and attention. Make appointments for a medical checkup and dental work to ensure that your body continues to function at an optimum level. Geminis who drive for a living or have a lot of errands to run should be alert in the vehicle as well as on foot. Minor accidents could befall those who display a careless attitude.

30. FRIDAY. Exhausting. Home and neighborhood affairs can cause conflict, particularly if you are trying to juggle too many demands from too many people. Delegate some of your routine obligations, or hire outside help to free up some of your valuable time. A discordant note is likely to ring loudly among certain members of your friendship circle. It would be wise for the ever friendly Gemini to stay neutral. Keep your mouth closed and mind your own business to avoid problems. A little soul-searching never hurt anyone, but do avoid a self-critical approach. Eat, drink, and be merry only in moderation so that vim and vitality are retained at a high peak.

31. SATURDAY. Stabilizing. Saturn, taskmaster of the zodiac, has set up home in Libra, your zone of pleasure, romance, and self-expression. Saturn in Libra over the next couple of years poses limitations as well as opportunities to build a solid foundation in these areas during that time. Gemini women could give birth to a child. Issues in a love affair may drag on. Many of you are likely to move in with a partner and make a permanent commitment. Today you might experience problems with members of a social club or political group. So it would be wise to back off and not get caught up in petty politics.

NOVEMBER

1. SUNDAY. Variable. Fun-loving Venus is in Libra, your house of pleasure and recreational pursuits, as the new month begins. So time spent enjoying yourself is well worth it now. However, you may need to curb the tendency to splurge on high-priced or luxury items if the bank account is leaning toward the low side. Your Gemini ability to articulate in a clear and concise manner is enhanced. Still, avoid acting as if you know everything and do not use sarcasm as a form of wit. Arguing with neighbors and siblings would be a no-no. Try to limit contact with people of a volatile nature. Retire early to bed this evening in order to recharge run-down batteries.

2. MONDAY. Sensitive. An emotional beginning to the day is foreseen. It would be best to tackle each problem as it arises. Logic and common sense are also required so that issues are kept to a minimum. The Full Moon culminates in the sign of Taurus, and this lunar cycle can bring an end to an old desire. Old wounds could be reopened and must be addressed before closure can come. Learning to let go of the past also means that you are willing to release things you have outgrown. Single Gemini should be prepared for an instant attraction. Although a love affair might be extremely pleasant, any chance of it lasting a long time is unlikely.

3. TUESDAY. Dreamy. Your head might be in the clouds today. If you have plenty of leisure time, exploring spiritual connections and New-Age topics can be a pleasant way to while away the hours. Your keen intuition should be used to ensure that you are on the right pathway. An individual or a situation from the past could return. Take care that you don't revert to old patterns. Instead, try to resolve the issue and move forward. An unusual invitation might be presented. Saying yes would provide an opportunity for you to move in different social circles. After a heavy day at work or at play, be wise and relax at home.

4. WEDNESDAY. Diverse. Wednesday is your ruler Mercury's day, and also the Moon is whizzing through your sign now. So you probably will be talkative and busy. Be careful about disclosing personal information. Make sure you trust people before revealing confidential matters. Inspirational Neptune begins going direct in Aquarius, your house of travel and education, which will help to remove delays in these areas. Any holiday plan or legal action that has been on hold could now move forward. You can expect to make a good first impression with your brilliant ideas and friendly manner. A creative streak should be utilized as a form of relaxation.

5. THURSDAY. Sparkling. The Gemini Moon guarantees a good day for you. But stop talking long enough to listen to what others say. Grasp opportunities as they appear, and they should lead to fine results. The Sun is merging with your ruler Mercury, making it a very busy time with lots of things to do and people to see. This is a favorable day to assess your employment choices and lifestyle routines. You will want to update your resume and obtain a clear picture of what lies ahead. Research all sources if you are looking for work or hoping to move up the corporate ladder. Employment interviews, staff meetings, and auditions should proceed smoothly.

6. FRIDAY. Nurturing. The Moon now glides through family-oriented Cancer, conveying a need to nurture yourself and loved ones. Make sure you don't spend money just to gain emotional comfort. Buying trinkets and treats could be a temptation, and later you might regret the cost. Mechanical breakdowns could loom on the horizon, and repairs might be an unexpected expense. Have an electronic diary close by, as an appointment could be overlooked in the course of a busy day. Joint finances are likely to bring tension to a committed partnership. Geminis who share expenses with roommates may run into a number of irritating obstacles.

7. SATURDAY. Productive. Under the Cancer Moon you have a strong desire for financial independence. You can assist this goal by regularly checking that passwords and bank pin numbers are safe.

Go over your credit card statements and look for errors. See that essential bills are paid on time. Venus, the lover of the good life stops, now visits Scorpio, your house of employment conditions, physical well-being, and the daily grind. Those of you actively trying to reform current working conditions are bound to attract supporters. Those of you unemployed should find it easier to settle into a new job of choice. Household duties could seem less of a chore now.

8. SUNDAY. Good. Rise and shine early on this foreseeably busy day. The Moon is sliding through dramatic Leo. So running errands, visiting, shopping at the markets, and playing or watching games are all satifying activities. This is an excellent period to help people who are experiencing a few problems. Your Gemini counseling and communicative skills are to the fore, but be assertive and not aggressive. If you don't agree with anyone's opinions, say so because you don't have to support everything. But say it gently and without arrogance. Promising more than you can deliver is a failing that needs to be guarded against.

9. MONDAY. Promising. Career and business possibilities indicate a financial boost. This is an excellent period to approach an authority figure for a pay increase, a promotion, or your own car park. The Moon in Leo is showering Gemini with amorous influences. Seductive Venus and passionate Pluto are happily entwined. Romantic desires move upward. If you are feeling a need for emotional comfort, arrange a special date with your significant other. Curb any jealous tendencies and make this a night of love and affection. A secluded setting under the stars, music for lovers, and a few delicious treats will help create an intimate ambience.

10. TUESDAY. Eventful. This morning the Moon moves into practical Virgo, accentuating your place of residence, family members, routine chores, and daily activities. Property matters are highlighted. Those of you who have been considering relocating can begin looking around for a new abode. Home improvement projects should proceed without snags as long as you are patient. Expanding or changing your living space can be an exhilarating experience. Meeting former coworkers for lunch or a shopping spree can also add a dash of excitement to your day. Tonight take your mate or favorite pet for a leisurely walk and forget about the cares of the world.

11. WEDNESDAY. Varied. Mixed trends prevail today as your ruler Mercury harmonizes with unique Uranus and challenges dreamy Neptune. Attempting honest and open communication could be fraught with difficulties and may be better left for another day. Distinguishing the forest from the trees may be impossible when confusion clouds the issues and the situations that are confronted. Restless tendencies might encourage reckless action because standing still isn't an option for the on-the-go Gemini. Implement relaxation techniques to help calm down anxiety and to reduce the chance of overload and meltdown. A few minutes of deep breathing can restore a sense of tranquillity.

12. THURSDAY. Constructive. Your home front takes priority this morning. An older family member may be required to make a major decision, so you should be on hand to provide support. It is a good day for those of you on the job. Put innovative ideas into a structured form so that colleagues will be impressed by your high level of expertise and productivity. Gemini sales representatives and commission agents can expect to receive a number of top leads that will yield financial gains. Someone eligible could appear on the employment scene, taking you by surprise when your heart strings begin to flutter.

13. FRIDAY. Active. If you are superstitious, don't fret about today's date. The stars are mainly swayed in your favor. As a Gemini, sitting still can be extremely difficult. Moving around is more to your liking. Being helpful is also very important, and for some of you there is nothing that irritates you more than people wasting time or doing nothing. Offer assistance to people who need help or who are struggling to keep abreast of their workload. Dinner for two and lots of good conversation could be the preference of committed couples. Singles may be in the mood for mingling and flirting. A letter from a lover stationed overseas will bring tears of joy and hope.

14. SATURDAY. Spirited. Resilience and determination will pave the way to successful outcomes now. Leisure, lovers, and children may take precedence today. Infants and the newborn could be the center of attention of Gemini parents. Dropping youngsters off at football, ballet, or the movies will keep you moving on foot and in the car. Impulsive behavior might lead you into a tight spot, so watch it. Have plenty of variety planned over the weekend to keep boredom at bay. Secure the enclosure of your favorite pets tonight and the next morning, or they may no longer be where they are supposed to be.

15. SUNDAY. Helpful. Implementing a responsible health and hygiene strategy will prove very successful. Be vigilant monitoring your diet and fitness programs. Your ruler Mercury slips into Sagittarius, your house of personal and business relationships. Sagittarius here boosts the flow of discussions between partners. Specialized counseling received now should be helpful. If you are unclear about what direction to take in life, you would greatly benefit from the guidance of a career or life-skills professional. Seek legal advice before signing a binding employment agreement. Thoroughly read everything contained in any important document.

16. MONDAY. Important. A major celestial influence is in play as serious Saturn disputes with powerful Pluto, creating stressful situations with love and shared finances. This is not the best time to take on extra responsibilities or any duties that would jeopardize a personal relationship or a business commitment. Borrowing money for a child or lover should be avoided. Refuse to guarantee a loan for anyone, or you might be left with a large debt to pay. A fresh cycle begins today with the Scorpio New Moon emphasizing health and employment. Now is an excellent period to consider the overall state of your physical fitness and to maintain the conditions that will help you live a long and healthy life.

17. TUESDAY. Supportive. The spotlight remains on relationships, including both intimate partners and professional partners. Getting everyone working as a team shouldn't pose too many problems. People will be more than happy to follow your lead. Close associates depend on your cooperation to get things moving. A significant other might need extra attention lavished on him or her, so turn on the charm and make up for past neglect. Keeping in top condition is often easier for the active Gemini than some sedentary individuals. If you intend to lose a few pounds, hire a personal trainer, purchase home fitness equipment, or schedule gym workouts to achieve a trim, taut, and terrific physique.

18. WEDNESDAY. Cooperative. Make cooperation the keyword for today. As you start, you might feel like it is one step forward and two steps back. Dealing with a cranky boss or authority figure can be challenging at times. But by day's end you will realize how much has been accomplished. Avoid hesitation, be prepared to take a leap of faith. If there is an important issue to be discussed with a partner, now is a favorable period to initiate open and honest communication. Ask another couple to join you and your lover for a night out. Unattached Gemini will have fun socializing with close companions.

19. THURSDAY. Manageable. Today you need to be scrupulous and discerning, particularly when it comes to matters involving your love life. Possessiveness and aggression should be avoided. Be realistic, Gemini. An overly indulgent lifestyle could jeopardize your financial status, causing economic problems and ever-increasing debt. Care is required with important financial and legal documents. Remember to check all facts and figures. An issue with a coworker that has been simmering on the back burner might come to the fore, ready for action to be taken. This is not a favorable day to purchase a new car.

20. FRIDAY. Challenging. Intensity mounts as the Moon zooms through the sign of Capricorn, your house of jointly owned assets and resources. Close associates could become envious without provocation, and there might not be much you can do to change the situation. Rather than arguing with those around you, set about organizing a new strategy to boost your financial status. A creative project will hit the right mark with people who have the clout to promote your work. This may mean the beginning of a successful career in public view. Studying the financial markets and how to invest can open up a new field of interest.

21. SATURDAY. Disconcerting. Past extravagant spending could catch up with you now, resulting in an argument with a partner. Self-employed Gemini should consider implementing a stock count or hiring an independent bookkeeper if you are not sure of the correct accounting figures. Seductive planet Venus is in dispute with jovial Jupiter, so don't expect much activity and passion to occur with a lover or in the bedroom. Over the next few weeks a significant new alliance could begin. Coupled Gemini might find yourself in the midst of the delightful task of preparing wedding arrangements. Changes in domestic plans may need to be made to suit the requests of relatives.

22. SUNDAY. Empowering. Overnight the Sun enters your opposite sign of independent Sagittarius, further accentuating your house of the other people in your life and just in time to begin celebrating the festive season. Happy news is likely to arrive for your partner, and you can expect to be sharing the good times with others. Energy applied to study can be of huge benefit. Gemini students need high marks to follow your dream. Foreign lands are in the frame. Travelers can expect most things to go to plan, except around lunchtime when risky action should be avoided. If you want to broaden your horizons, check out various travel options and begin plotting your journey.

23. MONDAY. Demanding. Your willpower might be very limited now. If so, moderation should be the day's guiding principle. Steer clear of department and specialty stores. The temptation to spend could be so strong that you buy impulsively without due consideration of how much you actually can afford. Expect travel to be exciting and adventurous. Still, tourists should beware pickpockets, street vendors, and sellers of pirated goods. Business operators importing or exporting products could run into problems with paperwork not filled out correctly or shipping containers stuck at the piers. Review plans for hosting a special function to ensure that costs have not surpassed the budget.

24. TUESDAY. Lively. Today is great for just about anything, Gemini. If you have plans set in motion or you want to get away from the everyday routine, consider acting now. The Sun and Saturn are making positive aspects to each other. So partnership affairs, legal issues, and professional consultations should progress favorably. A rough patch at work in late afternoon might mean that some of you are required to stay on the job rather than head home or take off to socialize. However, your departure is likely to be delayed only for a short time. It shouldn't take the organized among you long to resolve a problem and then finish off a task.

25. WEDNESDAY. Satisfactory. Make use of your artistic and innovative flair on the job. Thinking outside the square comes easily now. Once again, you should have problems solved in half the time it takes teammates to find an answer. Creative self-expression will win the day at work. This is your chance to finish off various tasks waiting for attention. When it comes to love, a few obstacles strew the roadway for singles seeking a commitment. Finding romance might not be difficult. But keeping the blinkers off will be the challenge because an enduring relationship is unlikely under current cosmic influences. Social events are highlighted, so accept invitations and have fun.

26. THURSDAY. Favorable. There can be a great deal of conviction behind your words today. Both speech and memory are apt to be sharper, and you may recall a lot of things that can assist your progress. Beware using sarcasm or appearing too forceful, as this behavior could work against you now. Geminis in a long-distance relationship should avoid too much socializing and mixing with singles if you value your current love affair. An assortment of tasks should be added to your list of things to do in order of urgency. Start with tasks that require mental application and concentration to detail because your focus is very strong.

27. FRIDAY. Fulfilling. Strong humanitarian impulses are likely to come to the fore now. Many of you may consider joining a group that aims to protect the environment in general and wildlife in particular. Gemini folk could also be the recipient of the generous spirit of others. Accept gracefully, then vow to help others in the same plight when you are back on your feet. An attraction to a like-minded group of people dealing with issues that stimulate the mind could see you becoming a member and an activist. If you are on the job today, put your head down and get moving to meet deadlines so that you are free from work this weekend.

28. SATURDAY. Happy. A pleasant day dawns when you should have a free schedule to relax and to focus on long-term personal goals. Typical Gemini folk have the wonderful ability to mix with various and diverse people. Attend a meeting of a local organization that deals with community issues and learn interesting things. Emotional comfort comes from good companionship. Socialize with friends who can introduce you to an assortment of lively individuals who will stimulate your mind. Don't be surprised if someone with creative ability suggests that you collaborate with them on a special project. It could lead to a lucrative partnership.

29. SUNDAY. Fortunate. This is a great day for anything but work, so it is just as well it is the weekend. Gemini confidence is high, and luck is on your side. Explore your daydreams and fantasies. These can be the source of creative inspiration. You could be asked to speak at a local place of worship or at a religious gathering. If public speaking is something you are not proficient in, don't stress. The words needed to convey a message will come as if by magic. Beware secrets, intrigue, and promises that have little hope of being kept. Travelers should choose sightseeing trips that feature notable monasteries and cathedrals.

30. MONDAY. Mixed. Proceed slowly. The cosmos is in favor of a quieter period today. It would be wise to rest and to review your thoughts. Talking business is unlikely to be productive. This is no time to take on competitors. Negotiations and transactions should be kept to a minimum, and impulsive action avoided. Gut feelings can guide you to opportunities for new projects, but be wary of whom you trust. Changeable influences are likely to create upheaval. The mix between your ruler Mercury and excitable Uranus impels you to be busy, chatty, sociable, and mentally stimulated, all of which will increase any restless tendencies.

DECEMBER

1. TUESDAY. Sparkling. If life has been very stressful for you lately, you can now look forward to a happier period arriving. Creative inspiration and artistic expression are high. First-time authors could finally see your name in print, while talented artists may be thrilled to have your work hung in a well-known gallery. Fun-loving Venus slips into your opposite sign of independent Sagittarius, encouraging you to put more effort and attention into a one-on-one relationship. A smart appearance and a change of style may be essential now. The outside facade can bolster inner feelings of confidence and self-assurance, so arrange an appointment for a new hairstyle and visit a favored boutique.

2. WEDNESDAY. Significant. Important cosmic patterns are to the fore today. For many Twins, various changes could occur that will be life changing. Both professional and personal goals remain at the forefront of your thoughts. Uranus, planet of chaos, is now moving forward in Pisces, your house of business and career. Uranus going direct can remove obstacles that may have been limiting your commercial success. Your enthusiasm and originality return to peak strength, aiding progress in making decisions about occupational interests. This morning's Full Moon in your own sign of Gemini places the accent on connections with other people. This lunar influence can either destabilize a romantic relationship or make it stronger.

3. THURSDAY. Tricky. Bringing stability to this day will be challenging. Heightened emotions could make you and other people quickly become rattled and agitated. If you are prepared for conflict at the onset, there is less chance of getting irritated and upset yourself. Patience will need to be exhibited when passions and desires run deep. But this might not apply to a partner who is too preoccupied to react to an immediate problem. Shop smart, preferably before lunch, and save your money. Later on, you may be tempted by sales signs and bargain prices. Although these may represent good buys, spending on them would strain the budget.

4. FRIDAY. Promising. It is a better day to head to the shops. You will be in a grounded and levelheaded mood. With an eye for quality at bargain prices, you will instantly know if you need something or not. The attitude of an associate or business partner could be subject to change, so hold off making final decisions until issues are clarified. Romantic trends are more subdued now. Your interests are focused on the practical side of a relationship rather than passion and desire. This is a favorable period for coupled Geminis to move in together, plan a wedding, or become engaged. Singles might meet an eligible newcomer who is older and more mature than you are.

5. SATURDAY. Reassuring. Endurance is the key to success today. Your empathy and compassion for the plight of others, as well as your ability to tune in to what is happening around you, are on the rise. Your ruler Mercury now takes up residence in the solid sign of Capricorn. A realistic approach toward love and romance continues. You can get right down to the nuts and bolts of relationship issues and goals. Curb your tongue, think before speaking. Words better left unsaid could tumble out, provoking discord. Unless you have a major social function to attend this evening, it might be a good choice to curl up with a good book or a lover and relax.

6. SUNDAY. Steady. A trip to the weekend markets to browse goodies on offer could be a delightful diversion and an occasion to buy gifts for the holidays. Geminis experiencing relationship problems should find discord beginning to disappear this morning. If you have pressing issues to discuss with a partner, do this now while the cosmos is supportive. Assuming the worst would be a mistake. Be patient, even forgiving, and maintain a tolerant attitude. Twins who need a break from weekend responsibilities could visit the local library, attend an interesting lecture, or participate in a community activity.

7. MONDAY. Uplifting. Seize the day and secure your future. An optimistic perspective and a positive attitude will enable you to assess any opportunities being presented now. Decisions affecting long-term investments can be made with a good chance of beneficial outcomes. Helpful advice and valuable information can also pave the way for a lucky break that will expand the bank balance. In-depth research carried out at this time should reveal everything you are looking for, and possibly more. Disputes relating to property, inheritance, or divorce should be settled in your favor. Geminis entering counseling will find comfort from the words of wisdom imparted.

8. TUESDAY. Varied. Gemini loves to gather knowledge whether it is trivial or probing. You can continue to broaden your horizons by listening to the news, watching and reading documentaries, and joining blog sites. Keep busy. If possible, steer clear of people who have a tendency to push your buttons. Your tolerance for close companions may be low, especially if their behavior rubs you the wrong way. Choose your words carefully. Try to work away from the hustle and bustle and noise of teammates. Take it easy while driving. Walk, don't run. Be more aware of potential injuries that could occur when traveling by bus or train.

9. WEDNESDAY. Fair. It should be a fairly quiet day on the work front. The festive season is coming closer. If you are hosting celebrations, set aside time now to make decisions regarding catering requirements. Cooking, cleaning, restocking the pantry, and preparing for guests are all chores that most of you will relish now. An awkward family situation might need to be resolved. But unless you are directly involved, remain neutral rather than becoming entangled in endless disputes that only drain your time and energy. An early night can help you maintain your physical reserves, also remove you from potential conflict.

10. THURSDAY. Vital. Energy is on the rise. This is the time to put special plans into action. Get an early start, and you can stay on track with allocated tasks and also reach a benchmark. People are likely to follow whatever direction you take, so lead by example. The Moon is gliding through Libra, enhancing your creative urges and your desire for love and romance. Social life should be on the rise as the weekend approaches. Expect to receive invitations to plenty of lively parties and celebrations. Attending children's concerts and plays should give delight. Participating in favorite pastimes will be both enjoyable and relaxing. A first date should prove successful.

11. FRIDAY. Bright. The pace continues to pick up, as does your creative streak and artistic flair. Instead of searching for special gifts for loved ones, consider making a few hand-crafted pieces with your own stamp of individuality. Besides, if you shop, you may be drawn to luxury items that will not suit the recipient. Conversation and discussion with a romantic partner should be kept lighthearted. Watch out for minor deception. Rely on your intuitive powers, your gut reaction. If you perceive that someone is telling you little white lies, they probably are. Tonight your guests should be impressed by your gracious hospitality and genuine friendliness.

12. SATURDAY. Accomplished. It is an ideal day to make handicrafts for the festive celebrations, volunteer for the school working bee, or rearrange the domestic environment. Get loved ones involved in preparing greeting cards and decorations. The kitchen of Gemini cooks could become a hive of activity. Goodies that tantalize the taste buds are churned out for all those lucky enough to sample your fare. If any health issues affecting someone in the household should emerge, you will take time from a busy schedule to focus on everyone's well-being. Plan to visit convalescent friends and relatives who need cheering up.

13. SUNDAY. Comforting. It is another day when preparing food could be on the agenda for Gemini folk. A new recipe book may be the inspiration needed to get you started. Healthwise, it may be time to cut back on rich and fattening food. If you have been overindulging recently, your stomach could be a little less tolerant now. Animals can be a source of comfort and love. Right now give extra back in the way of care and attention to your favorite pet. Dental problems can make life a little miserable for those of you who have been lax in keeping your teeth in good repair. If you experience even minor twinges, get an appointment sooner rather than later.

14. MONDAY. Lucky. Good fortune arrives today as well as a large dose of restless energy. Use a load of tact and diplomacy when dealing with the complaints and issues of clients and members of the general public. Success in a legal matter is more than likely. Gemini travelers should have a great day wherever you are in the world. Students can make progress, as distractions should be minor, and exams should be a breeze if you prepared. There will be lots of variety in your day to keep boredom away. A surprise incident with a partner could lead you to make a decision that has been long in coming.

15. TUESDAY. Liberating. Ambition on the job takes a backseat to your free-spirited creativity. If you haven't organized for the holidays, today you could be inspired to deck the halls with holly. Gemini folk are not known to be shy and retiring. But if you are one who is, abandon this approach now so that you can enter into party mode. Someone from overseas could spice things up no end, injecting excitement into home and hearth. A creative writing course explaining the basics of publishing your own novel would be an interesting experience. This is also a good time to send a manuscript to an editor or agent.

16. WEDNESDAY. Charming. Another great day dawns for Gemini to move special projects ahead. Those of you in retail sales, advertising, and public relations should experience better than expected profits. A New Moon in lucky Sagittarius this morning illuminates your horoscope zone of business partnerships, intimate relationships, and all contacts with others. Some lucky Twins are likely to receive a wedding proposal. Some of you may be in the throes of making preparations to walk down the aisle. Soft-pedal around any tricky situations to ensure that a happy atmosphere prevails around the home and working environment.

17. THURSDAY. Positive. Any Twins now experiencing a rocky patch in your relationship can utilize today's positive vibes to initiate honest and open discussion with a partner. Ongoing issues can be more easily resolved without tension or discord. As your creativity rises, those of you who write poetry or romantic stories should find that productivity increases. Gemini fashion and interior designers can also benefit, as inspiration flows and your ability to mix and match color schemes is high. Love and passion rule the nighttime, especially for young lovers and the reunited.

18. FRIDAY. Variable. Morning trends are not conducive for harmony and accord. Don't rock the boat or insist on having the last word, and you should make it through to more tranquil vibes around midday. Love remains a priority. The mood to make romantic plans with a significant other can be acted upon. A candlelit dinner for two and sweet anything's whispered will set an amorous scene. Geminis who haven't yet finished the festive shopping should make a start now. If a special gift for a lover needs to be purchased, you should find exactly what you are seeking. Lovely surprises can be expected, so be prepared to be pleasantly surprised.

19. SATURDAY. Disconcerting. Expect the unexpected. It is another day of surprises, but these may lean more toward shock and revelation than anything else. Upheavals are foreseen, especially in a romantic relationship or business partnership. The temptation for you or a partner to slip into old patterns of behavior can be over-powering. This could prompt you to end a permanent alliance or to seek some form of counseling. Solo Gemini seeking romance shouldn't have to look too far. Just enjoy the moment without ex-pectations, as your lover is unlikely to stick around for very long.

20. SUNDAY. Mixed. Weight watchers and those of you who have to stick to a diet for health reasons will need to exert extra willpower today. Communications with family or friends living abroad will be challenging when technology lets you down. It may be time to use your land-line phone to confirm holiday arrange-ments if cellular and Internet connections are lost. Your imagina-tion is working to capacity, urging you to put talents on display for all to see. Your interest turns to all things foreign, so plan to dine at a restaurant serving food with an exotic flavor. Then take in an art-house movie to round out an enjoyable cultural experience.

21. MONDAY. Easygoing. Energetic Mars has gone retrograde in Leo, which could help slow things down a bit. Even the most active Gemini should take a break and pace yourself as the countdown to the busy festive season begins. If the call of distant lands becomes stronger and louder, talk with a travel agent. Even if you can't go away right now, getting ideas for the future will be motivating. This is still a good period to hit the books and to join a discussion group that combines learning with socializing. At midday the Sun arrives in the practical sign of Capricorn, just in time to bring a thrifty ap-proach to gift giving and spending.

22. TUESDAY. Gratifying. Business and career matters rise to the fore today, so thoughts about the upcoming festivities should fade into the background. Commercial and professional opportunities open up now. Some of you could land a new and better job or a pro-motion at your current place of work. Mixing business with pleasure may provide a few laughs but might not be immediately profitable for the small or independent entrepreneur. Think long term, though. Establish new contacts. Build relationships with customers and clients. Such connections will be useful at a later time. Be vigilant guarding personal possessions when out and about this evening.

23. WEDNESDAY. Manageable. It is natural to feel a bit stressed at this time of year. Most Gemini people thrive on being busy and on the go. But you will need to keep emotions in check if you become a little frazzled. Satisfaction will come from working hard now to complete outstanding chores, to fill orders, and to make record sales. You could soon be taking a step up the career ladder occurs and receiving a bigger than expected bonus. Keep alcohol consumption to a minimum, especially if you have trouble curbing your tongue after taking a few drinks. A romantic dinner could be a perfect end to the evening.

24. THURSDAY. Spirited. With the Sun merging with intense Pluto, this is a great day to make solid plans for future happiness and financial security. The Moon dances to the tune of Aries this day before Christmas, so relax with family members, neighbors, and friends. A kind gesture extended now could make this a happy time for another who may be in need, lonely, or far from home. Consider offering hospitality to an associate or colleague who is unable to make it home for the holidays. You will feel the joy that comes from sharing. Join community carol and worship services this Christmas Eve.

25. FRIDAY. Season's Greetings! Today is likely to be what you make it. Those of you celebrating this special holiday will be happy if you remain cool and calm even when confronted by the usual array of mix-ups, delays, late arrivals, and badly prepared food. It can be an intense time, although peace will reign as people reach out to each other. Lovely Venus entering the sign of Capricorn today spreads an aura of harmony. Close and extended family mingling together will create new memories while talking about bygone days. Your energy may be at a lower peak than normal, so make sure you ask guests to help you with cooking, serving, and cleaning up.

26. SATURDAY. Quiet. This can be a day when enjoyment comes by relaxing alone or with friends and family. Group conversations should be spirited. You might decide to hit the post-festive sales. Or you could clean up the domestic environment, eat leftovers, and watch TV. If you have active plans, try to complete them before early afternoon. By then, your energy will become depleted. Listening to music might be the most appealing choice of amusement for tonight. Venus now visiting Capricorn, your sector of shared assets and resources, puts your focus on future financial security.

27. SUNDAY. Uncertain. Your ruler Mercury has now gone retrograde in Capricorn, which can pose delays to matters involving shared business and financial assets. Partnership funds are tricky. You could be a little battle weary and out of sync with people around you. If your plans are flexible, spend some time at home relaxing and recharging your energy. Be warned that minor quarrels could erupt with siblings, children, neighbors, or a lover due to crankiness or indiscretion when it comes to words spoken. Take care when sending e-mails that you say nothing to give offense.

28. MONDAY. Loving. The cosmos has swung your way when it comes to love and romance. Passion is intense. This is a perfect time to take off for a first or second honeymoon or to propose to a long-time lover. Gemini singles eager to meet someone should go slowly. Your burning desire might cloud your judgment. If possible, defer signing anything of importance for the next three weeks while your ruler Mercury is retrograde. But don't stop looking around for opportunities that could raise your financial status. A favorable period exists to catch up on paperwork, clean out your files, and remove clutter. Throw, sell, or give away to a charity things no longer in use.

29. TUESDAY. Productive. Relationships with intimate and professional partners remain in the spotlight. However, there is a more subdued atmosphere. This morning could be a case of whatever you do, be prepared for something to go awry. The Moon slips into your sign, which can be empowering as long as you focus and follow through. The good thing is that as a Gemini you usually learn by experience and are not prone to making the same mistake twice. You would do well to return to procedures that worked well for you in the past. Pay attention to share financial responsibilities, especially debts.

30. WEDNESDAY. Diverse. Gemini personal appeal is heightened, enabling you to persuade people that your way of thinking has merit. Take charge of shared funds if your partner is not thrifty. Be wary if shopping on line. So-called bargains could be misleading, and you might find the exact same product cheaper in a department store. If you are planning to travel with a group tour, make sure you take the required amount of spending money. Otherwise, getting cash through a foreign exchange could cost you in fees. Pack sparingly and keep your luggage weight under the limit to avoid extra costs.

31. THURSDAY. Good. An eclipsed Full Moon in the sign of Cancer can provide the encouragement you need to go through the attic, garage, and closets to remove old and useless items of clothing, furniture, and even out-of-date food stuff. Clear away the tired and useless things that are cluttering up your life. Make way for the new and the fresh. Geminis driving anywhere today should take care on the roads. Travel at a safe speed to avoid fines or minor traffic accidents. Mechanical breakdowns could also occur, so check tires and gas before going too far. New Year's Eve parties will be memorable for years to come.

GEMINI
NOVEMBER–DECEMBER 2008

November 2008

1. SATURDAY. Important. Geminis who are on the job this morning need to take extra care not to take out a bad mood on coworkers or customers, particularly if they are just innocent bystanders. If you go to a major shopping mall, resisting temptation will be difficult, but purchases need not be expensive. Choose a few economical items that catch your eye, but don't push your credit card to the limit. A relationship could begin to undergo an important transformation, possibly bringing both of you closer together as some recent obstacles are removed. You may not receive the answer you want to an important question, but don't give up.

2. SUNDAY. Edgy. You may be nervous and on edge today. People are likely to notice and comment on your changeable moods. Be kind to yourself over the next few days when it may not take much to put a damper on your outlook. Acting on the spur of the moment could cause financial embarrassment or lead to tricky issues in your love life. Neptune, the planet of illusion, begins tracking forward, which helps to remove any confusion surrounding upcoming travel or educational plans. Gemini authors who have been experiencing writer's block or problems getting published could find that obstacles begin to clear.

3. MONDAY. Troublesome. Do you best to keep activities light, fun, and in perspective even though challenging cosmic aspects prevail. Relationships are under close examination. You may feel neglected by a loved one, and boredom in a love affair is apt to lead to restlessness. This is not the day to express dissatisfaction. What you say might cause an immediate backlash that will be difficult to repair in the future. This is not the best time to seek a loan because banks are likely to be strict with their lending policies. Self-employed Geminis should be concerned if business sales are slow. This might require immediate action to make improvements.

4. TUESDAY. Unsettling. As a Gemini you normally have plenty of common sense, but right now it might be difficult to figure out what is going on due to the confusing influences that prevail. Your ruler Mercury transits mysterious Scorpio, joining the Sun and Mars there, until November 23. This encourages you to ponder ways to improve job prospects and general health. Secretive or unexpected communication may come to light, which could be exciting while forcing sudden changes to your plans. Put greater emphasis on communicating, writing, studying, and paperwork.

5. WEDNESDAY. Upbeat. Imagination and creativity are enhanced. Geminis who are creative for a living should find inspiration flowing freely. Widening your horizons always brings pleasure to those born under the sign of the Twins. Exciting opportunities surround you. This is an excellent time to plan your next vacation or holiday getaway. Streamlining employment procedures and methods can help restore motivation and lead to increased satisfaction on the job. If involved in a professional partnership you may not be given the support at work that you need now. As a consequence you might now have to go it alone. Stay home tonight and relax in a soothing bath.

6. THURSDAY. Distracting. It is essential to vary your routine activities in order to fight boredom. Change your means of transportation or your route this morning. Continue to switch duties to keep mentally alert. Be flexible and try to adapt readily to changes imposed on you, especially if these occur on the job. It won't help if you are worrying and wondering, so try to remove anxiety and concentrate on taking positive action. Resist any urge to make critical comments. You might think these are constructive but other people could find them disparaging. For Gemini singles, someone new and very different could come along and have a very profound effect.

7. FRIDAY. Beneficial. Most of the day should proceed smoothly. With the Moon sailing through your Pisces career sector, your boss might be inclined to increase your responsibilities on the job and to take notice of your ideas and opinions. Although you may prefer to stick with what has been working well so far, this is a good time to adapt to a new set of employment conditions. Working with colleagues can bring out the best in everyone. You and other people are each willing to pull your own weight and make the team experience a positive one. Don't be surprised if someone asks for guidance. They may have realized that you have the knowledge, expertise, and common sense to provide sensible assistance.

8. SATURDAY. Opportune. Lucky vibes reign. Like other signs of the zodiac, Geminis occasionally experience periods of self-doubt and confusion. Generally you lead by example, and again today other people are apt to be clamoring for your advice and assistance. Work hard to achieve your own goals and to get a record of solid accomplishments for your resume so you can move higher on the ladder of success. You are up for any challenge confronting you now, which is just as well. Work-related travel, although exciting and possibly profitable, could be forced on you at the last minute, throwing your social plans into chaos.

9. SUNDAY. Lucky. Good fortune continues to beam on those born under the sign of the Twins. Enjoy an extra long stay in bed this morning, especially if you have someone with whom to share this pleasure. During the next few days expect powerful emotions and a compelling romantic desire to get up close and personal. All of your relationships are likely to intensify, and you will need to guard against your own manipulative tendencies or a bossy attitude. Support for some of your aspirations may come from someone who is in a position to help you materially. Friends could also be an invaluable source of backing. Show appreciation by inviting them over to share your hospitality tonight.

10. MONDAY. Auspicious. Grand cosmic patterns have formed, with plenty of good fortune again coming your way. Just be aware that you could be an easy touch. Energy, optimism, and self-confidence are high. Unexpected and exciting benefits or opportunities can occur through friends, societies, or associations. This is a time when you will be inspired by new ideas and creative themes. These will produce easy access to networking with similar-minded people, leading to significant progress toward the achievement of goals. The atmosphere on the job and with fellow employees should be friendly, providing an opportunity to spend some time with workmates you don't know very well and get to know each other better.

11. TUESDAY. Excellent. Seize opportunities as they arise. Your skills and expertise allow you to take on important challenges. With the Sun and Saturn in a helpful aspect, you will be in an efficient and practical mood. This is a starred day to get things done. Work your way through papers that have piled up on your desk, do the filing, or generally straighten up and organize. If you work from home, reorganize your space, improve your surroundings, and update equipment needed to carry out moneymaking duties. If you are struggling in some way, take any assistance that is offered to help you change direction. Don't wait to investigate ways to begin your own investment portfolio.

12. WEDNESDAY. Good. There are days in the month when it is advisable to take a backseat and let other people run the show, and today and tomorrow fit that category. Conserve your energy until the weekend, when you will feel like stepping back into the limelight once more. Venus is very active, moving into your Capricorn zone and enhancing a desire for pleasure and affection until December 7. A highly seductive setting prevails. Geminis in a committed union can rekindle the glowing flame of love, longing, and lust. Establishing intimate rapport with that special person is often difficult for Geminis, but this will be smoother and easier now.

13. THURSDAY. Liberating. Lady Luck continues to make her presence felt. Many cosmic influences light up your life today, including a Full Moon in the seductive sign of Taurus. Expect a high level of emotion, with the possibility of disagreements erupting suddenly. During the next two weeks your challenge will be facing up to insecurities and putting these into proper perspective. If you suspect that you stepped out of line over the past few days and alienated someone, this is a good time to make amends and admit that you were wrong. This is unlikely to be as hard as you might think, and other people will respect your courage.

14. FRIDAY. Positive. Expect another fairly good day ahead. An idea playing in your mind could pay big dividends if developed sufficiently. Don't be discouraged if other people are not as impressed or as enthusiastic as you are. Having faith in your own abilities is half the battle. Although you might want to help others, you will realize that this may be difficult. Don't feel bad if there is nothing you can do except offer comfort and support. An active social life as well as mixing with family and friends can have you in a whirl, and this is unlikely to let up for some time. Guard against a tendency to overextend yourself and to believe that you are capable of doing more than you actually can.

15. SATURDAY. Mixed. Hasty words spoken today can easily wound people's feelings. You will feel better if you set time aside for yourself. Forget about cares and worries for a short period and just relax. Gemini folk are usually outgoing and love to talk, attributes that can bring positive gains for those who communicate for a living. This afternoon it could be a case of have money, will spend. You may be more concerned with the pleasure gained from shopping rather than how much is disappearing from your checking account. A new job offer or improvements to your daily routine might be offered.

16. SUNDAY. Stimulating. Cosmic aspects featuring your ruler Mercury indicate that you will be mentally alert, sharp, and ready for anything that happens. With the festive period drawing closer, this is the time to begin thinking about all the preparations needed to make your celebration a success. If you haven't already started shopping, write out a list of needed food supplies. Also prepare a budget to cover expected expenses so you know how much you can afford to spend. Dynamo Mars now enters the fun-loving sign of Sagittarius, your zone of relationships, and will imbue passion and desire into Gemini lovers.

17. MONDAY. Confusing. Difficulties will be hard to avoid today. Your ruler Mercury has a big say in dictating the outcome of daily events. Confusion, illusion, and unrealistic thinking are possible scenarios. You will also have to deal with being exposed to misunderstandings or untruths. Intellectual disagreements or differences of opinion might arise. If you go out doing errands and are driving a car or bike, be sure to maintain your concentration to avoid a minor accident or other mishap. Failing to double-check arrangements could find you becoming lost, turning up late, or not arriving at all for a social function.

18. TUESDAY. Unstable. Restrictions, duties, and responsibilities will make you impatient. If you are stuck in a rut, the opportunity to break out continues. Geminis who are involved in a school debate, political discussion, or lecture presentation should perform superbly. Your ability to think on your feet and fluently express ideas is at a peak. Writing also comes easily. This is an excellent time for would-be authors to finish a manuscript that has been languishing half-completed for some time or to finalize a thesis waiting for further research. Take care not to become embroiled in a neighborhood or work-related dispute. Let other people fight their own battles.

19. WEDNESDAY. Challenging. Dealing with customers and coworkers might pose a few difficulties. Mix-ups and misunderstandings are likely to increase your stress. Separating fact from fiction will not be easy because information received now could have some glaring omissions or distortions. Be extra diligent when handling paperwork or you may miss something important. If you are drowning in a multitude of duties, tackle tasks in order of highest priority. Tracking down and identifying accounting errors or technical mistakes will be harder at a later time so take extra care now.

20. THURSDAY. Satisfying. Your mood should be secure and stable. The Moon is sliding through Virgo, the sign of perfection, so home comforts and family matters are in focus. You may feel far shyer than usual, which can be a welcome change for the normally outgoing and restless Gemini. There may be a delay if you are waiting to hear about a job interview or a medical issue. If you are temporarily unemployed, use this time to update your resume and source out prospective employers. You are an effective communicator with the ability to successfully convey information. For singles, a romantic encounter could lead to a major change in your life.

21. FRIDAY. Stable. Steady progress can be made now due to the happy connection of abundant Jupiter and disciplined Saturn. Long-term desires can move closer to realization. Branching out in a new direction or expanding an established business is favored. This is a terrific day to spend time with a variety of people. Go out of your way to be friendly and accommodating, displaying your best attributes to good advantage. The Sun enters freedom-loving Sagittarius, positively accentuating your personal and professional partnership sector for the next four weeks. During this period there may be times when you will not enjoy being on your own and will crave companionship.

22. SATURDAY. Helpful. Many house-proud Geminis will wake up this morning with an urge to clean or to take care of minor household repairs and maintenance work. Those in the midst of renovations should help the project along by painting or removing debris as a way to forget about the delays or current mess left by paid workers. It is a good time to consolidate your assets. You might decide to purchase land or acquire property as a way to enhance your financial stability. You can be very supportive of your mate or partner's needs at this time, although you will expect similar treatment in return. Limit alcohol intake if socializing.

23. SUNDAY. Promising. Your ruler is on the move again, now visiting outgoing Sagittarius and joining the Sun, Mars, and Pluto there. With four planets placed in your relationship house, partnerships, public relations, and advisers are in focus. Geminis searching for a mate or partner should find this task easier now. Expect increased contact with people, loads of conversations, and plenty of social invitations. If involved in a personal or professional partnership, take steps now to settle any differences. To improve rapport, thrash out disagreements once for all. Begin putting a small amount of money aside for a future vacation or major purchase.

24. MONDAY. Renewing. Partnerships are to the fore. Take the opportunity to share mutual interests and to find satisfactory solutions to problems that have been causing concern. Lack of joint finances might need to be addressed in order to avert tension. Misunderstandings and a few minor problems dealing with customers or workmates can be cleared up fairly quickly if common sense is applied. Becoming involved in deep emotional issues can make many Geminis feel uncomfortable, as it is like delving into the unknown. Consulting a professional counselor can be a positive step if you are trying to cope with ongoing problems.

25. TUESDAY. Eventful. Look forward to a busy day. A positive attitude provides a clearer picture of where you are heading in life and how you personal aims can best be achieved. This is an excellent day to make decisions, particularly those concerning partnership issues and legal matters. Whether you are working on the job or around the home, achieving expected results is more than likely. Focus and concentration should be strong, and any work that requires attention to detail can be successfully completed. You could be unusually opinionated and prone to speaking or blurting out ideas before thinking them through.

26. WEDNESDAY. Revealing. Listening as well as talking can test your resolve. If you are planning to move to another location, details can be finalized now. If you are involved in a secret love affair, be prepared for your secret to be revealed. Pluto, planet of power, has now moved forward into Capricorn, bringing into prominence shared resources, your partner's income, and money you have not had to actually earn. Applying for a mortgage or arranging for a personal loan should be easier. Personal and professional partnerships may go through a transformation due to changing conditions confronting your mate or partner.

27. THURSDAY. Significant. Only a few insignificant matters are likely to test your resolve. For most of the day a great mood prevails, and you should be feeling confident and happy. Anything seems possible. Be prepared to make a fresh start or to take a few chances to hasten progress. Today's New Moon in optimistic Sagittarius brings a change of cycle and can have a beneficial impact on close personal and professional relationships. Take the initiative. Plans can now be carried out to your advantage. Venturing into a new undertaking or beginning a new partnership is a positive step that can lead to future happiness.

28. FRIDAY. Spirited. Ample planetary activity indicates that it might be hard to remain on an even keel today. Prepare to face argumentative coworkers or bad-tempered customers. Be vigilant when handling knives or any sharp object. You should be well compensated for any difficulties you confront. Unexpected luck and pleasant surprises are likely to put a smile on your face. Erratic Uranus is moving forward in Pisces, your vocation sector, which increases your chances of obtaining an exciting promotion, new employment, or an unexpected business contract. Social activities this weekend should be more stimulating than usual.

29. SATURDAY. Encouraging. Initiating unusual ideas and plans can bring you to the notice of supportive people and help keep you one step ahead of business rivals. Sharing good fortune and companionship with a friend can be rewarding for both of you. Minor irritations and annoyances can create frustration. Watch where you park the car. Slow down driving since there is a chance of receiving a speeding ticket. A romantic relationship that begins now has an increased chance of enduring. If single you could opt for a partner who is considerably older or younger than you are.

30. SUNDAY. Bright. Mental energy is high. Geminis who are delivering a sermon, presenting a workshop, or addressing a forum can expect a good reception from the audience. If you have nothing special on your schedule you might prefer to kick back and relax by taking a long nap, catching up on your reading, or working on your favorite kind of puzzle. Taking care of important family business might include sorting through current financial obligations, revising the household budget, or writing down a list of personal valuables for insurance purposes. Practical as well as tasteful aesthetics can be easier to design for those with an urge for home remodeling.

December 2008

1. MONDAY. Liberating. This is a great day to hit the shops early and avoid the crowds. Your judgment regarding the purchase of presents is outstanding right now. Make sure your mate or partner has a say if joint funds are being spent. It might be time to reveal a secret you have been keeping to avert possible embarrassment if it is uncovered and discussed. If a partnership or romantic liaison needs to be repaired or improved, this is a good day to make overtures intended to restore harmonious vibes. Gemini singles may announce an engagement, or wedding bells could soon be ringing. You will feel like celebrating, so have fun.

2. TUESDAY. Helpful. You might be tempted to take on too much, especially activities demanding physical exercise. Cut back on time spent at the gym or with home exercise. Participate in a more gentle form of fitness to conserve your energy. Recently there has been a strong emphasis on personal and professional relationships, and you might identify some partnership patterns that can benefit from adjustments to increase harmony. You could be under siege from bothersome people who are trying to sell you something or want you to participate in some type of mutual effort. Decline politely. You may be eager to travel but will have to put up with small setbacks.

3. WEDNESDAY. Buoyant. Today's burst of energy will help you stay on top of things. Enthusiasm regarding a program that can assist your career progress could find you working hard to learn new techniques and procedures. Avoid becoming rivals with a colleague. Even if this is friendly competition, it may backfire at a later time. Associating with people who have the same interests as you or study similar topics can be exhilarating as well as informative. If you have been hoping that a colleague will notice you in a romantic manner, you might let it be known how you feel today. Dress properly; there is a chance of coming down with a cold.

4. THURSDAY. Opportune. This is a day to experiment with new themes, ideas, and plans. The ambitious side of your nature is on display and you will be intent on doing things your way. Just try not to talk only about your own ventures and enterprises. Allow other people the chance to share information about their projects and you could learn something advantageous. When it comes to dealing with others, including clients and business associates, be ready and willing to cooperate and compromise. Moderation is the key to avoiding excessive behavior. Overdoing even the good things of life can be bad in the long term.

5. FRIDAY. Uneasy. You could wind up in the wrong place at the wrong time. With your ruler Mercury challenging erratic Uranus, you will be in a restless and unpredictable mood. It will not take much for you to become bored. Take care not to do and say anything that is not in your best interests. Obtaining cooperation from other people may not be easy. Geminis who are involved in a club or association could become entangled in controversy or infighting that is difficult to resolve. If you are looking for a new job or want to make changes in how work is performed, begin to implement plans now. Friends make the best companions tonight.

6. SATURDAY. Creative. Your life ruler Mercury forms mixed influences today, creating both positive and negative trends. You may experience anxiety or nervousness due to insecure or unstable feelings. You could be tempted to withdraw a little and opt to be alone. With your imagination highly stimulated, use it in a creative manner to ward off any thoughts of doom and gloom that may surface. Participate in an artistic enterprise that is of interest. Even though you might be more critical of your work than usual, you will not have as much time to be pessimistic. Benefits can come from inspired and practical thinking. The easiest way could well be the best.

7. SUNDAY. Enjoyable. Venus, planet of love and money, enters your Aquarius house of travel, distant matters, philosophical interests, and plans for the future, and remains there until January 5. This is an excellent period to plan or to go on vacation. Significant benefits can come from overseas contacts and connections. You could also benefit from spending some time thinking and rethinking about your current relationships with loved ones. This is the time to seek out people who can offer a more diverse way at looking at or dealing with situations. Advantages can come from involvement with a religious, university, or cultural institution. Delve into what is different and challenging.

8. MONDAY. Successful. An expensive or beautiful gift could be given to you with love. The atmosphere on the job should be friendly, with colleagues in a talkative and pleasant mood. Career and job prospects look promising, with the possibility of receiving advance notice of a promotion or change of employment duties.

You will be full of ambition and anxious to take on duties that are more demanding than those you are currently performing. Take the initiative and ask the boss for some challenging assignments that provide increased scope for advancement. A recent addition to your social circle could become a new romantic potential.

9. TUESDAY. Tricky. Over the next few days a potentially accident-prone period is in force, warning Geminis to take particular care around the work environment. You could also be more impatient, irritable, or inclined to behave impulsively. A competitive attitude, although probably leading to increased productivity, could create hostility and antagonism with colleagues. If it can be arranged, working alone or independently from other people would be a wise option. If you are the boss, beware favoring a particular employee, which is bound to arouse jealousy among other staff members. Include activities in your leisure time that refresh and rejuvenate.

10. WEDNESDAY. Unpredictable. Unusual stars prevail today, creating the possibility of some upsets or surprises. Agitation and tiredness might make many tasks on your agenda seem like a huge effort. You are apt to be reluctant to do much at all, especially if this involves working for a living. Other people, including fellow employees as well as a superior, might expect you to have all the answers when it comes to finding solutions on the job. This could be difficult if you have far more interesting tasks on your agenda than worrying about the dilemmas facing other people. Involvement with a large institution could bring benefits your way.

11. THURSDAY. Variable. The need for variety and change remains in force. The ability to be adaptable is a strong Gemini attribute, and today you will need to go with the flow in order to keep nervous tension from arising. Plans are unlikely to turn out as expected, and changes might need to be implemented at the last minute. If you have been feeling alienated from anyone in particular, this is a good time to get back in touch and renew the bonds of friendship. Sending a greeting card or e-mail could be the best way to break the ice. A compliment received now can boost your waning ego. Your social calendar should begin to get very crowded.

12. FRIDAY. Sensitive. This is a very active day in the skies, with the Full Moon taking place in your sign of Gemini. Although it is never good to bottle up emotions, try to keep a lid on any feelings of anger. Instead get involved with some project that keeps your mind off stressful situations. The atmosphere between you and your mate or partner could leave a lot to be desired. You need to retain a sense of perspective in order to keep on top of everything. Your loved one may feel that you have pulled away from the relationship due to outside involvement. Plan to spend quality time together, restoring feelings of love and companionship.

13. SATURDAY. Accomplished. Geminis have the power of persuasion right now, and selling or debating should go well. This influence can be particularly effective for those of you in volunteer work or fund-raising activities. Whatever you say can convince other people to donate money or time or both. If a need for greater freedom in your personal relationships emerges, handle it carefully. A night out with just the girls or guys might be enough to make you realize that you miss having your mate or partner around. Geminis with creative talent could save money by making original gifts for loved ones or workmates.

14. SUNDAY. Cautious. Aim for moderation and balance in everything you do. When it comes to gift giving and purchasing hospitality items, don't let your generosity severely deplete your bank balance and perhaps your mate or partner's as well. Money might slip through your fingers with no effort at all. Take special care if you are on an economy kick since you might not know when to call a halt to spending. Misunderstanding the intentions of other people could put you in an embarrassing situation. If painting, cleaning, or redecorating around the house or your working environment, take care to avoid accident.

15. MONDAY. Uncertain. This is not an auspicious start to the new working week. You may feel tired and listless and could also be bad-tempered. It may not take much for an argument to develop out of nowhere or over nothing. Feelings of inadequacy and a lack of self-confidence might make it difficult to get your views across effectively to other people and in particular to your mate or partner. Contending with interruptions, disruptions, and possible equipment failure that is beyond your control could increase your frustration. This is not a favorable time to obtain price quotes or hire someone to make household repairs.

16. TUESDAY. Mixed. A lack of ambition and assertiveness is likely. Geminis are usually the social butterflies and love communicating with other people. Today, however, mixing with those who talk a lot could be irritating, especially if you need to keep an eye on the clock. If you have an important deadline looming, don't put it off until the last minute. Start work well in advance so you can pace yourself. Imagination is enhanced, assisting Geminis who are employed in creative fields. Conditions favor a cultural activity, inspirational movie, or romantic dinner with someone special this evening.

17. WEDNESDAY. Upbeat. If your patience has been tested by glitches at work or around the house, expect a better day. Prepare for a busy social period as the festive season moves closer. Today marks the beginning of hectic activity. Your home could be buzzing with noise, excitement, and guests. Sort out winter clothes or blankets you no longer use and donate these to a local charitable organization. If you are expecting visitors for the holidays begin making arrangements now. Prepare the room where they will sleep, and stock up the pantry. Your guests could make a surprise arrival. Enjoy loved ones this evening, particularly youngsters.

18. THURSDAY. Good. Home comforts and domesticity will be the preferred option for Twins who are not going out to work. Enjoy cooking and preparing festive foods, decorating the tree, or wrapping presents. Later in the day listen carefully to an older relative who has information to share. Be careful if involved in any serious discussion. Stand your ground if necessary but without being aggressive. If trying hard to establish a business but not receiving expected support from your mate or partner, don't be too judgmental. Perhaps they are concerned about the lack of social and family time available due to the long hours you are working.

19. FRIDAY. Festive. You are in the mood for some fun and frivolity. If you have been working long and hard on the job, consider taking time off away from the hustle and bustle. Enjoy some quiet relaxation with your significant other. Social and artistic activities are important. A creative project could be completed with real style. Helpful people may cross your path and lend a hand with a career project. Now is the time to get in the holiday spirit around the workplace. If attending an office celebration this evening you should have plenty of fun. Just be sure to arrange a ride home with a nondrinker or call a taxi.

20. SATURDAY. Happy. Having fun will be on the top of your agenda, and you won't expect anything else. If you don't have any exciting social plans, try to arrange something at the last minute. Your creative abilities are likely to be sparked by past and present experiences. News from a distance might involve a child or a newborn-to-be. Children may be very fussy and hard to please, possibly causing petty disagreements at home or while out visiting. If you have left shopping to the last minute you might find that bargains are not plentiful this year, forcing you to pay more for your purchases. That is not good news.

21. SUNDAY. Surprising. A family member or friend may surprise you with an unexpected gift or invitation. If hosting a get-together, you can make your catering arrangements all the more special by featuring a few gourmet foods that are not too expensive. The Sun now moves into Capricorn and visits there until January 19. During this transit your thoughts are likely to turn to financial security and shared assets. If you have been hitting the credit cards particularly hard, this transit might bring you to your senses. Geminis who go out socializing might spend a lot of time with someone who just wants someone to talk to. Listen attentively and keep your promise not to reveal what they say or how they feel.

22. MONDAY. Energetic. Energy is at a peak. Be prepared for a number of challenges to come your way. On another level you are capable of very profound insights. Whatever you do will be more intense and deeply thought out than normal. Guard your health since you might be tempted to overdo. Your ability to impress other people, especially those in positions of power, could put you ahead of the crowd but might also increase rivalry with business colleagues or competitors. Research is likely to reveal significant information that will aid whatever you are involved in. Steer clear of dangerous areas. A windfall could give you possibilities.

23. TUESDAY. Pleasant. Extra energy in reserve will help you complete last-minute shopping and take stock of preparations carried out so far. Write down what still needs to be done, and enlist the help of other household members if you are running short of time. A desire for greater stability and security remains strong. This is an excellent period to discuss or request financial assistance, a bank loan, or insight from an accountant. Geminis who have been through a period of stress can look forward to some relief and the likelihood of a positive outcome to any outstanding issues. Listen to uplifting music, invite friends over, relax with an intimate.

24. WEDNESDAY. Fortunate. It might be difficult to concentrate on routine chores if your mind leaps from one thing to the next. Holiday shopping could prove very expensive if you do not keep emotions in check. Your ruler Mercury, planet of news, is conjunct with Uranus, planet of the unexpected. This happy link opens the door to pleasant surprises and sudden benefits. A better than expected bonus, a promotion, or a commission check can put you on top of the world, making this a very special day. Friends may drop by for a drink and some reminiscing. Ensure that all home security measures are in place to deter unwelcome visitors.

25. THURSDAY. Merry Christmas! Expect a busy day that will be anything but dull or boring. Have your camera ready. Today's activities will be very pleasing memories tomorrow. Pull out all stops to make this a joyful and happy time, spreading the message of peace and goodwill. Be sure to offer thanks for any and all gifts. A religious service this morning will give you reason to sing and also to meet up with family and friends. If sharing hospitality at your home, ask for some help with preparations so you do not end up doing all the work. Keep the conversation light and happy despite a recent upset.

26. FRIDAY. Gratifying. Gemini people are likely to remain in a happy mood from yesterday. Make an extra effort to get along well with everyone you mix and mingle with. A practical mood assists those who have to clean up leftover litter from yesterday's festivities. Take care of chores early so you have the remainder of the day to do whatever you enjoy most. If seeking to put a deposit down on a new house, a serious discussion with parents or other older family members might provide you with advice or funds. Issues about commitment could interfere with relationship harmony tonight. However this is not the right time to discuss this delicate problem.

27. SATURDAY. Fruitful. An idealistic atmosphere prevails. You might have a tendency to daydream or escape into the realm of fantasy. Romance, music, and artistic forms are enhanced. Inspiration is likely to come easily, providing pleasant relaxation. The New Moon in the sign of Capricorn opens up the chance of financial opportunities that may bring a dream closer to reality. The next two weeks is the time to make something happen. Self-employed Geminis or those who operate a business can begin new enterprises or ventures now. You have an excellent chance of a successful outcome. A partner could receive a thrilling surprise.

28. SUNDAY. Vibrant. Motivation, drive, and desire are at a peak. You have plenty of energy at your disposal, leading to many achievements. This is not the day for any sort of impulsive behavior that could put your physical safety and well-being at risk. Impatience could cause an accident if you are not vigilant. Assertive Mars and passionate Pluto merge now, and a tense atmosphere could pervade the air at times. Socializing with those who enjoy lighthearted conversation and have a great sense of humor can cheer you up. Steer clear of financial discussions. Conflict with a person you share resources with could become very heated.

29. MONDAY. Lively. Do not act in a risky manner. Be extra careful with personal safety again today. Inattention during your daily routine might cause a mishap or accident. With six planets congregated in your solar house of financial resources and shared assets, your motivation to acquire investments geared for long-term gains is strong. Use this to build a solid foundation for future economic stability. Opportunities to bolster your bank account are likely through confidential dealings currently being negotiated. If you are back at work be vigilant when handling money and possessions belonging to other people.

30. TUESDAY. Positive. If end-of-year sales are calling loudly, work out what you need and how much you can afford to spend before heading to the stores. Opt for quality over quantity, and you should do very well. This is a fine day to review what you have accomplished throughout this year and to begin implementing plans for 2009. Self-employed Geminis and small business operators who are struggling with monetary decisions can obtain excellent advice from a financial counselor, banker, or accountant. Make an appointment now to restore peace of mind.

31. WEDNESDAY. Spirited. Happy trends prevail as the year comes to an end. If you purchase a lottery or raffle ticket or enter competitions, you could come out a winner. You might be thrilled by your achievement on a recent examination or the successful conclusion of an apprenticeship or training course. Justice and a sense of fair play are heightened, allowing for a realistic approach to outstanding legal matters. If you haven't made plans for a vacation, this is a favorable period to research possible destinations. You will want to celebrate tonight as you head into a happy new year.

WHAT DOES YOUR FUTURE HOLD?

DISCOVER IT IN *ASTROANALYSIS*—

**COMPLETELY REVISED THROUGH THE YEAR 2015,
THESE GUIDES INCLUDE COLOR-CODED CHARTS FOR
TOTAL ASTROLOGICAL EVALUATION,
PLANET TABLES AND CUSP CHARTS,
AND STREAMLINED INFORMATION.**

ARIES	0-425-17558-8
TAURUS	0-425-17559-6
GEMINI	0-425-17560-X
CANCER	0-425-17561-8
LEO	0-425-17562-6
VIRGO	0-425-17563-4
LIBRA	0-425-17564-2
SCORPIO	0-425-17565-0
SAGITTARIUS	0-425-17566-9
CAPRICORN	0-425-17567-7
AQUARIUS	0-425-17568-5
PISCES	0-425-17569-3

Available wherever books are sold or at penguin.com

#1 *New York Times* bestselling author
Sylvia Browne

Book of Dreams

Sylvia Browne takes us on an
unprecedented journey through the
world of dreams—and reveals how they
can influence everything from health
and careers to love and happiness.

Available wherever books are sold
or at penguin.com

#1 *New York Times* bestselling author
Sylvia Browne

Visits from the Afterlife

With her sixth sense, coupled with stirring true
encounters, Sylvia Browne describes visitations
with ghosts, in-transition spirits, and other
troubled souls seeking peace and closure.
Through these spiritual visits, Browne explains
the reasons behind many of the world's most
bizarre and mysterious hauntings.

Available wherever books are sold
or at penguin.com

FREE
PARTY LINE

Make new friends, have fun, share idea's never be bored this party never stops! And best of all it's FREE!

Never Any Charges!
Call Now!

775-533-6900

Only Regular Low Long Distance rates apply where applicable